ALFRED

&

AGNES

The Story of My
Immigrant Parents

Frieda Fritz Stiehl

ALFRED & AGNES
THE STORY OF MY IMMIGRANT PARENTS

Frieda Fritz Stiehl

Library of Congress Number: 2016914535
International Standard Book Number: 978-1-60126-526-5

Masthof Press
219 Mill Road | Morgantown, PA 19543-9516
www.Masthof.com

This book is dedicated to my parents,
so that they might be remembered,
and to their grandchildren,

Kathy Lydia
Renee Anna
Lois Anna
Wendy Toni
Linda Dee
Steven Eric
Laura Bonnie
Anthony Norman Alfred
Jerrold Kevin
Rudy Alfred
April Elise
James Jeffrey

. . . so that they might know.

There are no ordinary lives.

—KEN BURNS

CONTENTS

FRITZ AND BREDEHÖFT

A recent search of the German national telephone directory for the surname "Fritz" shows over 13,800 listings, with the largest concentration in the German State of Baden-Württemberg in southwestern Germany, where there are 1,466 private listings within a thirty-mile radius of the village of Heutensbach, my father's birthplace.

A similar search for the surname "Bredehöft" shows only 225 listings, most located in the state of Niedersachsen in northwestern Germany. A majority (160) are within a thirty-mile radius of the town of Sittensen, my mother's birthplace.

CHAPTER 1

*How do you know who you are,
if you don't know where you have come from?*

M Y FATHER was born in 1904, in Heutensbach, a small farming village of around 250 inhabitants, located near Backnang, some 30 kilometers northeast of Stuttgart, the capital of Baden-Württemberg, a German state bordering France to the west and Switzerland to the south.

Historically, the inhabitants of this southwest region of Germany are descendants of an ancient Germanic tribal group known as the *Alemanni* or *Suebi*. In medieval Germany, the region became known as Swabia, and its inhabitants were known as Swabians ("Schwaben"). "Schwäbisch" (Swabian) is still the spoken local dialect.

Schwäbisch is a much softer language than *Hochdeutsch* or standard German. To my ears, it sounds so friendly and cheerful, and growing up in America, I remember it was always lots of fun listening to my father and my aunts and uncles speaking in melodic *Schwäbisch*. For speakers of *Hochdeutsch*, *Schwäbisch* is difficult, if not impossible, to understand. They say you cannot learn it, but have to be born into it.

As an ethnic group, Swabians are well-known for certain cultural characteristics, or ways of life. There is even a popular *Schwäbisch* slogan which has become synonymous with the personality of the *Schwaben*:

"Schaffe, schaffe, Häusle baue!"

"Work, work, build a house!" expresses one of the leading life mottos of the *Schwaben*, who are known to be the most frugal, thrifty, entrepreneurial and hardworking of all the German people. My father, a true descendant of that frugal race, was especially thrifty and hard working – *"immer am Schaffen"* (always hard at work). Forever striving to get ahead, he found it almost impossible to relax or take it easy. "Work and save…work and save!" That is how my father lived his whole life.

You might say that frugality was seared into my father's Swabian soul. He never bought anything he could not pay for, and he always watched where his money went. He especially hated waste. Lights were turned off; heat was conserved, and only as much water was used as was needed for basic cleanliness. Ingenious at repairing, re-using and recycling, he considered it shameful to pay money for something you could do yourself. Of course, all that frugality was not merely for its own sake. He saved for a new car, or for new farm equipment, and for acquiring more land.

Swabians, however, are not ostentatious. My father would never have dreamed of flaunting or displaying his wealth, rather, the *Schwäbisch* orientation is to "have it, but not show it," as opposed to people who "look rich" but might be up to their ears in debt.

The hard-working *Schwaben* are often accused of being stingy, but this is not true. They are simply notoriously frugal, and this also includes being thrifty with words and cautious in conversation. Ask a true *Schwab* how he enjoyed his meal and his highest praise will be *"nicht schlecht"*, "not bad", when what he actually means is fantastic! I never heard my father praise anyone, and as a kid growing up, I was never praised, never told that I had done a good job. After all, there is always room for improvement. How does the *Schwäbisch* saying go? *"Net gschimpft isch gnuag globt"* – meaning not to be criticized is praise enough. This saying is sure to keep you modest.

In the *Schwäbisch* culture there are many songs and jokes about themselves, about them being deliberate, slow and stubborn. But *"die dummen Schwaben"* are anything but stupid. They are, on the contrary, thoughtful, reflective and shrewd. It's just that they are not very talkative.

My father was not much of a talker. It would take him forever to reply, having first to deliberate and thoughtfully weigh his answer. He might then utter a reply, condensing whole sentences into one or two words, especially if he was in one of his darker moods, and then expect you to understand. Even in the best of times, I cannot recall him ever speaking more than a few full sentences at a time to anyone. He may have been a bit in awe of people who had a way with words, but at the same time, also contemptuous. Why did they need so many words to express what they had to say? Maybe they had nothing to say, but were speaking just to say something!

Descended from a long line of Swabian peasants, my father's ancestors had lived in the same area of Württemberg for centuries. Through church registry and LDS (Latter-day Saints) genealogy records we are able to trace direct line ancestry back many generations to the late 16th century, to my father's sixth great-grandfather, Peter Fritz, born 1596 in Mannholz, a rural hamlet (even today it has a population of only fifty) near Welzheim, about 35 kilometers east of Stuttgart.

Although the town of Welzheim itself dates back to the Middle Ages (1266), the history of Welzheim reaches back to the time of the Roman Empire, to the first century AD, when the area was occupied by the Romans. Welzheim was once a Roman colony, and remnants from Roman times – the reconstructed ruins of a Roman fort and the

Roman *limes*, the old Roman fortification wall built to keep out the marauding Germanic tribes (the *Alemanni* and the *Suebi)*, can be seen on display there.

Early in the third century, the *Alemanni* drove out the Romans, but in 500 AD the *Alemanni* in turn succumbed to and were then Christianized by the Franks. In the High Middle Ages the area became part of the Holy Roman Empire, during which time Württemberg developed as a powerful political entity in southwest Germany, with its core set up around Stuttgart by Conrad I, Duke of Swabia (died 1110). His descendants, the various counts (*Grafen*) of Württemberg, gradually expanded Württemberg while all the while surviving Germany's religious wars, changes in imperial policy, and invasions from France. In 1495, Württemberg became an imperial fief (*das Herzogtum Württemberg*) and remained a dukedom or duchy for the next four centuries until 1806, when Napoleon elevated it to a sovereign kingdom (*das Königreich Württemberg*). The Kingdom of Württemberg lasted until 1918, until the end of World War I, although it became a State of the German Reich in 1871. Thus, my father was born both a subject of the King of Württemberg and a citizen of the German Reich.

In 1539, Luther's Reformation came to Welzheim, and our Swabian ancestors converted to Protestantism. One hundred years later, many would perish in the Thirty Years' War (1618-1648) when their farmlands became a war zone. Württemberg, a central battleground of the war, with various marauding foreign troops and warlords repeatedly ransacking and pillaging the area, lost almost three-quarters of its population, so that by the end of the Thirty Years' War, the Duchy's population had declined from 415,000 to 97,000. Whole towns were burned to the ground, the surrounding farmland plundered and laid waste. Entire villages were deserted, with terrified peasants fleeing for their lives. Hiding out in the forests, many died of starvation and disease.

Pestilence and the plague soon came to the town of Welzheim and the adjacent villages. In 1630 our earliest traceable ancestor, Peter Fritz, married Anna Hoersel. In 1635 their son Georg was born. [The name Georg or Jörg (*Schwäbisch Jerg*), is the Swabian form of the Latin name *Georgius*, meaning "earth-worker" or farmer.]

That same year, eight hundred of the town's inhabitants died of the plague. (It would take a hundred years for the population of Welzheim to recover to its 1630 level!) The misery of those that lived through this brutal and horrific time is hard for us to imagine. But somehow Peter Fritz and his family managed to survive both the plague and the devastations of the Thirty Years' War.

Around 1660, Georg married Anna Maria Kaufmann. There was a serious shortage of peasant farmers in the aftermath of the Thirty Years' War, with some rural areas even more severely depopulated than others. Perhaps that is why Georg and his wife relocated to Althütte, a village some 13 kilometers northwest of Mannholz, or a good day's journey by oxcart along rutted roads. Their son Peter, named after his grandfather, was born in Althütte in 1676.

This second Peter Friz (that was how the name was then recorded) married Anna Margaretha Eisenmann around 1700. All thirteen of their children were also born in Althütte. (In those days couples had large families, if only to help scratch out a mere existence, and also because the infant mortality rate was very high.) Their tenth child was Johann Thomas Friz, born in 1720. Our direct line ancestry can then be traced through the following marriages:

1748	Johann Thomas Friz, Althütte, and Maria Sara Fellmeth
1789	Johann Michael Friz, Rudersberg, and Anna Maria Luzey
1821	Friederich Friz, Heutensbach, and Christina Barbara Krautter
1847	Matthäus Fritz, Heutensbach, and Christine Fiechtner
1893	Christian Fritz, Heutensbach, and Luise Pauline Kopf

Our Fritz ancestors were *Bauern*, small-scale peasant farmers who grew enough to feed their families, to meet their obligations (in goods and services) to whatever prince, duke or nobleman owned the land, and to have enough seed grain for the next year's planting.

Historically, a peasant, or *Bauer*, was someone who was bound to the land, a serf. Serfdom went hand in hand with feudalism, the political and agricultural system in Europe during the Middle Ages, where peasants, the lowest-ranking members of society, made up ninety percent of the population. Peasants did not own land, but were bound to a hereditary plot of land owned by a feudal lord. As the lord's subjects, they were under his absolute control, but the lord, in turn, was obligated to provide protection in exchange for labor and goods.

Over the centuries, farming continued to be the work of peasants who paid rents and obligatory services to a landlord – typically a nobleman. Since the land they farmed was hereditary in nature, so long as they were able to meet their obligations as tenants, they were able to pass down their allotted plots of land to their descendants.

It was an agricultural way of life and a farming system that only disappeared with the coming of the Industrial Age in the mid-19th century. In the Kingdom of Württemberg, personal freedom, or emancipation from serfdom, was granted in 1817, but it was not until the land reforms of 1848 that peasant farmers were given the opportunity to actually own their land. Even so, it could take years before a poor *Bauer* could afford to purchase the land his ancestors had cultivated for centuries.

Often, a small-scale *Bauer* (*Kleinbauer*) had barely enough land to feed his family, along with a pig and maybe a cow. In order to make ends meet, he had to have a second way to make a living. Thus, over time, some of our ancestors became skilled craftsmen – blacksmiths (*Schmiede*), cobblers (*Schuster*), barrelmakers (*Küfer*), or winegrowers and vintners (*Weingärtner*). In the mid-19th century, with industrialization and the coming of the railway, several became skilled bricklayers (*Maurer*).

In 1847, Matthäus Fritz, my father's paternal grandfather, a *Kleinbauer* and a *Maurer*, married Christine Fiechtner, whose ancestral lineage can be traced back to mid-17th century Austria.

The Fiechtners were Protestant religious refugees fleeing from Catholic Austria. They had been forced to leave their home in Gramastetten in *"das Ländlein Ob der Enz"* (the principality above the River Enns) in today's Upper Austria.

Luther's Reformation movement came early to Gramastetten; already in 1539 there were many converts to the Protestant faith, so that by the end of the century, most of Austria had converted to Protestantism. But a counter-reformation then took place, and in the early 1600s the Hapsburg dynasty declared the country's religion Catholic again. All those who refused to give up their Protestant faith were forced to leave.

It is estimated that upwards of 15,000 Protestants left Upper Austria as religious exiles. Seeking asylum in the (Protestant) Duchy of Württemberg, their names begin to appear in church records at the end of the Thirty Years' War (1618-1648) where they are listed as *"Exulanten"*.

Arriving in Württemberg, the exiles would have found a countryside devastated by war – burned out villages, farmland laid waste. They were therefore welcomed with open arms. After all, the *Exulanten* would help repopulate and rebuild, and they were potential taxpayers!

Andreä Fiechtner and his family were among the religious refugees fleeing Austria. Exactly how and when he settled in Unterweissach, a farming village five kilometers north of Heutensbach, is unknown, likely sometime around 1657. Upon arrival, he, like others, was perhaps offered a ransacked, abandoned farmstead, its previous owners having been either murdered or having died of starvation or the plague.

The church registry in Unterweissach notes many marriages between local women and Austrian men. On February 26, 1661 the following entry, the very first written record of the Fiechtner family in Unterweissach, was made by the pastor officiating at the wedding of Abraham Fiechtner, son of Andreä Fiechtner:

"Abraham Fiechtner of Unterweissach, originally of Grammenstetten, *Ländlin ob der Entz*, Austria, and Maria Kleinknecht, daughter of Sebastian Kleinknecht, Judge in Wattenweiler."

Christine Fiechtner's paternal grandfather, Johannes Fiechtner (1750-1819) was a *Schultheiss*, or mayor, a prominent member of the community. A *Schultheiss* was appointed for life. His was the most important post in the village, and this position of honor can be traced back through the generations all the way back to Abraham's son, Hans Michael Fiechtner (1664-1742) who was both a district judge in Ebersberg (*Amtsrichter* von Ebersberg) and the mayor or *Schultheiss* of Wattenweiler for thirty years (and was married for fifty-five years!) His father, Abraham, who died in 1716 at the age of eighty-eight, even lived to witness that festive day when his son was appointed mayor.

These bits of information are fascinating when we consider that the average length of a marriage in the late 1700s was seven years, before one or the other of the partners expired – usually the wife, in childbirth. And for Abraham Fiechtner to have lived to the advanced biblical age of eighty-eight is definitely noteworthy, as our life expectancies now are more than double that of our ancestors in the 1700s.

My father's maternal grandmother was Rosine Barbara Falkenstein. Her ancestral line is also traceable back to the time of the Thirty Years' War, to a Georg Falkenstein (Falkhenstein?), born Easter Monday 1625, who hailed from Bünzwangen (near Göppingen) and who in July 1655 married Anna Hess of Uhlbach. Succeeding generations of the Falkenstein family were *Bürger* (freemen, as opposed to serfs) and winegrowers in Fellbach and Neustadt.

Born June 8, 1834 in the village of Neustadt, near Waiblingen, the sixth of nine children, Rosine Barbara Falkenstein married quite late in life; she was already thirty-six when on May 15, 1870 she became the third! wife of Andreas Kopf, *Schneidermeister* (master tailor) in Waiblingen. Ten months later, on March 29, 1871 she gave birth to a daughter, Luise Pauline Kopf, my father's mother.

Just one year after the child's birth, however, on March 13, 1872, Rosine was granted a divorce. Rosine's escape from an unhappy marriage was very unusual, since for most of the 19th century, everything to do with marriage, including the divorce laws, was based in favor of men. A woman wishing to divorce her husband was almost unheard of and a very bold step. In this regard, Rosine was far ahead of her time. In fact, the right of a woman to divorce her husband in a German court of law had only been passed into law one year earlier, in 1870. I suspect Rosine had good reason for wanting a divorce. The tailor Andreas Kopf (who received permission to remarry) then went on to marry a fourth and even a fifth time, siring a total of fifteen children altogether!

It was left to Rosine to support herself and her child. It would have been very difficult for her. Both fatherless (her father died when she was only twelve) and motherless (her mother died one year after Rosine's divorce), what would become of her? We know that Rosine returned to using her maiden name. We do not know, however, by what means she, a divorcee and no longer young, managed to provide for herself and her child. Perhaps she went to live in Neustadt, where one of her married siblings may have taken her in, in exchange for manual labor – assisting with household chores, working in the fields and vineyards. Perhaps she went to live with her brother, Karl Falkenstein, in Zuffenhausen, just north of Stuttgart. Leaving her child in the care of one of her siblings in Neustadt, she would have joined the growing ranks of women factory workers in Germany's burgeoning industrial revolution, toiling long hours in the spinning mill in Zuffenhausen.

One thing is certain, however. Rosine managed to provide well for her child. We know that when her 22-year-old daughter Luise was married to Christian Fritz of Heutensbach on March 25, 1893, the young bride did not enter the marriage empty-handed. According to the then obligatory *Beibringens-Inventarium*, a detailed inventory of the possessions of the bride and groom, Luise contributed a great deal more to the marriage than just her prayer book! Indeed, the bride's inventory states that Luise owned land valued at 1,300 marks: a wooded meadow(10 *Ar*) from her aunt Carolina Falkenstein in lieu of wages; plus a wooded plot (15 *Ar*) and a narrow garden plot (1 *Ar*) from her mother. Luise's dowry included also a sizeable trousseau: a bedstead and bedding, both top and bottom featherbeds (stuffed with goose feathers she had gathered over the years from plucking geese), two large down pillows, a straw mattress, plus an assortment of linens including 10 coverlets, 10 full-sheets, 2 mattress covers, 20 pillowcases, 5 tablecloths, a dozen towels, and 12 chemises! In addition, the bride listed among her worldly possessions her prayer book, several outer garments (her own, plus those passed down from her mother), a golden ring (her wedding band), plus two pieces of jewelry passed down from her mother: a golden brooch and a pair of gold earrings.

Marriage required government approval; permission to marry would not be granted unless there was "proof of sufficient means" so as not to become a burden upon the *Gemeinde,* or local community. Fortunately, the groom, 24- year-old Christian Fritz, had not only completed his military service obligation, but was also able to show that he had sufficient means to establish himself and to support a family.

Christian would not have chosen his future wife lightly. Social and economic factors, more so than "romantic love", would have influenced his decision. In 19th century civil society, marriage had a certain (property-centered) transactional quality to it. People didn't marry for love; they married for advantage and inheritance. Indeed, there were only two situations in life where a person might have a real chance at improving one's livelihood: marriage and inheritance. As we shall later learn, Christian had already received his inheritance. Now he would further improve his circumstances by selecting not only a young, healthy woman of moral virtue, but also preferably someone who might add to the "family" property in the form of her dowry. It would then be up to him to "husband" his wife's property.

Marriage expectations were not the same as today. Nowadays; we no longer marry for economic reasons; we marry because we like each other. Christian and Luise might well have been attracted to each other, but their outlook on marriage was not the same as ours today. Theirs was a pure patriarchal society; women's rights were severely restricted. Church law regarding marriage, as well as German state laws pertaining to the rights and duties of man and woman in a marriage, stated clearly that the man was the "head" of the family. The woman took his name. Men were considered superior and were in charge of everything. German law gave the husband the right to decide where they would live, to make decisions about the home and to make all other decisions regarding married life. There was no gender equity; all power belonged to the man. A woman submitted to her husband in order to gain his protection as well as financial security for herself and her children. As women were not allowed into higher education, there were no professions open to women. Only marriage would assure a woman of her proper place and status within society.

Thus, today's notion of marrying for love is a new one. The modern idea of marriage based on mutual emotional attraction, on friendship and a companionship of equals between the spouses did not come about until much later.

At the time of her daughter's marriage, Rosine Barbara was already sixty years old. She would spend her remaining years living with her daughter and son-in-law, helping with the work and looking after the many children. Nothing was too much for her. She gardened and cooked, fed and bathed the babies, and washed their soiled diapers in the stone trough in the kitchen. Her grandchildren called her *"die Ahne"* and took her for granted, as children do. She was simply there, a quiet old woman who lived and died without ever telling her story to anyone. It seems nobody ever bothered to ask. She died peacefully in 1917 at the age of eighty-three.

The old grandmother was no sooner dead than word spread that she was descended from the nobility! The rumor began immediately upon the issuance of her death certificate. To everyone's surprise, her surname, as noted on the certificate, was preceded by the preposition *"von"* – "Rosine Barbara von Falkenstein!" Surely German bureaucracy, known for its efficiency and accuracy, would not confuse a commoner with a person of rank!

Such a rumor was not entirely implausible. Germany did not exist as a single nation state until 1871, when Wilhelm I of Prussia became emperor (Kaiser) of a united German Empire. Before unification in 1871, Germany was not a country at all, but rather a collection of thirty-nine independent states, and for hundreds of years it had consisted of an even more bewildering collection of small duchies, dukedoms and kingdoms, all with separate borders, and each governed by its own regional aristocracy. Aristocratic dynasties had ruled Swabia for centuries. The old grandmother, it was now being gossiped, was descended from minor nobility!

Indeed, Rosine Falkenstein did have amongst her few possessions a wax seal bearing a coat of arms. Now her son-in-law recalled the seal and examined it more closely. Did the seal belong to an aristocratic ancestral family? Before long, Christian began to use the seal in his commercial transactions, impressing it onto his business correspondence and other documents to make them appear more "official" in order to lord it over his business associates and competitors. Nor did he lose any time instructing his children that they were of aristocratic lineage. The children (Karl and Elise could vividly recall "playing" with the seal) bought into the story and later carried it with them across the Atlantic, in time passing it on to their own children in America.

"Your great-grandmother was a "von", my Onkel Karl enlightened me one Christmas Day when I was thirteen years old. My mother, however, overhearing the conversation, pooh-poohed my uncle's story. Confused, skeptical, yet wishing it to be true, I recall being secretly thrilled at the idea.

Even today there are family members who, having heard the story from their parents, are quite certain that they are descended from German aristocracy. The myth of the "von", of being descended from nobility, still persists. Although *wahrer Adel liegt im Gemüte und nicht im Geblüt* ("true nobility is more a reflection of character than of blood lineage"), we in America, in what is supposed to be an egalitarian society, relish the thought that there might indeed be a drop of "aristocratic" blood in our veins!

My father's peasant roots ran deep; countless generations of his Swabian ancestors had lived out their lives within a few kilometer radius of his home village. A time would come, later in his life, when the longing he felt for his homeland would completely overwhelm him, causing him to grow increasingly nostalgic for his *schöne Heimat,* the beautiful Swabian homeland to which he was so deeply bound.

And "das Schwabenland" truly is a postcard-pretty countryside, a rolling, idyllic countryside of picturesque villages tucked into valleys, each village surrounded by a patchwork of tidy, cultivated fields, lovely orchard-meadows (*Streuobstwiesen*), vineyards and woodlands – of course, everything much smaller, more cramped together, but also more neat and tidy than in the U.S. In the spring, the surrounding orchard-meadows with fruit trees of apple, pear, plum and cherry burst into bloom, and in the fall, grapevines

Signpost for the village of Heutensbach

heavy with ripened fruit stretch from the steeper hilltops down to the road. Aside from the farmland, villages and towns, there are many streams, rivers and lakes (beautiful natural areas with hiking trails), and large forests (*Schwäbischer Wald*). Directly to the south are mountains of over 700 meters in the *Schwäbische Alb*, a forerunner of the Bavarian Alps, with picturesque meadows filled with wildflowers and herds of grazing sheep.

The beauty of my father's 'Heimat' took even the conquering Americans by surprise. During the Allied advance through southern Germany in the closing weeks of World War II, at dawn on the morning of April 20, 1945, an advance battalion of five hundred soldiers belonging to the 397th Infantry Regiment of the 100th Division approached the Weissach Valley from the south. The American commander was so taken aback by the springtime loveliness of the scenery opening up before them – the fragrant green meadows with their fruit trees in full bloom, all bathed in the early morning sunlight – that he was said to have given the memorable order: "What a beautiful valley! Boys, hold your fire here!"

Springtime idyll. A shepherd guides his flock through a blossoming orchard-meadow. (Heutensbach, 1990)

In fact, in my father's youth, the early part of the 20th century, the area where he grew up would not have appeared that much different than today, some hundred years later, except for increased industrial growth and the expansion of the towns. Heutensbach, at the southern

edge of the Weissach Valley, backs right up to the edge of the Swabian Forest, and although today the road through town is paved and more heavily trafficked, the peaceful charm of Heutensbach has been preserved. Instead of plodding oxen or straining horses pulling loaded carts, cars now slow down as they pass through the village, but then quickly accelerate as they leave the last few fields and meadows behind before entering the trees and beginning the steep ascent through the dark forest and up over the ridge towards Rudersberg and the next valley beyond.

The major crops were wheat, rye, oats, barley, potatoes, fodder beets and clover. Rye and wheat were the staple grains used to make bread, with rye flour added to the wheat flour. Barley was widely grown not only for livestock fodder, but for human consumption as well – in the form of barley soup and porridge, and, of course, as the main ingredients in making beer! Oats and meadow hay, along with fodder beets, were fed to the horses and other livestock, and boiled potatoes to the hogs.

The system of farming was similar throughout southwestern Germany. The farmsteads were clustered together inside villages, surrounded by fields, meadows and woodlands. There were no houses, barns or sheds outside of the village, nor were there any fences or hedges. The farmers lived inside the village and walked out each day to farm their plots of land scattered throughout the *"Gemeinde"* (village community with its adjacent land).

Their cultivated strips of land were long and narrow, often not much wider than was necessary to turn a plow. This farming practice was the logical outcome of the arrangement of medieval days, when all the land belonged to a noble lord who ruled over the *Gemeinde* and who rented out plots of land to the peasants for yearly tenancy. Rather than one continuous plot of land, each peasant received a proportion of good land and a certain proportion of inferior land, so that a family might end up with a dozen or more plots in various areas within the *Gemeinde*. By degrees, it became customary for the same plots to be allotted to the same families each year. In this way, over generations, individual custody of the land was established.

But in contrast to northern Germany, where it was the rule that one heir alone (usually the eldest son) inherited a family's property and possessions, most of southwest Germany for a long time did not have any set inheritance law or custom. The parents' property was inherited more or less equally by all of their surviving children (partible inheritance). The lands were divided among all the children and the plots became smaller and smaller. Eventually the plots became so divided and subdivided until there was no room left to divide. It then became customary for only one son (usually the eldest son) to inherit; the remaining sons would have to seek their fortune elsewhere, many of them as *Tagelöhner*.

Tagelöhner, landless farm laborers, stood on the lowest rung of the social ladder. Claiming no land beyond that on which their tiny, wretched dwellings stood, they had to "sell" their labor by the day or by the week. They could only secure a small part of their food from the tiny garden plots surrounding their shabby huts, and the best they could afford in the way of domestic animals were a goat, some chickens and a few rabbits. *Tagelöhner* lived from hand to mouth and in great uncertainty. In times of economic crisis and crop failure, they were the first to be in trouble. From there, the way to the poorhouse for the whole family was not far. Day-laborers did not have much hope for the future; usually they could not even afford to marry. For that reason many children from day-laborers' families emigrated to America in the second half of the 19th century.

My father was born into a world totally different than today. Life in the German countryside was for the most part quiet and uneventful. In those days, people hardly ever left their villages. But if you did need to go to the next village or town, you walked. If you were rich enough to afford a horse, you could travel on horseback or in a horse-drawn cart or farm wagon. Automobiles were almost unheard of; it was a rare sight to even see one, much less an airplane! There was no electricity and thus no refrigeration, no washing machines, no central heating, etc. There was, of course, no television; there wasn't even radio. The cinema was still unknown at that time. There were no telephones. Even a photograph was something very special and limited to the hands of a few experts.

Indoor plumbing was non-existent; there was no running water from faucets. Water mains were just beginning to be laid in the towns, but in rural areas, people still drew water from a well. In Heutensbach, each family had its own well, plus there was also a common well whose water was extolled for many years for its medicinal properties!

There were eighteen farmhouses in Heutensbach, most with red-tiled roofs, clustered together on both sides of a narrow dirt road leading through the village. These were mostly *Fachwerk* in design, the typical German half-timbered style, medieval in its origin, and were constructed so that family and livestock were both housed under one roof. Usually, the family lived on the second floor, and the first floor, at ground level, was used to house the livestock. This was a throwback to medieval times when peasants, inside their huts, shared their living space with their animals. It was an arrangement that served them well, since the heat of the animals helped to keep them warm.

My father's family lived in a type of *Bauernhaus* (farmhouse) where house and barn shared a common roof, but with the family occupying one side of the structure and the animals housed on the other side. A hallway separated the family's living quarters from the cow stall and stable. You entered the barn through a connecting door leading from the hallway.

Stacked up outside each *Bauernhaus*, and serving as a status symbol, was the *Misthaufen* – the larger the manure pile, the more prosperous the farmer!

Inside the *Bauernhaus*, the bare wooden plank floors throughout were swept daily and scrubbed every Saturday. There was very little furniture. The *Bauernstube*, or family room, was defined by a long heavy wooden table in the middle of the room – two sides with benches and two sides with a mix of wooden dining chairs – used for many of the family's activities such as sewing, reading, knitting, and eating. A massive wooden cupboard stood against one wall. A treadle sewing machine was placed under the window.

Heat was provided by a large, ceramic tiled wood stove (*Kachelofen*) built into the adjoining wall between the kitchen and the *Stube*. The firewood was added from the kitchen end. The *Bauernstube* and the adjoining kitchen, which had a separate cookstove, were the only two rooms heated during the winter.

There was a third room downstairs, the front room, the so-called *"gute Stube"* (parlor room), which contained a sofa, a few good pieces of furniture and a harmonium. *Die gute Stube* was unheated and kept closed except on special occasions, such as a wedding, a funeral, or a visit from the pastor. Later on, the Fritzes were the first to have a telephone in the village, and the telephone took its place of honor in the *gute Stube*!

My father's boyhood home was a half-timbered farmhouse in which the family and animals shared the same roof, if not the same living space. It was built in 1905, after the previous structure was destroyed by fire. (Photo dated 1963)

Architectural rendering dated 1905

Of course, there were no modern conveniences, no indoor plumbing – no piped water. All the water for washing and cooking had to be hauled in by hand from the backyard well and then heated atop the cookstove in the kitchen.

Toilet facilities were located inside the house in separate toilet alcoves, one upstairs and one downstairs. They were not water closets ("WCs"), but rather non-flushing toilets, where water from a bucket was used to manually rinse the toilet bowl and flush the waste down the hole. This type of toilet, which worked through gravity rather than water, was called a *Plumpsklo* ("plop-toilet"), and especially in the summertime it did not smell very pleasant. Of course, the rinse bucket then had to be refilled at the well and carried back inside.

From the hallway, a set of stairs led to the second floor. There were three bedrooms upstairs. The children under ten years of age slept in the same bedroom as their mother and father – in separate "quarter" beds – two children on either side. The baby slept in-between the parents on a special baby cushion. The remaining children slept in the other two bedrooms, boys in one room and girls in the other, always three to a bed. There was also a closet-sized room downstairs just off the kitchen where the old grandmother slept. After her death, the boys used this space as a second bedroom.

Also upstairs, above the kitchen, was a storage room containing chests of flour and other foodstuffs, as well as a large bin for storing firewood. Here the hams and *Würste* (sausages) were hung after butchering, and it was also a general storage space for the few items of food that farm people purchased in those days – salt, sugar, salad oil, vinegar, and coffee, although housewives also made their own salad oil, extracted from poppy seeds or rapeseeds, and vinegar and yeast were often homemade as well. Sugar had to be purchased, but lots of times, honey or beet syrup took the place of sugar.

The Fritzes regularly brought their sacks of wheat and rye to the mill to be ground into flour – small batches at a time, since the wholegrain flour would otherwise quickly grow rancid. They also brewed their own coffee from roasted barley. Genuine coffee from coffee beans was considered a luxury and seldom purchased, reserved for special occasions such as a confirmation, a wedding, or a baptism.

The attic and the cellar also served as storage areas – the attic for miscellaneous tools, old bits of harness, chains, etc., but mainly for the storage of dried seeds for planting and also as a storeroom for the bags of grain and animal feed. In the cellar were stored the barrels of *Sauerkraut, Most* (fermented apple cider) and grape wine, along with dried plums and pears. Apples, potatoes, and turnips were stored in a separate "root cellar."

*   *   *

O N JULY 19, 1904 an eighth child was born to Christian and Luise Fritz. Actually, my father was their seventh surviving child, since their first-born, also a boy, had died two days after birth. In all, Luise would give birth to fifteen children, twelve of whom would survive infancy and childhood. Of these twelve, seven children would later emigrate to America. The names of the twelve surviving Fritz children, in the order of their birth:

Rudolf	1895	Emma	1901	Elise	1910
Frieda	1897	Hedwig	1902	Johanna	1912
Theodor	1898	Alfred	1904	Erika	1914
Berta	1899	Karl	1907	Margarete	1916

Although it was common in earlier times for people to have large families, the Christian Fritz family was prodigious indeed! Many years later, while Erika was visiting her brother Karl in Pennsylvania, she attended a German *Volksfest* in Philadelphia where she met another German emigrant from the Backnang area. The man recognized Erika immediately as an offspring of Christian Fritz of Heutensbach, declaring "I know a Fritz when I see one!" and adding, *"Er hat ja einen ganzen Hasenstall voll gehabt!"* ("He [Christian] had sired more offspring than a rabbit!").

It is difficult to write much about my father's mother, Luise. She was an only child, three years younger than her husband. Although she had her mother to help her, Luise probably didn't have time to think much about anything other than helping with the farm work plus looking after the daily needs of her ever-growing family. During the first twenty-three years of her married life (from 1893 to 1916), she bore her husband fifteen children, which means she gave birth every year-and-a-half! Her first-born, Christian, died shortly after being born, in 1894. Two more children, Helene (born 1906) and a second son called Christian (born 1908), also died young. Baby Helene died of diphtheria when she was only six months old; there was still no remedy against it. Young Christian died of scarlet fever at age four.

As was customary in that part of Germany, women were expected to help alongside the men in the fields. Luise would have had a physically draining life – long hours of laboring from dawn to dusk, since most of the drudgery of farm work would have fallen upon her (and her children).

Farming was very labor-intensive. Instead of tractors, they used draft animals – horses, oxen, even cows! And such everyday, old-fashioned farming tools as the scythe, the sickle, the hand-rake and the hoe had not yet been supplanted by mechanized farm machinery. Thus, while men normally handled the horses and oxen, and plowing and planting were primarily a man's work, both men and women went out each day to tend their plots of land. Women hoed the crops, raked hay, helped harvest the grain, and dug potatoes. Women also milked the cows, watered the animals and brought in the daily green fodder. (Since their fenceless system of farming precluded the pasturing of cattle, the cows never left the barn and were stall-fed, winter and summer. During the summer, the cows got fresh meadow grass cut and gathered by hand.

Women were also responsible for the large vegetable garden beside the house where they grew all the food for the family – cabbage, carrots, onions, beets, spinach, lettuce, beans, peas and lentils.

It was not unusual for a farmer's wife to perform strenuous manual labor right up until the time she delivered. More than once I was told how a woman would be working in the fields (usually during an especially critical time such as haymaking or grain harvesting), and her baby would be born right there in the field. The next day, she would be back in the fields, working!

A farmwife's lot was a harsh one; most of her work was outdoors, it was hard, and it was never-ending. What I found particularly infuriating: Although both men and women shared in the farm work, "real" work tended to be defined only as caring for the animals or doing the heavy tasks of the field. Housework, or "minding the house," was considered a "light" duty (lighter than outdoor work) and so didn't really count!

Grain harvest – 1950s. The man mows with a scythe, while the woman binds the stalks of grain into sheaves, using wisps of grain stalks to hold the sheaves together.

Bringing in the sheaves

Thus, traditionally, housekeeping was not Luise's first task; she always had to share the farm work, and when her husband later spent more and more time away from home on business, most of the responsibility and drudgery of the farm was transferred to her and the children.

Of course, levels of personal and domestic cleanliness were more relaxed than today. Dirt was integral to their labor-intensive, non-mechanized way of farming. With no piped water, with farm animals sharing the family's accommodation, and with manure piled up in front of their farmhouses, folks had a different attitude toward dirt and dung and did not live in the aseptic way that we live today. They did not mind the livestock smell or the straw and dirt that were dragged into the family's living quarters from the cow stall and stable or from the yard outside.

Nor did people bathe or change their clothes often, since there were no bathrooms or washing machines – no such thing as taking a quick shower or doing a quick load of wash. In fact, doing the family laundry was one of the housewife's most strenuous and time-consuming chores. Washday was once a week, always on a Monday, and it took the whole day. On that day, there was no time for much else, including preparing meals. Starting very early in the morning, buckets of water had to be hauled from the well. Meanwhile the kitchen stove or a wood-fired wash boiler had to be heated, and the water brought to boil in which the bed linens and undergarments (the whites) were first set to boil before being transferred to a wooden washtub where they would be scrubbed and washed, followed by the rest of the dirty laundry, before being wrung out, transferred to a galvanized washtub filled with clean water for rinsing, rinsed and wrung out, rinsed again, and lastly, wrung out one final time – all by hand – before being hung out to dry.

Doing the family washing took at least one full day, and it was a particularly exhausting day for all the women involved. A woman had to be strong to lift heavy, wet sheets in and out of the various washtubs. Plus, standing up and bending over a washboard all day was very hard work.

As to bathing, with twelve children plus two grownups, try heating enough water atop the stove to give everyone a bath! In fact, Onkel Theo told me in all sincerity that during all his growing up years, he could not recall ever having taken a real bath! People normally stood, half-naked, in front of a washbasin and gave themselves a sponge bath in cold or lukewarm water. They changed their clothes only on washday. On Sundays, they wore their Sunday best, but only to go to church. Once home from church, they changed back into their everyday clothes.

It was said that Luise had the finest nightgowns, since the Fritzes grew their own flax – to make into linen cloth for bed linens, undergarments, dress fabric, etc.

The actual process of converting flax straw into flax fibers is tediously demanding in its preparation, as many different actions are required to separate the flax fibers from their woody stems and soften them enough for spinning. The first step, I learned, involves soaking the flax straw in water. The story goes that Christian was able to purchase a water-logged parcel of wetland very cheap, since nobody else wanted it. Then, in a separate field, he planted flax. Flax grows tall – and quickly. It can be sown one month and harvested the next. Once harvested, Christian had his children cart the flax straw to the newly acquired wetland where they spread out the straw, allowing it to soak in the stagnant, but clean pools of water. Of course, the villagers were more than a bit envious of Christian Fritz for making "valueless" marginal land profitable.

"Whatever he touched turned to gold," they grumbled.

Once a year, a seamstress came to the house to sew new dresses and undergarments for Luise and the older girls, and shirts for the boys. All their clothes were made from homespun linen cloth. A tailor came to measure Christian, and each boy, once he turned fourteen, was measured for his first suit of clothes, the so-called confirmation suit.

Each family member had two sets of clothes (so that they could change off on washday) plus a set of Sunday clothes worn only to church and on special occasions. Each had one pair of shoes – sturdy leather shoes, made by hand, by the village cobbler. Clothes were made to last. Dresses, shirts, trousers, even undergarments were patched and darned, let out and taken in, and then passed down to the next child in line. In the evening, Luise and the girls sat around the table sewing, mending, or knitting stockings and warm outer garments.

Christian and Luise had acquired their small farmstead in Heutensbach in 1895, the same year in which Rudolf, their oldest surviving child, was born. Their land holdings at that time totaled just 14 *Morgen* (approx. 9 U.S. acres). Their acreage, however, was fragmented. As explained earlier, each villager owned plots of meadowland, woodland and arable land – not contiguous, but distributed over a wide area in the *Gemeinde*. Since some of the parcels of farmland, separately owned and cultivated, were quite narrow, one had to be careful not to trespass on the strip of land adjoining one's own.

The unit of measurement *Morgen*, meaning "morning" in English, was still in use at the turn of the century, before Germany converted to the metric system. In Austria they used the term *Joch*, meaning "yoke." (The yoke is the wooden bar by which two oxen are joined at the head or neck for working together.) Both words are interchangeable and were used to designate the amount of land that could be plowed with a team of oxen in the course of one morning.

Nowadays Germans measure their land in Hektar:

1 Ar	= 100 square meters (10m x 10m)
1 Morgen	= 25 Ar (25m x 100m)
1 Hektar	= 100 Ar = 10,000 square meters = 4 Morgen
1 Hektar	= 2.471 U.S. acres

Farmsteads in Germany are much smaller than in the United States. In all of Germany, the average size of a farm in 1949 was 6.9 *Hektar*. In 1960, this figure was 8.0 *Hektar*. [Note: By 1999, the average farm size (in the former West Germany) was 27 *Hektar* (67 acres)].

Christian's original acreage, 14 *Morgen* (9 acres), a hodgepodge of arable land, woodland and meadowland, was considered a decent-sized holding at the end of the 19th century – the second largest in Heutensbach. More remarkably, by the time of his death in 1933, Christian had increased his total acreage to 9.2 *Hektar* (23 acres), thus almost tripling its size. His was a large farm indeed by German standards!

In southwest Germany, there were three distinct classes of farmers: *Kuhbauern*, *Ochsenbauern* and *Pferdebauern*.

The poorest (*Kuhbauern*) used their milk cows as draft animals, while those better off financially used oxen to pull their wagons and plow their fields. The possession of a horse was a status symbol, as only well-to-do farmers could afford to keep them. Although by the beginning of the 20th century, horses had replaced the ox teams, most small-scale farmers continued to use their cows as draft animals until well after the Second World War.

Kuhbauer using his milk cows as draft animals. (Cottenweiler, 1966)

Kuhbauer with grandchildren

Accordingly, a villager's wealth could be determined in three ways: the number of acres he owned; the type of animal he worked with (whether cow, ox or horse); and the size of the manure pile heaped in front of his house.

Christian Fritz was considered a *Pferdebauer*. As such, he had no need to be embarrassed by the size of his manure pile, since in his stables, stalls and pens he kept a total of six horses, three or four cows, along with their calves, three or more pigs, as well as a flock of hens.

He was also an important and influential man in the village. Not only was he a member of the *Gemeinderat*, or village council, but he also headed up the local fire brigade, and from 1923 to 1924 he even served as Chairman of the Board of Directors of the *Spar- und Darlehenskasse*, the local cooperative lending bank.

Although a *Bauer*, Christian was first and foremost a businessman, a clever entrepreneur who during his lifetime was involved in many business enterprises, structuring and assuming the risks of various profitable ventures before the First World War and then prior to and after the Hyperinflation of the 1920s. He was intelligent and extremely ambitious. Talented in business, he was eager to try his hand at anything, although it was his children who ultimately were stuck with doing the work. Always on the lookout for new business opportunities and ways to turn a profit, his motto was "*Ein bissle gfuggert ischt besser als g'schafft!*" ("It's better to use your head than your hands!")

As an example, the right to hunt was severely restricted, leased out by the *Gemeinde* on a limited basis. But Christian usually outbid the other men in the village for hunting privileges. As a *Jäger*, ("huntsman"), he was allowed to own a rifle and to hunt for boar, deer and rabbit, thereby earning good money from selling wild game meat.

Everyone automatically assumed that he was wealthy. After all, at one time, he had half the men in the village working for him! That was prior to the First World War, or the Great War, when he became the proprietor and operator of a small *Steinbruch* (stone quarry) which in turn led to his involvement in the transport business – hauling gravel and carting logs: *Streuführer* and *Langholzführer*.

Christian then bid on and won the contract to lay the railway bed for the rail line between Schondorf and Welzheim. During this time, he had three men in his employ, and the job kept him away from home most of the week, except on Sundays.

Next he won the bid to construct the *Waldstrasse* from Allmersbach to Hertmannsweiler. Since in those days all hauling and carting was done using horses, three separate teams were needed to haul the gravel and stones used in the road construction. Laborers were needed not only to work in the quarry and to drive the teams of horses used in transport, but also for unloading and crushing the stones. Thus, Christian really did have at least half of the men in Heutensbach in his employ at any one time!

But then came 1914 and the outbreak of the War. Christian's horses were soon requisitioned for military purposes. The children gave them one last lump of sugar and watched sadly as their horses were led off to war…

Without horses, Christian was forced to abandon his many ventures, including the various road construction projects. He also lost the help of his eldest son, Rudolf, who was soon called up to serve the Kaiser. Two years later, in 1916, Theo turned eighteen and was also conscripted into military service. Thus, the Great War put an end to Christian's business ventures for its duration.

The Great War would take a heavy toll. By the end of the four long war years, the population of Germany was half-starved and completely exhausted. Already two years into the conflict, the military situation had begun to deteriorate; the Kaiser's generals called upon German citizens on the home front to send any last reserves of manpower and materiel to the front. Farmers had to register the total number of livestock owned and deliver up any livestock the government deemed expendable. They were also allowed to keep only a small portion of their harvest; the major portion was requisitioned for the war effort.

But as the war grew increasingly unpopular, many disgruntled farmers found ways to cheat the authorities by hiding their crops and surrendering as little as they could get away with. It was during this time that Christian was jailed for six months in the nearby town of Backnang.

The story goes that he and his children had just finished cleaning out the pigeon roost in the attic, shoveling the pigeon droppings into sacks, to be used later as valuable

*Uncle Emil
Heller and
fellow German
soldiers in
World War I*

fertilizer. Unfortunately, the sacks filled with pigeon dung were still stacked alongside the sacks filled with grain on the day that several members of the military commission showed up at the farm. They were there to inspect whether the amount of harvested grain conformed to the quantity that Christian had dutifully reported. Unfortunately, the sacks of pigeon dung were counted along with the sacks of grain!

Christian was charged with willfully undermining the war effort. The stubborn officials refused to accept an explanation. As penalty for the crime of withholding surplus food, the family's entire grain harvest was confiscated. The Fritzes were left with no grain at all – none to sell at market and none for their own consumption, for grinding into flour.

Furious at being penalized unjustly, Christian decided to take revenge by genuinely cheating the authorities, resorting to illegally butchering at night, under cover of darkness, and then selling the meat on the black market. But the military authorities were on to him. He was eventually caught and hauled off to jail.

Poor Luise! She soon exhausted her remaining supply of flour! Her family would now go hungry for lack of bread, since bread was a food staple, "the staff of life", a main source of sustenance. Nowadays, we have lost the sense of what real bread is – dense, coarse peasant bread that bears no similarity whatsoever to that bleached, pre-sliced, fluffy white stuff found on store shelves.

Deeply ashamed, Luise tried to hide her humiliating and embarrassing situation from the rest of the villagers who remained unaware of the family's plight until the Fritz children began fainting from hunger in the fields. The neighbors then came to their aid as best they could....

Never anticipating that the conflict would last more than a few months (German soldiers were assured that they would be home by Christmas!), the government had failed to ensure domestic food production. As a result of the inadequate food supply (caused mainly by the British naval blockade), people in the cities were starving, and the population was becoming increasingly disaffected with the war. People began to distrust their government, to question the reason for the mass slaughter on the battlefields and for the suffering at home. They began to demand an end to the senseless war. In the end, the generals did finally capitulate. Kaiser Wilhelm II was forced to abdicate as part of the armistice, and eventually a German republic was established, the Weimar Republic.

During the war years, and then during the civil unrest and economic chaos that followed the collapse of the German empire, Christian stayed close to home, focused on preserving what he had. But as soon as the economy began to improve, he embarked on what would turn out to be his most successful business venture ever.

Christian became one of three partners in an extremely profitable distillery, a *Schnapsbrennerei* that produced *Schnaps,* hard liquor, along with fine liqueurs such as *Kirschwasser and Pflaumenschnaps,* cherry and plum brandy. The distillery was located in Schorndorf, south of Rudersberg.

The Schorndorf distillery eventually became so profitable that Christian decided to open a second distillery in Heutensbach, although the construction plans for its expansion were never approved. However, during the brief time that the make-shift facility in Heutensbach was in operation, close to a hundred pigs were kept in an enclosure nearby, fed on the mash from the distillery.

The story goes that one morning, in a fit of anger, Christian beat a young nursing sow when he discovered that she had smothered and killed most of her litter by lying on top of them. From then on, he could not go anywhere near the enclosure. No sooner would the sow catch sight of him than she would go crazy. Grunting and squealing wildly, she would break through or climb over any barrier and chase after him. Christian would have to run to get away as fast as he could. What a comical sight for the children, watching their father being chased by a pig!

What kind of man was Christian? Who was the man behind all that business acumen, who was this clever, entrepreneurial person who succeeded in so many business ventures and then relied on his *"Kaninchenstall"* – his batch of obedient, disciplined and hard-working children – as a source of unpaid labor?

Christian with business partners, distillery workers and family members pose before the farmhouse in Heutensbach.

My grandfather, Christian Fritz, was born in Heutensbach in 1868 and lived there most of his life. His father, Matthäus Fritz (1819-1889), was a *Kleinbauer* and a *Maurer* (bricklayer), as was Matthäus' own father, Friedrich Friz (1797-1869). Both ancestors lived during the time of Germany's Industrial Revolution and witnessed the advent of the railroad. In 1861, the Remsbahn line out of Stuttgart was laid, which ran through

Waiblingen, Schorndorf and Gmünd, and in 1876 the Murrtalbahn line out of Stuttgart was extended to Backnang. Railway stations had to be erected all along the newly laid rail lines, as well as *Bahnwärterhäuser*, signalman's cottages, constructed every few kilometers along the tracks. Thus the great need for bricklayers.

Christian was the youngest of six children; he had three older brothers and two older sisters. He never even knew his eldest brother, Johann Gottlieb (born 1847), who emigrated to America in 1867 (a year before Christian's birth) and was then never heard from again. His sister, Karolina (1853-1927), who was fifteen years older, was married to Jacob Wilhelm Stecher, a blacksmith in Neustadt, near Waiblingen. Another sister, Eva Friedrike (1857-1920), emigrated to America in 1887 with her husband Johann Adam Wurst and their three small children. The Wurst family homesteaded in Kansas. Another of Christian's brothers, Jacob Friedrich (born 1860), was a bricklayer in Stuttgart. He never married, and in mid-life committed suicide. Gottlieb, the brother closest to him in age (1863-1938), was a blacksmith by trade.

As the youngest child, Christian lived at home and helped support his aging parents. He may have learned bricklaying from his elderly father; most likely he also hired out as a *Tagelöhner*, or day laborer. He was only twenty years old when his father died at the age of seventy-two, his mother having passed away just a few months earlier. Universal military training was then the rule, and so Christian, now an orphan, then spent the next three years of his life in compulsory military service.

We know from the details of the *Beibringens-Inventarium* that Christian inherited 2,623 marks, and that at the time of his marriage in 1893, at the age of twenty-four, he had savings of 2,336 marks. His wife, Luise Kopf, was from Neustadt, near Waiblingen. It is thought that the couple met after Christian had already been discharged from the army. With both parents dead, Christian may have gone to live with his married sister Karolina in Neustadt.

During his three years of active military duty with the Württemberg Corps of the Imperial Army, Christian served in the heavy artillery, where he trained to position and to fire the heavy battlefield cannons. Christian wholeheartedly embraced the ideas and ideals of the Prussian military tradition, and he would remain a military man in spirit for the rest of his life. His well-groomed mustache conveyed an air of distinction, and there was a certain military appearance in his movements and in his bearing, which was always straight and erect. He never walked or strolled in a leisurely manner; wherever he went, he marched – left, right, left, right – emphasizing the left, so that even at the age of fifty, he would still wear out two soles from his left shoe before the shoemaker would have to replace the sole on the right. Disciplined, strict and authoritarian, he would later demand respect and absolute, Prussian-like obedience from his children.

Christian was a whistler. They say you could hear his whistle in the next village. Even if you couldn't see him, you could hear him, and the children knew to get busy with their chores whenever they heard their father's approach.

He became very religious after the death of his young son, Christian. The little boy was his second son to die (the first having died shortly after birth), and both sons had borne his name. Little Christian died of scarlet fever in January, 1913 at the age of four. There was no medicine to save him. It was a time when children still died of childhood diseases, and where every illness, every cut or open wound could lead to infection, and every infection could lead to death.

Christian subsequently began to occupy himself with religion. After a dispute with the Lutheran pastor of St. Agatha's church in Unterweissach, he left the *Evangelisch-Lutherische* church and joined an *Evangelisch-Methodistische* congregation, which in those days was considered a Protestant sect – not a part of the established church. On Sundays the entire family, Christian whistling in the lead, would walk to Cottenweiler, the next hamlet over, to attend worship services there. Methodists were very strict; the Fritz children were not allowed any "frivolous" amusements such as dancing, or playing cards on Sundays, although they found ways to circumvent these rules.

Joining the Methodist church was considered a radical move; there were only two other Methodist families in Heutensbach. But the church became an important social outlet for the Fritz children. They sang in the church choir, and several of them learned to play musical instruments: Rudolf played the trumpet, Karl the cornet, and Elise played the guitar and the harmonium. There was also a *Musikverein*, a music club where the young people would get together to sing *Volkslieder*, traditional German folksongs.

Although a strict Methodist, Christian was not averse to imbibing in alcoholic beverages. He would generously extend an invitation to potential business partners to join him in the village tavern where he would often get his guests inebriated while discussing and finalizing various transactions, Christian all the while knowing full well that he could drink any man under the table. In this way, he would often gain the advantage in negotiations.

Christian's "flaw" was his weakness for the opposite sex. With his mustache neatly trimmed, his face freshly shaven, often smartly dressed for business in a suit, he cut a handsome figure much admired by the ladies. My grandfather, it seems, was a philanderer who sired at least two illegitimate children as a result of his infidelities.

Through the mist of time, we may now revisit two of these events as they happened over a century ago.

First there is the "alimony" story, which was told to me by Onkel Theo. There lived at that time in Heutensbach a young woman, the "village hussy," who had already given birth to one illegitimate child. She was three years older than Theo, and according to him, really lusted after men! In fact, while Theo was on home leave from the front, he was able to enjoy a week's worth of romantic nights with her, but "was careful not to get her pregnant." Young Ted had barely rejoined his unit when his superior officer informed him that a young woman had written, requesting that he (Theo) be given special leave to return home at once to get married. After recovering from the initial shock, Theo informed his superior in no uncertain terms that he had no intention whatsoever of going home to get married!

At war's end, Theo was more than a bit hesitant to return home, since in the meantime the young girl in question had given birth and the whole village assumed that he was the child's father! How could he prove it was not? To make matters worse, Christian and Luise were very much in favor of a match between the two young people – apparently the bride would bring a good-sized property into the marriage. Theo, however, adamantly refused.

Years later, while Theo was in the process of applying for an immigrant visa, his visa petition was initially refused. Apparently, the girl's parents had accused him of failure to provide child support. It was then that Christian stepped in and 'graciously' agreed to compensate the girl's family on behalf of his son, paying out 750 marks in child support, after which all charges were dropped and Theo was allowed to emigrate. Years later, on his deathbed, Christian confessed to his eldest son, Rudolf, that he was the actual father of the child!

The second story is that of "Onkel Otto." In 1897, the same year as Frieda was born, the neighbor lady across the way, Wilhelmine Esenwein, also gave birth – to a baby boy. She named him Otto. Otto Esenwein, the kid next door, grew up to be a fine boy who later married a lovely girl from Unterweissach, Pauline Haegele. By the time Otto and Pauline (Päule) left Germany in 1927 to make a new life for themselves in America, seven of the Fritz children had already emigrated.

My story now skips to the summer of 1948, over twenty years later. Onkel Theo from Nebraska was visiting relatives in Pennsylvania for the first time. As always on such occasions, everyone would get together. Now they were gathered for a picnic at Otto Esenwein's farm: Theo's two brothers, Alfred and Karl, plus close friends from Philadelphia, all former neighbors from Heutensbach, everyone speaking in the familiar *Schwäbisch*, delighted to see each other again.

That is when it happened. Theo had just arrived at Otto's house and was stepping inside when he suddenly stumbled and almost fell; he was that startled, certain that he had seen a ghost! What he saw was an apparition of his own father, dead these many years, descending the hallway stairs toward him!

In that brief moment, the sight of his dead father almost gave him a heart attack! In reality, it was Otto, now in his early fifties and middle-aged, coming towards him to greet him. But for an instant Theo could have sworn it was his father who was now standing before him!

That is when Theo was let in on the family secret that everyone else assembled on that day already knew, namely, that Otto Esenwein was his half-brother. It was extraordinary how much Otto resembled his father – Christian Fritz!

*   *   *

M Y FATHER was born at home in the late afternoon of July 19, 1904. The arrival of a new baby was not a big deal, since by that time his mother already had six other children to care for – three young ones: Hedwig (2), Emma (3) and Berta (5), in addition to three older children: Theodor (6), Frieda (7), and Rudolf (9). Another baby was sure to follow in another year or two.

Four days after my father's birth, Christian dropped by the *Standesamt* to register his birth under the name Karl <u>Alfred</u>, with Alfred his *Rufname* (called name), the name by which he would be known.

In many ways, and judging by today's standards, my father never had a childhood, much less a "happy" childhood. The Fritz children were not 'spoiled' with love and attention. There was never any fondness shown, no hugging or kissing – no displays of affection of any kind. The children simply "grew up" taking care of each other, the older children looking after the younger ones. Viewed as cheap labor, children were thought of (if they were thought of at all) as short adults with inferior skills. They were taught how to work from an early age. Work, after all, was what determined whether the family would survive economically. Even toddlers were exposed to work. At around age three, they would begin to tag along with their older siblings while they went about their tasks (after all, they had to be looked after!), and around five or six years of age they would be assigned their own chores. Their hands could be very small, but their parents still found work for them to do, and in no time at all, they became fully integrated and productive members of the farm's labor force.

Christian demanded of his children that they prematurely behave like grown-ups, and they were also expected to work like grown-ups. Childishness, or nonsense of any kind, was not tolerated – no horsing around, no acting up, no making noise. Early on, the childrens' actions were expected to reflect maturity and good judgment, and upon their father's return home, the performance of their chores would be controlled and evaluated.

Of course, children had always been a vital part of the farm labor scene. In the 19th century, if a farm family did not have enough children of its own, it would take on an extra child or two, children that were hired out by their poorer parents to work for meager wages. Such a youngster was called a *Kleinknecht* (little servant) or a *Hütekind* (child who herds animals). The practice of poor parents hiring out their young children as child-laborers on farms during the summer months would continue into the early 20th century.

Although children belonged to their parents' household, they were, unlike today, not that necessary to their parents emotionally. The relationship between parent and child was more on an objective, rather than on an emotional level. In an agricultural household, a person was judged on the basis of his usefulness, his ability to work. Children might not have had the feeling that they were emotionally needed, but they knew full well that they were needed for their labor. It is the exact opposite of the situation today. In today's world, simply having a child in itself affords pleasure to the parent, and children are no longer needed by their parents for the work they can perform.

Thus, given today's understanding of childhood, it is true that most farm children back then, and well into the 20th century, did not have much of a "childhood." However, all social criticism to the contrary, we cannot always be certain that children back then were not sometimes quite happy in the grown-up role they played in the workplace.

Christian Fritz ran his family in a military, authoritarian manner and demanded strict obedience. The children never once dared to question their father's authority, nor did they ever dare to talk back or, God forbid, tell a lie. For a time, young Theo considered himself his father's "favorite," but even so, when he was six years old his father once slapped him in the face because he thought he was not telling the truth. His father hit him so hard that even as an old man, Theo could still feel the sting of his father's hand. Elise vividly recalled the time when her father walloped her simply because she did not obey him quickly enough!

Of course, corporal punishment was nothing unusual in those days. It was socially completely acceptable for parents to thrash children in the name of discipline. Children were taught disciplined obedience beginning in childhood. In fact, the basic rules within the German family were identical to those of the German state: obedience and respect. Any hint of individual autonomy, any form of rebellion would be punished, and any kind of backtalk or protest against any type of perceived injustice would not be tolerated.

The Fritz children were there for one express purpose only – to work! They all had their regularly assigned chores. In fact, most of the drudgery about the farm fell to the children, since their father was often absent, tending to his many businesses. The children had to work, but it was not a situation where they had to be constantly reminded or coerced. Rather, they accepted the strict performance of their duties, their responsibilities, as a matter of course. Work was simply a part of life. They were serious about it, and even if they sometimes goofed off, no sooner did they hear their father approaching – you could hear him whistling, even if you couldn't see him – than they knew to get busy in a hurry.

By all accounts, Luise was not an especially warm or loving mother; it was the older children who nurtured their younger siblings. Nobody expected to be fussed over. There was even a saying that a sick cow was worth more effort than a sick child! If you were lucky, you might be treated to a soft-boiled egg on your birthday, and although Christmas was observed, there was no Christmas tree, and certainly no presents, except that the children might each receive an orange, which was considered a rare treat in those days. The family attended church services on Christmas; the holiday was otherwise distinguished by the fact that there was less work, and meals were more elaborate on that day.

But even though daily life consisted mainly of hard, routine labor, life was not entirely without its pleasures; it also had its brighter moments and amusements. The children belonged to the local *Gesangverein* (choral society) and enjoyed singing. They also managed to sneak away to the village dances. On winter evenings, the children gathered around the table under the oil lamp to play *Mühle* (Mill), an ancient board game my father taught us as children, *Dame* (Checkers), and a card game called *Schwarzer Peter*.

It seems the Fritzes seldom, if ever, went visiting, and whenever guests did arrive, their father simply motioned for the children to disappear. Thus, they were seldom able to listen in on 'adult' conversations and were left largely in the dark about many things. For instance, they knew very little about their aunts and uncles, nor did they know much about their grandparents, except, of course, for "*die Ahne*" who helped to rear them.

Eventually it was revealed that their father had a brother living in Stuttgart who was a heavy drinker and who in mid-life had committed suicide by hanging. The children were not even aware of a second uncle until Rudolf learned of his existence when his regiment was posted near Esslingen, where the uncle was working as a blacksmith.

Elise could vaguely recollect that soon after the war's end, several parcels arrived by mail. Only nine years old at the time, Elise recalled that one of the parcels from America contained, among other things, a pair of narrow high-top leather shoes that nobody could fit into because their feet were too wide. She vaguely recalled hearing about an aunt who had gone to America... (We now know that Christian's sister Friedrike and her husband, Adam Wurst, had a farmstead in Kansas and that Friedrike Wurst died in 1920, shortly after the last parcel arrived. With Friedrike's passing, she and her descendants in America were then all but forgotten...)

Given the constant work, the children had little time for themselves – little or no time to play. In reality, there was no such thing as "free time," since, after all, children were supposed to be useful. There were always chores that needed to be done. While the older boys were either assisting their father with his many business ventures, caring for the horses and oxen or helping their younger siblings with the fieldwork, the younger children were kept busy feeding and watering the livestock, cleaning out the manure from the cow stalls, the horse stables, the pigpen and the hen house, hoeing the garden, harvesting fruits and vegetables, and performing a myriad of other chores. Wood had to be chopped, as the kitchen stove was always in need of firewood. Potatoes for their daily meals (and for boiling as feed for the pigs) had to be brought up from the root cellar. The fodder turnips had to be chopped up for the cows...

Just to water all the animals was a big job! Each cow alone drank upwards of three bucketsful of water – three times a day – and since they were watered by hand, one child could be kept busy just carrying all the water from the well that was needed to water the livestock and for use inside the house. The grandmother would bang loudly on a kitchen pot for one of the children to run and fetch a bucketful of water whenever she ran low on water for cooking or washing up. With the older children busy with their various chores, the younger children were placed in charge of caring for their even smaller siblings. Nobody ever just sat around doing nothing…

During the summer, the potato and turnip fields required constant hoeing. Also, since the livestock was kept inside yearlong, fresh grass had to be cut and brought in for fodder each day. I suppose that is how my father learned to handle the scythe so well – tough work even for a grown man. He would have had plenty of practice from a young age, since during the six months of the growing season, two or three children had to go out early each morning to mow with the scythe enough fresh meadow grass for the cows and horses to eat, then rake it together and cart it home.

During haymaking season, their father would knock on the children's bedroom doors at dawn, even before the rooster began to crow, and while the ground was still wet with dew. Half asleep, the children would stumble out of bed, throw on their clothes, and, carrying their haymaking tools, they would file out the village until they had reached the parcel to be mowed. Mowing grass with a scythe is easier when it is damp, and so hay-making traditionally began at dawn and stopped a few hours later, the heat of the day being spent flipping the mown grass over with hay-forks or rakes to allow the air and sun to dry it. When the hay was dry (usually the hay that had been cut the previous day), it was carted home for winter storage in the hayloft.

In July and August, the ripened grain would be ready for harvesting – again by hand, with the entire family helping – the men cutting the grain (rye, wheat, oats and barley) with a sickle, with the women binding the cut stalks into sheaves, using wisps of stalks to hold them together. Then the children helped stack the sheaves into shocks. The shocks were left to dry for several days before bringing them in from the field and stacking them in the barn's mow. Later, the bundles of grain would be hauled down to the threshing floor where the grain would be separated from the straw.

During the summer, there was always an abundance of cherries and plums and garden vegetables to be harvested and preserved. In the fall, there were pears and apples to be picked, the apples made into *Apfelmost* (fermented apple cider) or hauled to market. Later in the season, there were fields of potatoes to dig up. The work was never-ending.

Village women baked bread once a week in a communal bread oven. The day before, Luise and the older girls prepared the dough at home using rye and wheat flour milled from their own grain. Then, on baking day, the sourdough loaves of bread, each weighing between four and five pounds, were carried to the *Backhaus* (community bake house) on wooden pallets with handles. Since there were so many mouths to feed, the Fritzes would always have two racks of bread to be baked, the other families in the village only one!

Grain harvest. Wooden farm wagon loaded with sheaves of barley and pulled by a team of cows (Mittelbrüden, 1933)

Meals were extremely frugal; they ate like poor peasants. Breakfast consisted either of oat and barley porridge or a type of thickened soup, *Brotsuppe*, made from crumbled-up, coarse rye bread mixed with boiled milk and water. There were also cooked potatoes.

The main meal was eaten at noon, or *Mittag*. The *Mittagessen* (noon meal) consisted of anything and everything the farm produced: *Bratkartoffeln* (boiled potatoes sliced and fried in fat) or *Kartoffelsalat* (warm potatoes sliced and mixed with diced onions and poured over with warm broth, vinegar and oil); garden vegetables in season, *Sauerkraut* (fermented cabbage), cooked dried beans and lentils, and hearty rye bread topped with *Wurst* (sausage meat) or spread with *Schmalz* (rendered pork fat). There was an occasional omelet, and in summer fresh green salad and cucumber and green bean salad with diced onion. Lentils and *Spätzle* (homemade noodles made with flour and eggs) was a favorite dish.

Sometimes the main meal consisted only of potato soup, made with bacon, onions, potatoes, flour, butter and milk.

During the week, meals were usually meatless unless they had recently butchered, although there was always meat on Sundays and on holidays, usually stewed meat served with *Spätzle* and potatoes. *Apfelmost* (hard cider) was the drink of choice.

Supper, the evening meal, was always the same: a large pot of boiled potatoes placed in the center of the table. Each person then helped himself and peeled his own potatoes. The older children added buttermilk to their potatoes; the younger children took fresh milk.

Christian sat at the head of the table, and before each meal said the blessing: *"Komm, Herr Jesu, sei unser Gast, und segne, was du uns bescheret hast. Amen."* ("Come Lord Jesus, be Thou our guest, and let these gifts to us be blest."). Then the children, one by one, each repeated a short prayer, beginning with the oldest child and ending with the youngest: *"Abba, lieber Vater, Amen!"* (The same prayers would later also be spoken at our table.) Meals were eaten in complete silence, not only out of fear of their father or out of respect, but because each child concentrated on getting his share of the food and filling his belly.

After the noon meal, Christian would read a short selection from the devotional reading, a slip of paper that was torn off the bottom part of a small calendar each day. In fact, that was how Theo came to his name: The name "Theodor" happened to appear in the devotional reading on the day he was born, so Luise decided to give him that name. When Christian arose from the table after the devotional reading, it was the cue for everyone to get up from the table and return to their work.

In my father's generation, village children in Heutensbach attended *die Volksschule* (elementary school) for seven years. The eighth school year was only introduced at a much later date. In 1927, an attempt was made to introduce an eighth school year, but the two most influential men in the village, Messrs. Häusser and Fritz(!), were opposed, arguing that given the economic uncertainty of the time, the introduction of the eighth school year should be postponed, since parents were economically dependent on the labor of their children!

For the most part, village children enjoyed going to school (a chance to sit and rest!) and paid close attention to the schoolmaster who instructed them in reading, writing and arithmetic. My father, good at figures, had a special talent for mental arithmetic. But school could not have been easy for the village children. Their schoolmaster, who had upwards of sixty pupils to instruct, at seven different grade levels – all in one large schoolroom – was strict and did not tolerate any nonsense. And although the children spoke in the *Schwäbisch* dialect at home, at school they had to speak *Hochdeutsch* (Standard German), which to them was like learning a foreign language.

In the morning, the children were each handed a still hot potato from the stove to keep their hands warm on their way to school and to eat during the morning recess. School lasted all morning. Two or three times a week there was afternoon instruction as well, in subjects like history, geography and religion, in sewing and needlework (for the girls), and in agriculture (for the boys). Village children all went home for the noon meal.

On Sundays they attended church and church school where they received religious instruction in the Protestant Christian faith and were prepared for confirmation. By the age of fourteen, a child would have completed seven years of formal schooling and would then be confirmed into the church. Confirmation was a rite of passage.

Once confirmed, you were no longer considered a child, but a grown-up, expected to assume the role of a working adult – to earn your keep. For example, during the winter, when there was less work about the farm, the older Fritz siblings might find work in the nearby town of Backnang, either in the *Spinnerei* (spinning mill) or in the *Lederfabrik* (tannery). Often village girls would hire themselves out as *Mägde* (maidservants), the boys as *Knechte* (farmhands).

Rudolf and Theo, the two oldest boys, had either to manage the farm in their father's absence or to assist in his various business ventures. One of Christian's many enterprises consisted of selling apples and apple cider. In the fall, when his apple trees were heavy with the ripening fruit, Christian would have his two teenage sons, Rudolf and Theo, load up a farm wagon, hitch it to a team of horses, and drive all the way to Stuttgart to the farmers' market. (This was prior to the war, when they still had the horses.) Theo and Rudy would drive a team of horses to Stuttgart three times a week, traveling through the night in order to arrive at the open market in Stuttgart at dawn to sell their apples and cider. This routine would continue for three months in the fall, and it was very hard work, with little or no sleep for the two boys, since by the time they returned home, it would be time to load up the wagon with apples and set out for Stuttgart all over again. The boys never received any pay for their work – all the profits went to their father, of course.

No distinction was made between the girls and the boys – all had to work equally hard, the girls alongside the boys in the field or wherever their father happened to have use of them. If, for example, as a girl you might not be quite as strong, it was no excuse for you to slacken your pace of work. Elise, for example, told the following story:

One day, when she was fifteen years old, she was standing atop the large manure pile in the front yard, flattening it out, when a passing neighbor remarked to her father that his daughter was finally filling out. Whereupon Christian replied: "Ja, I make her work hard. *Entweder wird etwas aus ihr gemacht, oder sie wird untergehen.*"

Feeling degraded as well as humiliated, Elise never forgot her father's remark that all the hard work would either make or break her! This one small example pretty much sums up what the Fritz children were up against every day of their young lives, under the watchful gaze of their father…

By the time Alfred began attending school, his two older brothers, Rudolf and Theo, had already been assigned their regular tasks about the farm where both of them had their work cut out for them, as well as assisting their father in his various businesses. During the war, however, both were called up for active service, first Rudolf, and two years later, Theo. The war also forced Christian to halt or postpone any business ventures, so he stayed close to home, working the farm with the help of his daughters.

When the world went to war in 1914, Alfred was ten years old; he was fourteen when it ended. With his two older brothers in the army, he was the only male at home except for Karl, who was three years younger and thus still too young to be of much help.

It was around this time that Christian began establishing a flock of sheep – eventually growing in size to anywhere from 250 to 300 head! (Could the army's need for wool [for military uniforms] have had anything to do with this sudden interest in sheep?) One day, Christian looked at Alfred, his third eldest son, and saw in him the ideal candidate to tend his growing flock. Thus was established Alfred's future role in the family.

Young Alfred's assigned task of herding sheep would not only determine his immediate future, but would impact the rest of his life. His whole way of being – his character, his personality, his social outlook and attitude toward life – was inevitably and unavoidably the product of the lonely and isolated years (shaped by physical, emotional and psychological trauma) that he was destined to endure as his father's shepherd.

His "career" as a shepherd boy began at a very early age. Already as an eight-year-old his father would "arrange" with the schoolmaster for Alfred to be granted special permission to leave the classroom earlier than the other children due to his status as *Hütejunge* (boy shepherd or herder). (The schoolmaster would have been reluctant to protest, since his own appointment and income depended on the goodwill of the village school board, of which Christian was an influential member…).

The farmer who made the highest bid to the *Gemeinde* would acquire the privilege of letting his sheep graze on that part of the village (common) land that he had bid on. Christian would usually make the highest bid and thus obtain full grazing rights. He would also obtain grazing land from private sources. Beginning in the fall, farmers who wanted their fields fertilized would pay to have sheep come onto their land to graze on the stubble fields and the harvested fields of potatoes and fodder turnips. Sheep droppings were considered a valuable source of fertilizer and also a very effective deterrent to the potato beetle and other destructive insects. The shepherd would put up a *Pferch* for the sheep, a makeshift enclosure that could be moved frequently across a field to attain maximum grazing and fertilization. During the night, the shepherd would have to get up at least once, preferably several times, to move the enclosure in order to prevent over-fertilization. The *Pferch* consisted of several wooden posts with pointed tips to which wires were attached. The posts would be pounded into the ground and the wires stretched between them to form an enclosure. To change the position of the enclosure, the shepherd would allow one section to remain stationary while he alternately moved the position of the other posts. This procedure would be repeated until the entire field had been covered.

The farmers to whom the sheep were rented out were responsible for providing food for the shepherd and his dog. They also would assist in moving the *Pferch* from one field to another. The *Schäferkarren* (shepherd's cart) also had to be moved. This

Schäferkarren (shepherd's wagon) on a wintry field

A shepherd leads his flock through the village of Oberweissach

was a small, lightweight, two-wheeled cart, a very primitive contraption in which the shepherd would sleep. It was furnished only with a small, narrow mattress placed upon a built-in bench along one side, and underneath which the shepherd would store his few clothes and his stash of provisions: coarse dark bread; *Speck* (bacon); *Schmalz* (lard, or rendered pork fat) to spread on the bread *(Schmalzbrot)*, onions, and an occasional crock of pickled tongue *(Ochsenzunge)*, my father's favorite.

When the sheep and Alfred were stationed at home, his little sisters would play in the cart. A *Schäferkarren* was not high enough for an adult to stand up in.

Alfred was only a child! But although still a child, when he tried to go home in the beginning because he was afraid, or simply because he was painfully lonely, his father would beat him and send him back out to the sheep. It was almost as if the young boy was being banished from his family, with no claim whatsoever to sympathy or understanding. As time went by, Alfred felt that he was alone and completely forsaken. He grew ever more solemn, unsmiling and bitter. To his classmates at school he seemed unfriendly and bad-tempered. How little they knew what was really going on inside his mind! They were not with him out there in the fields! Nobody was around to notice when, alone and lonely, a deep sadness would settle upon him, sadness so deep that it had to finally burst and he would break down and cry from loneliness.

Often he was frightened. Alone at night, he was afraid of being attacked by wild dogs. At times it was so dark that he couldn't see anything when he got up in the middle of the night to change the position of the enclosure, and often when he returned to his cart he was so cold that he couldn't go back to sleep. Sometimes at night, especially when the sheep were grazing near a cemetery and he had to get up to move the posts, he would be so scared that he would almost go in his pants…

As he grew older, Alfred assumed more and more responsibility for the flock, until he was hardly ever at home anymore. The sheep were on the go most of the year, except during the cold winter months when the flock was kept at home, especially during the lambing season, so that some of the ewes and their lambs could be brought inside to be kept warm. But during the summer months, Alfred would be gone for weeks at a time. Try to imagine a young boy in this day and age, out herding sheep, alone, all summer long!

Once Alfred had turned fourteen and had completed his seven years of formal schooling, he became a full-time shepherd, traversing through distant villages with his bleating sheep, wandering with his flock through the fields and grazing lands of southern Germany, past the *Fränkische* and the *Schwäbische Alb* and as far south as the *Bodensee* (Lake Constance) bordering Switzerland. Now a full-fledged shepherd, his brothers and sisters rarely saw him; they barely knew him. He remained a shepherd until the age of twenty-one when his father suddenly summoned him home. He was to take the place of his brother, Theo, who was planning to emigrate to America.

Christian selected his son, Alfred, as shepherd because he was the obvious choice at the time. I doubt very much that Christian gave any thought as to the boy's inclination for the job or whether his character and personality were predisposed to shepherding. A former classmate in Heutensbach recalled that Alfred never associated with the other boys; he always remained aloof from the rest of the children. It seems that Alfred was difficult to get along with – sullen, withdrawn and stubborn.

But of course, the games and pranks of his classmates must have seemed silly to him! As a shepherd boy he had a great deal of responsibility placed upon him at an early age. His daily routine was completely different from that of the other children; their youthful perceptions of life entirely different. Thus Alfred either lost, or never had the chance to learn to communicate or interact socially with his classmates. From the tender age of eight, he spent the majority of his afternoon hours, when he was not in school, mostly by himself and apart from the other children, tending to his father's flock.

We now know how crucial childhood experiences can be in contributing to personality development. As a shepherd, Alfred was mostly excluded from society. He hardly ever needed to talk with anyone; probably he talked to himself at first, but after awhile the spoken words lost their importance. There was no need for him to speak. He only needed his tongue for whistling to the dog and his vocal chords for calling to the sheep or to chase away any intruders. When he had to speak with his father, whom he feared, or with other villagers, he was inhibited. Mostly he would quietly observe people from a distance, how they behaved, how they interacted with one another...

The ways of the shepherd and the farmer are intimately linked with each other in the course of the yearly farm cycle and the four seasons. The shepherd has to know when he may cross a farmer's field without damaging the crops, when to take his sheep to higher pastures, when he must take them down to a warmer area for shelter, and when the farmers will again welcome his coming. He also has to know how to assist with the lambing and how to care for the sick animals. Because he is alone and entirely self-reliant, he must be able to handle crucial and unexpected situations, must learn to follow his own intuition, to be quiet and observe things. A shepherd must have an extreme sense of duty and responsibility. Rain or shine, the work is unremitting, with no time off, no opportunity for fun or amusement. Shepherding is a 24/7 job; in the evening, a shepherd cannot simply go home and call it a day, nor can he take Sundays or holidays off.

Unfortunately, Alfred was not always on good terms with his herd dog, and for a shepherd, who has only his dog for company and who relies heavily on his dog to do most of the legwork, he was not always on the best of terms with his four-legged companion, especially when he was in one of his dark moods and the animal was being disobedient or unhelpful. One time, the dog ran away, returning home to Heutensbach, hundreds of kilometers distant from where Alfred was stationed with the flock. The dog suddenly showed up at home! Christian easily surmised what had happened. To teach his son a lesson, Christian kept the dog at home for a few days, letting Alfred run after the sheep by himself before shipping the dog back to him.

So it was that Alfred stood alone in the fields and meadows, separated from society. Often he was alone with his flock and his dog for weeks on end, day and night, traveling hundreds of kilometers on foot, far away from home, eating whatever provisions he had. He was alone not only in a physical sense, but also psychologically; having only himself to rely on, feeling many times that he had been deserted. It must have been in these times of extreme loneliness and self-reliance that my father's strongest inherent character traits emerged, were shaped and reinforced.

We know that human behavior is a nuanced mixture of environment (family background, early childhood experience) and genetic predisposition. In my father's case, I believe it was his lonely existence as a shepherd that most shaped his personality and behavior.

When an individual is kept away from society and the world around him, there are certain benchmarks or reference points he lacks by which he can orient or compare himself. An isolated human being runs the risk of reacting improperly or inappropriately, even in a grotesque manner. In later years, my father was quite unable to "connect" with others, to "fit in" socially. Sometimes he would embarrass those around him with words or actions totally inappropriate or out of place in any given moment or situation. His social ineptness, his clumsy, awkward behavior and his generally anti-social mind-set, even among family friends and acquaintances can undoubtedly be traced back to his lack of socialization, to his lonely, isolated boyhood and formative teen years as a shepherd.

In World War I, both Rudolf and Theo were conscripted into military service. Neither was sorry to leave home! Rudolf was assigned to an artillery division where teams of horses were used to move and position heavy machine guns and light cannon on the battlefield. Theo was assigned to a cavalry or mounted infantry (dragoon) unit used in flanking maneuvers. Initially garrisoned in Ludwigsburg, Theo was proud to have his own horse and thoroughly enjoyed the camaraderie of his comrades in arms.

[On mobilization in 1914, the regiment included 37 officers and 683 non-commissioned officers and men. By the end of the war, only eight officers and 262 non-commissioned officers and men were still alive.]

The German generals signed an Armistice with the Allies in November, 1918. After the Armistice, the remnants of the German Army straggled home from the Front. By Christmas, Rudolf and Theo had also made their way home to Heutensbach, where, according to Theo, their father was not particularly thrilled with their homecoming and greeted his sons' return with near indifference. How could Christian not have been overjoyed that both his sons had returned unharmed, that both had miraculously survived the carnage, when so many young men would never come home again! (Germany alone had lost over 1.9 million men!)

With the abdication of Kaiser Wilhelm and the collapse of the Monarchy, Germany was now a republic. The German Empire, founded by Bismarck in 1871, had come to an end.

Given his father's less than enthusiastic welcome, Theo decided to return to his barracks in Ludwigsburg, voluntarily re-enlisting. However,

Stylized photo of Private Theodor Fritz of the Dragoon-Regiment Queen Olga 1st Württemberg Nr. 25 (Dragoner-Regiment "Königin Olga" (1. Württembergisches) Nr. 25)

Weltkrieg 1914-19.

Gefreiter Fritz

1. Württemb. Dragoner-Regiment Nr. 25 Ludwigsburg

DRUCK u.VERLAG v. AUG.WOLF, KUNSTANSTALT, ULM GESCHÜTZT.

with his former regiment now tasked with civil policing and security, Theo found that he no longer enjoyed military life. In 1920, he had his father petition for his premature discharge, stating as a reason that Theo was needed at home to help with Christian's recently acquired business – the distillery in Schorndorf.

The Schorndorf distillery turned out to be extremely profitable. Things were looking up again! By 1921, Christian was even able to finance and oversee the construction of a new house at the edge of the village (later Rudolf's home). Theo and Rudolf were once again helping him run his various businesses, Alfred was out herding sheep, and Karl, his youngest son, was at home with the girls.

Christian was at the peak of his farming and business career. In 1921, on the occasion of Karl's confirmation, he lavishly had each family member outfitted with a brand new set of clothes and a new pair of shoes. He then hired the services of a professional photographer to take a family portrait.

It was the first and last time they would all pose together. Not long afterwards, the German economic situation would worsen, dramatically…

At War's end, Germany had been forced to sign the Treaty of Versailles, which was a sham, as Germany was forced to accept sole responsibility for causing the war and had to pay huge war reparations for all the damage. Germany was required to make large yearly payments to the Allies as "reparations." But the new German government, the democratically elected Weimar Republic, with its badly damaged economy, was unable to meet the impossible demands of the reparations payments. France then charged Germany with willful default under the Treaty. In January 1923, French troops moved in and occupied the Ruhr region, the industrial heartland of Germany, with the idea of extracting the reparations payments due from the steel industries located there. The German steel workers countered with passive resistance and strikes. All production came to a halt, further damaging Germany's ability to make reparations payments. The strike lasted for more than eight months.

Since all production in the mines and factories had ceased, Germany no longer had sufficient exports to back up its currency. Plus, all the striking workers and their families had to be supported, since the government itself had encouraged them to strike. And so, the government of the Weimar Republic began to spend money it did not really have.

In order to deal with the growing economic crisis, it decided to pay its war debt by printing more banknotes. But the more money was printed, the less it was worth, resulting in uncontrolled inflation. The whole monetary system began to collapse. There was more money, but it bought less and less, and before long, the German people discovered their currency had no buying power. Their money was totally useless!

Prior to the outbreak of the war, the value of the German mark was 4.2 per dollar. But now, it fell in value from seven thousand marks per dollar in January 1923 to one

The Christian Fritz family of Heutensbach – 1921. Back: (left to right): Alfred (17), Emma, Berta, Hedwig, Theodor. Center: Johanna, Frieda, Luise, Christian, Rudolf, Elise, Karl. Front: Gretel, Erika (The dog's name was Stumper.)

million marks per dollar in August 1923 to four trillion marks per dollar in November 1923. In short, it became utterly worthless.

The Hyperinflation of 1923 would cause terrible suffering. The banks all went bust; anyone who had their life savings in a bank lost everything. The worst hit, of course, was the working middle class, who were paid in wages, and the elderly, who relied on a monthly pension. They were no longer able to purchase anything with their now worthless wages or monthly pension checks.

It was at the very onset of the inflation that Christian and his Schorndorf partners were made an offer too good to resist from a buyer interested in acquiring their profitable distillery business. Christian and his two partners never dreamed they would be offered such a good price! Christian came home with a suitcase full of money – over one million

Christian and Luise Fritz – 1921

marks! – for his share of the business. Needless to say, he was ecstatic. "My children and their children will never have to labor again!" he proclaimed. "They will all be able to attend university!"

But instead of immediately cashing in his marks and exchanging them for dollars, Christian followed the advice of his banker to hold onto the money for a few days longer, since the value of the mark was fluctuating wildly, and the speculation was that it was about to increase in value again. Unfortunately, just the opposite occurred. Christian's suitcase full of money was now next to worthless.

From that time on, Christian Fritz became known as "*der Millionen Fritz.*" Or perhaps he had been assigned that name previously, since the villagers had always considered him wealthy? At any rate, since many people in the surrounding villages had the same last name, in order to distinguish one person from another, it was customary to assign a nickname or a name derived from one's occupation or other circumstance. Decades later, in the 1970s, when a visitor from the States inquired about where Mr. Fritz used to live, the locals asked which Fritz he meant – *der Millionen Fritz?*

In July 1923, in the midst of the Hyperinflation, Christian was appointed chairman of the board of directors of the *Raiffeisenbank*, the local credit union or cooperative lending bank. The *Raiffeisenbank* at that point was struggling with crisis management; the hard-earned savings of every farmer in the village were at stake! Hoping to exert damage control, Christian struggled to keep the rate of return equal to the rate of inflation, raising interest rates on depositor accounts to 20% in July, and in September again to 50%. But alas, he was unable to prevent catastrophe. Soon all was lost, the savings of the entire village simply vanished! The following year, in the fall of 1924, a defeated Christian resigned his position as chairman of the board. In just one year he had gone from success (as "millionaire" businessman and chairman of the board of directors of a thriving cooperative lending bank) to complete and utter ruin.

Those who lived through the hyperinflationary days of the Weimar Republic of 1920's Germany related such fantastic stories as needing a wheelbarrow full of money just to purchase a loaf of bread! It would then take an hour or longer just to count it!

Young farm girls who had hired out as maidservants and who had worked all year barely had enough money to purchase a pair of stockings from a year's wages! The same pair of shoes that cost thirteen marks in 1913 now cost more than a year's salary! Onkel Theo told of selling apple cider at the farmers' market in Stuttgart in the spring of 1923. As soon as he and Rudolf had sold their cider, they immediately had to run and purchase something with their profit before the money was further devalued. Theo told me how at that time he was "in love" and contemplating the purchase of two plain wedding bands. But the rings would have set him back sixty-eight million marks!

Against this backdrop of economic collapse it is easy to understand how many young people would have come to the realization that there was no future for them in Germany. In 1923, sixty-eight thousand people emigrated from Germany to America. In 1924, seventy-five thousand people left for America, and in the years from 1925 to 1929, fifty thousand Germans emigrated to America each year!

But the United States had begun to restrict immigration. The Emergency Quota Act of 1921 limited the number of immigrants to the United States by imposing quotas based on country of birth. Only a prescribed number of people from each individual foreign country were permitted to enter the United States in any given year. In 1923, under the quota system, the maximum number of immigrants laid down for Germany was sixty-eight thousand. In that year, Germany exhausted its quota within six months!

The first of the Fritz children to leave home was the oldest girl, Frieda. Frieda emigrated in August 1923, sponsored by Mrs. Carrie Pfaender, the aunt of her friend and next-door neighbor, Pauline (Päule) Pfaehler, who had left home several months earlier. Frieda found a job as *Kinderfräulein* in Philadelphia.

Five years later, Frieda's friend, Päule Pfaehler, would make the acquaintance of Gottlieb Haegele, a baker (*Bäcker*) by trade. Although Gottlieb hailed from Unterweissach, just three kilometers from Heutensbach, oddly enough it was in Philadelphia where he and Päule first met! Gottlieb and Päule Haegele later owned and ran a successful German bakery at 6101 Lawrence Street.

Back in "the Old Country", Gottlieb Haegele's sister (her name was also Päule) was already married to Otto Esenwein of Heutensbach. Thus, the two Päules became sisters-in-law. In November 1927, Otto and Päule Esenwein and their five-year old son, Erich, emigrated to Philadelphia, sponsored by Gottlieb Haegele.

These three related families, the Pfaehlers, the Haegeles and the Esenweins, would later play a prominent role in my father's life.

Berta was the next to leave, sponsored by a Methodist congregation in New York. After Berta's arrival in early October 1923, Frieda came up from Philadelphia to join her in New York. Both sisters readily found employment in the homes of wealthy, upper class German/Jewish families. At the time, German maids, as well as German cooks and *Kinderfräulein,* were in high demand. They were valued especially for their cleanliness, efficiency and strong work ethic.

Next was Theo, the first of the Fritz brothers to leave. During the winter months, Theo worked at the tannery in Backnang, commuting to and from work by bicycle. He was by all accounts a very handsome young man, exceptionally good-looking, and a real dandy. At the time when he left home (he had just turned twenty-seven), he had more hand-tailored suits than he could ever wear! (Later on, his Nebraskan wife, a practical woman, would cut up his suits and use the fabric for quilting material, since "he wouldn't need all those fancy suits anymore!")

Theo's sponsor was a wealthy widow who had emigrated to Nebraska years earlier and who was visiting relatives in Heutensbach in the summer of 1925. Frau Lanz took an immediate liking to Theo and was keen on having Theo marry her daughter, Tilly. Theo was also interested, and so he applied for an immigrant visa to the United States.

Many years later, when he was an old man, Theo could still recall the exact travel dates that marked his journey: Leaving Heutensbach on December 9, he traveled by train north to Bremerhaven where he boarded the steamship *America* on December 12, arriving in New York ten days later, on December 22. At Ellis Island he was met by his sister, Frieda, and they were able to spend some hours together. On December 23 he boarded a train heading west, and three days later, on December 26, 1925, the day after Christmas, he arrived at Holdrege, Nebraska, his final destination. Unfortunately, in the meantime, Tilly had married someone else!

Theo's first instinct, he later confided in me, was to turn around and go back home. His arrival in the land of his dreams was not quite as he had imagined it. But Frau Lanz had paid two hundred dollars for Theo's passage, and since Theo didn't have any money, he would first have to stay and repay Frau Lanz by farming one of her properties (half of a quarter-section, or eighty acres) for a year. Handsome young Theo soon became a hit with the local girls, and one of them in particular caught his eye – Miss Dora Meyer, daughter of August Meyer. One fine morning after church, young Dora invited Theo home for Sunday dinner to meet her folks...

Theo and Dora were married on New Year's Day 1927. They began their future married life together as tenants on a farm belonging to Dora's grandparents.

With Theo in the process of finalizing his plan to emigrate, Christian realized he would soon need someone to replace him in his newest venture: He was by then heavily involved in the brick-manufacturing business and had his own operation. He

Theo and Dora were married on New Year's Day 1927

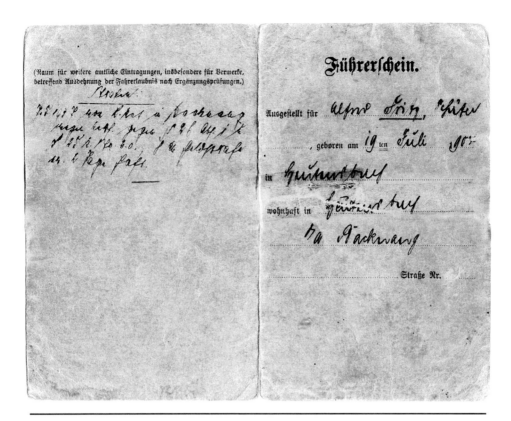

Drivers license (outer cover) – September 1925

Drivers License with photo I.D.

also wanted to expand into manufacturing roofing tiles. Thus, in the fall of 1925, after years of shepherding, Alfred was summoned home. He was needed in his father's business to drive truck (the horses having since been replaced by motorized vehicles).

Less than a year later, Alfred wrote to his brother in Nebraska asking if he couldn't find a sponsor for him as well.

What prompted Alfred to want to join his brother in Nebraska? He must have anticipated a bleak future for himself in Germany, and Theo's letters home sounded very promising. It must have been the same drama playing around in the heads of a lot of young men in those days. The villagers often spoke about those who had emigrated – about their luck as well as their misfortunes. Any letter from America, any news from abroad, would be strangely agitating, would stir their imaginations...

Alfred Fritz at the age of twenty-one

In his letters, Theo wrote that farm workers were in great demand in Nebraska, and that a farmhand could earn good money. Tired of slaving for his father, the thought of emigrating became a fixed idea that would not leave him in peace. It kept hammering in his brain. Emigration meant freedom, no matter what hardships would await him. And in moments of despair, the thought of leaving and going to America became the only weapon he could use against his father. It was the one possibility open to him – to turn his back on his *Heimat,* to leave his homeland forever.

CHAPTER 2

"Aller Anfang ist schwer."
-popular German saying

T HE IMMIGRATION ACT OF 1924 placed further restrictions on immigration to the United States by establishing a consular control system. Ellis Island would no longer be used as a clearing station. Instead, prospective immigrants now applied for their visas at American consulates in their countries of origin. The necessary paperwork was completed at the consulate, and a medical inspection was also conducted there.

In order to secure a visa, prospective immigrants had to present a large number of documents for inspection: Passport, birth certificate, marriage certificate, police certificate of good conduct, military record, and income statement. Furthermore, immigrants had to pay upfront for their passage, and once in the U.S., they were not permitted to become a burden on the public welfare. Thus, sponsorship had to be guaranteed.

Alfred's visa petition was processed through the American Consulate in Stuttgart.

Departing from Bremerhaven aboard the "President Roosevelt" on March 23, 1927, Alfred arrived in New York ten days

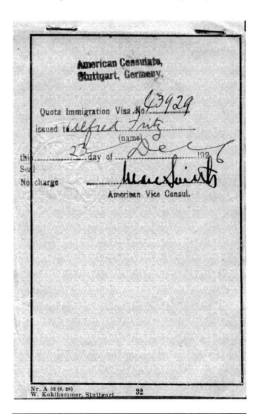

Immigrant permit (visa) dated December 23, 1926

later, on April 2, 1927, with $80 in his pocket, more than enough to buy a train ticket to Nebraska. The ship's manifest lists his occupation as *"Landarbeiter"*, or farm laborer, and his final destination as Smithfield, Nebraska.

So it was that Alfred arrived in Holdrege, Nebraska on April 5, 1927, a young man full of expectation, just three months shy of his 23rd birthday. Theo had paid his ship's passage, and Dora's parents had kindly agreed to be his sponsors.

Not long after Alfred had left home, his younger brother Karl had a major altercation with their father. The quarrel began over something quite trivial, but soon escalated. Christian was forever complaining about Karl's bicycle blocking the passageway leading from the hallway to the cow stable, and one day he exploded in rage, furiously hurling the offending bicycle out the front door and into the yard, then chasing after Karl and threatening him with bodily harm. With that, Karl decided he had finally had enough, and so he fled his home and moved in with married sister Emma in Cottenweiler. By day he bicycled to his job at the tannery in Backnang, and in the evening after work he secretly helped his sisters in the fields. Karl knew how desperately they needed his help; his four younger sisters (Elise, Johanna, Erika and Gretel) were now the only ones left on the farm.

Christian was indeed upset! He had lost his best workers! Rudolf now had his own start-up trucking and hauling business, Emma had married a young farmer in Cottenweiler, and all the other older children (Frieda, Berta, Hedwig, Theodor and Alfred) had gone to America!

It wasn't long before Karl decided to join his two older brothers in Nebraska. When Christian learned that Karl, too, was applying for a visa to emigrate, he was furious. He realized that he no longer had enough "manpower"; the only children left at home were girls – two of them still in school! Initially, he flatly refused to sign the parental consent form (Karl was still underage). In the end, however, he relented, angrily signed the visa form, and then threw his youngest son out of the house for good. Not one penny did Karl ever receive from his parents!

Karl was twenty years old when he left home. Sponsored by Theo and Dora, he arrived in Nebraska in early December. Thus, by year's end 1927, seven of the Fritz children were in America:

Theodor (Theo) was married to Dora Meyer in Nebraska. The young couple were tenant farmers on a farm belonging to Dora's grandparents.

Alfred and **Karl** were both working as 'hired men' in Nebraska.

Frieda and **Berta**, both formerly employed as *Kinderfräulein* in the homes of wealthy New Yorkers, had decided to exchange life in the large metropolis for rural life in Nebraska. Theo had recommended his sister Frieda to Paul Kleinknecht, a bachelor farmer, whom she married in March 1927. Berta would marry bachelor farmer Emil Heller in July of the following year.

Hedwig had married Gottlob Schwarz in March 1923 against her parents' wishes. Christian and Luise were dead set against their daughter marrying a mere tailor, the son of a *Tagelöhner*. They wanted Hedwig to "marry up" and they already had a well-to-do farmer for her in mind. But strong-willed Hedwig prevailed. Her audacity to marry the man she loved was a brave, almost revolutionary act.

Initially, Christian refused to give his consent, and Hedwig, still a minor (not yet twenty-one), could not marry without it. In vain did she attempt to persuade her parents that Gottlob Schwarz from neighboring Wattenweiler, a decorated war veteran and *Meisterschneider* (master tailor), was a suitable marriage partner. But Christian, then at the height of his business success, was in no mood to see his daughter marry beneath herself.

Hedwig, however, was every bit as strong-willed and stubborn as her father. The months went

Berta and Emil Heller (July 1928)

by, until one day Hedwig announced that she was pregnant. In order to avoid further gossip, and not wanting his grandchild to be born illegitimate, Christian finally gave his consent. In March, Hedwig and Gottlob hastily married, and daughter Almida was born three months later, in May 1923.

Hedwig's defiance resulted in lasting hostility. Christian never fully accepted his daughter's marriage to the tailor, and eventually the young couple moved to Ludwigsberg in order to get away. From there they emigrated to New York and were living in Brooklyn.

Elise left Germany a few weeks before Karl. The feisty young girl had already placed her name on the immigrant visa waiting list when she turned fourteen! She had had it with her father and wanted out of the farming life. She had a feeling that if she stayed, she would end up marrying a farmer and be trapped into a life of hard work and drudgery, working her fingers to the bone from dawn to dusk. Hedwig, in New York, had agreed to sponsor her. As she impatiently waited for her name to clear the list, Elise was nevertheless glad not to miss the wedding of her oldest brother.

When Elise announced to her father that she too was going to America, he glared at her incredulously, then silently shook her hand and handed her a ten-dollar bill (which she used aboard ship to get a haircut).

During the ocean crossing, by pure coincidence, she was assigned a berth in the same cabin as Frau Bitsch, the now destitute widow of her father's former business partner in Schorndorf.

Hedwig and Gottlob Schwarz with daughter Almida prior to emigrating to America in December 1926.

Wedding of Rudolf Wilhelm Fritz to Helene Schiefer (June 1927). Gretel (11) is standing at the far right. In the second row, from left, are Erika (13), Johanna (15) and Elise (17). Karl (19) is directly behind Johanna. Married sister Emma (26), dressed in black, is standing at the right rear window.

*Elise at her
confirmation (from
left: Helene Schiefer,
Luise, Erika and
Gretel, Rudolf, Elise,
Karl (behind Elise)
Johanna, Christian)*

Herr Bitsch had made the same mistake as her father – holding on to his share of the proceeds from the sale of the distillery until its value was totally lost in the inflation. Unable to cope with financial ruin, Herr Bitsch had committed suicide. His young widow, previously accustomed to a certain lifestyle, had been left entirely without means. Reduced to poverty, the poor woman was now on her way to America to find work as a housemaid.

Elise was only seventeen when she arrived in New York in mid-November 1927. She had never been anywhere outside her village before. Hedwig, her hair smartly bobbed, dressed in the latest fashion, wearing a fur coat and dark lipstick, was there to meet her little sister at the dock. But Elise did not recognize her. She had never seen anyone in her family dressed like that. Focused on Hedwig's ruby-red lips, she initially took her for a loose woman, a prostitute!

Elise stayed with Hedwig and family for a short while before going out into the wide world as an *"au pair"* for a Jewish family with two children. Although she spoke no English, the children taught her quite a bit. In-between jobs, she would move back in with Hedwig, who in the meantime had moved from Brooklyn to Ridgewood, Queens.

Just two years after arriving in America, and three weeks before the stock market crash of October 1929, Elise would marry Henry Frank Wagner, the handsome young man who lived with his parents across the street. Henry was in the business of buying, selling, and repairing printing presses and bookbinding machinery.

The Fritz children had arrived in America!

*   *   *

Elise and Henry were both only nineteen when they were married.

ALFRED ARRIVED in Nebraska in early April 1927, shortly after Frieda's wedding. Initially, he stayed with Theo and Dora before beginning work as a hired man on a farm five miles distant. On Saturday afternoons he met up with his brother and sister-in-law in town and then went home with them, staying overnight and spending Sundays with them.

In those days, folks took their weekly bath on Saturday morning, before going to town. Then everyone would drive to the nearest town in either their farm wagons or their Model T's ("Tin Lizzie's").

By the mid-1920s, most everyone already owned a car – a Model T Ford. Cost: $290 new. The average annual income for someone working in agriculture was only around $300, but Fred Hueftle, owner of the Eustis Mercantile (cars, machinery, hardware, home furnishings, etc.) made sure that all the young men coming from Germany would have a car, arranging for them to pay "in installments." The Model T was very durable. In fact, Henry Ford believed the Model T "was all the car a person would, or could, ever need." (The Model A was then introduced in 1927. An old-timer explained the difference between a Model T Ford and the Model A: The Model T was made with more wood and cloth; for example, it had wooden wheel spokes, whereas the Model A had more metal.)

Going to town was a weekly event everyone looked forward to. Farmers from miles around came to town with their families to shop, run errands and tend to business. It was a day-long ritual that filled the stores with people and jammed the town square with their farm wagons and Model T's that had brought them on journeys of an hour, two hours, or more. Farmers brought their containers of cream to the creamery and sold their butter, eggs, and even live chickens to the grocer in exchange for much needed cash in order to purchase the few things they needed. From the grocer, where items were sold in bulk in barrels or sacks, they purchased salt, sugar, flour, rice, coffee, tea, dried beans, potatoes, dried fruits, crackers, vinegar, oatmeal,

Model T Fords parked at the Eustis Community Fair in 1925

etc. At the mercantile, they purchased kerosene for lamps and lanterns, shoes and boots, ready-made work clothes (for the men), and sewing notions and dressmaking fabric sold by the yard as well as linen yardage for making sheets, tablecloths, and pillowcases.

While the women were busy with their purchases, the men folk would discuss crops and prices, rainfall and the weather. Saturday night was THE big night; for most folks it was the only time they got a chance to socialize. Occasionally (if you had money and could spare twenty-five cents) you would go to see a silent picture show on a Wednesday night, but Saturday was the big night in town.

On Sunday morning, everyone attended church, and often people went visiting on Sunday afternoons. But although Alfred spent Sundays with Theo and Dora, he would seldom go along with them to church or accompany them when they visited Dora's parents in the afternoon. He was a loner who avoided people and conversation. Once Karl arrived from Germany, Dora just couldn't get over the difference in their personalities. She was so relieved and delighted to discover that Karl, although also a man of few words, liked to laugh and even joke!

Alfred began work as a hired man for a Swedish immigrant farmer/blacksmith who had two sons. That first summer in Nebraska, he labored very hard, becoming familiar with a different style of farming than he had known back home in southwest Germany and learning especially about growing corn, which at that time was still an unfamiliar crop in Germany. In the short time he had been in Nebraska, he had already learned that corn was a mid-western farmer's most important crop. Without corn, you couldn't feed the livestock, and without the farm animals, you would have no milk, no eggs, no meat, and you'd have to pull the plow yourself! Corn, along with wheat, was also an important cash crop.

That fall, around the time of the first frost, the corn was ready for harvesting, which in those days was still done by hand. One chilly morning he watched as the farmer's sons added a couple of boards to a farm wagon, then hitched up a team of horses and headed for the cornfield. While the team of horses plodded slowly through the field, straddling a row of corn, the two men went down through the field, picking corn. Taking two rows at a time, they used a special peg to open the shucks, twisted the ears free of the stalk, and then tossed the ears into the wagon.

Throughout the year, a farmhand would receive regular wages; however, at corn-husking time, a hired worker would receive ten percent of whatever price the corn was selling for on the market. In other words, if corn was selling for eighty cents a bushel, a hired-out worker would receive eight cents for every bushel he harvested.

Now, Alfred had never husked corn before in his life. He had never even seen corn before coming to Nebraska! But when he saw that the farmer's sons, using a husking peg, could each husk up to eighty bushels in a single day (if the corn stalks were tall and stood close together), he was determined to do the same. It was hard work! You had to put in long days, and of course, in the beginning, try as he might, he could not keep up with the other men. But he tenaciously persisted, and after awhile he achieved his goal – working late into the evening, until it got too dark to see, and getting up before sunrise to begin all over again.

Alfred continued to be a loner and a stubborn fellow who had his difficulties relating to other people. Not long after he arrived, Eustis resident and former immigrant Karl Haegele spotted Alfred standing on a street corner in downtown Cozad. Karl Haegele couldn't quite trust his eyes! He thought he recognized Alfred, a former schoolmate whom he had not seen since boyhood. He at once approached Alfred, greeting him warmly and introducing himself. Alfred just stared back, stubbornly pretending not to know him. But Karl Haegele, not one to be put off that easily, persisted and eventually succeeded in eliciting a response. After all, as Alfred's former schoolmate, Karl Haegele not only knew everything about him, but "he was certain he knew a Fritz when he saw one!"

Alfred simply did not know how to behave around people, and he often came across as coarse, crude, and altogether impolite. Incapable of making small talk, he was unsociable and aloof. Later on, he and Karl, both bachelors, would often spend Sunday afternoons with Karl Haegele and his wife at their home in Eustis, playing cards. Alfred hardly ever spoke a word. Karl was just the opposite – always in a good mood, ready to laugh and joke. One time he had to be operated for appendicitis. After the procedure, the doctor cautioned him to take it easy for a while and not do any heavy lifting. But Alfred did not follow the doctor's advice, and while loading manure onto a wagon his incision tore open and had to be re-stitched. But a couple of days later, he was back out loading manure. He was just too stubborn to listen to anyone.

But of course he had to work! He worked day and night, whenever and wherever hired help was needed – plowing and sowing, harvesting with the threshing crews, husking corn, and all the while saving every penny in order to get ahead, so that he could advance from hired man to tenant farmer. And his hard work paid off. Already by Christmas of the first year he had paid off his debt to his brother, and by the spring of 1930, Alfred had sufficient savings to begin farming on his own.

He found a farm for rent "on the Valley", midway between Eustis and Cozad. The fact that he could advance from hired hand to tenant farmer in just three years was nothing less than amazing – clear proof of just how hard-working and industrious he was.

A tenant farmer in the late 1920s and early 1930s had to supply his own farm implements as well as the horses that were needed to farm the land. From six to eight draft horses were needed so that you could change off, plus their work harnesses.

Box wagon filled with husked corn – Emil Heller (left) with hired man, Cozad, Nebraska, ca. 1932.

The main cash crops grown were corn and wheat, but oats and hay were also grown. A farmer plowed, disked, harrowed, sowed, cultivated and harvested. To accomplish that, he needed a plow (called a "lister" which preserved the sod), a disc-harrow, a corn planter, a grain drill for planting wheat and oats, a cultivator, a mower, a grain binder; hay racks, and, of course, a box wagon.

A tenant farmer would also have to keep some livestock – a few cows, hogs and chickens – to provide him with milk, eggs and meat. Much needed spending money came from the sale of calves and hogs, as well as from the eggs, cream and butter that he might sell in town.

There were always tenant farms available IF you could manage to provide your own equipment. In fact, during the 1920s, almost half the farmers in Nebraska were tenants who did not own their land. This was due in large part to the fact that so many farmers had over-extended themselves during World War I and later had either been forced into foreclosure or were deeply in debt.

During World War I, the federal government had subsidized farms and paid absurdly high prices for wheat and corn, encouraging farmers to buy more land and to produce more food. Many farmers had gone head over heels into debt in order to purchase more land, in the expectation that prices would remain high. But as soon as the war ended, the federal government stopped its policies to aid farmers. Where, during the war, the government had paid an unheard of $2 a bushel for wheat, by 1920 wheat prices had fallen to as low as 67 cents a bushel. As farm prices tumbled, the same farmers fell into debt and were stuck with mortgages they could not repay. That is why there were so many "deserted" farms available for tenant farming.

Alfred, had now been in Nebraska for four years, and for the last year or so he had lived a very lonely existence indeed as a bachelor tenant farmer. As such he would have had a very difficult life, having to look after himself, to do his own food preparation, washing, mending, as well as tending to the livestock and caring for the horses – doing all the work by himself. It seems unlikely that a man could go on managing for himself for any length of time.

Six-horse team hitched to a disc-harrow – Gotlob Heller, ca. 1932

Sure, he was resourceful, plus the many years he had lived as a shepherd in Germany had taught him how to withstand loneliness and deprivation. But running a farm alone was just too much, no matter how competent. What Alfred especially needed was a cook. How he would look forward to those times when he would be helping out on another farm and be served a delicious, home-cooked meal!

No, loneliness was not Alfred's problem. He was used to being alone. What he needed was someone to look after him, to cook for him, to be supportive of him, to bear him children. He needed a wife, so that together they could make a go at farming. That was his dream and his ultimate goal – to own his own farm.

At the age of twenty-seven, just four years after arriving in Nebraska, he was ready to take a wife.

Alfred Fritz as a young bachelor tenant farmer in Nebraska (1928).

CHAPTER 3

Amerika liegt ja gleich um die Ecke!
[America is just around the corner!]

M Y MOTHER was born in 1906 in Sittensen, a small town located in the North German Lowland (between the Weser and Elbe rivers) in the upper part of what is now the state of Niedersachsen. Niedersachsen (*Nieder* means "low-lying" in a geographical sense) is bordered by the North Sea to the north and the Netherlands to the west. Sittensen lies mid-way between the two great port cities of Hamburg and Bremen, with Hamburg located approximately 70 kilometers to the northeast and Bremen equally distant to the west.

Today, the town of Sittensen has over 5,500 inhabitants, but back then, Sittensen was a small farming community with a population less than 800. Sittensen is where my mother's roots lie. For centuries, her ancestors were at home in the neighboring rural hamlets to the west and northwest of town. We are able to trace them back to the time of the Thirty Years' War (1618-1648) and even earlier. Thus, the area's history and topography sets the background for understanding their lives.

Historically, the inhabitants of this low-lying region of Germany are linked by a common ancient Saxon origin and by the use of the Low German language known as *Plattdüütsch*, a dialect that has more in common with other Germanic languages (Dutch, Swedish and English) than with Standard German. When my mother first arrived in America, some English words would have sounded quite familiar to her, such as *lütt* for little (German has *klein*), *wief* for wife (German has *Frau*) or *süük* for sick (German has *krank*).

The Saxons, who inhabited the northern Lowlands for thousands of years, were first conquered and then Christianized by the Frankish emperor Charlemagne (*Karl der Große*) in 804 AD. Over the centuries that followed, the region would be invaded, occupied, and consequently influenced by several different nationalities. In the Middle

Ages, Sittensen belonged to the Prince-Archbishopric of Bremen (*Erzstift Bremen*), an ecclesiastical state within the Holy Roman Empire, established in 1180. During this time, Dutch settlers, skilled canal builders, came to build dikes to control the flooding and to drain and reclaim the marshland north of the Elbe. The land was recovered in stages, with the area first completed designated "das alte Land" as opposed to the new land more recently drained. "Altes Land" still bears the same name today, and city dwellers from Hamburg travel there on weekends to enjoy the beauty of the countryside.

In 1638, during the Thirty Years' War, the Northern Lowlands came under the rule of Sweden. The Prince-Archbishopric was then transformed into the Duchy of Bremen, a secular monarchy ruled in personal union with the Swedish crown. The Swedes remained in control for over half a century, until 1712, when the area was briefly occupied by Denmark. In 1715 the Danes handed the Duchy over to the House of Hanover. The Duchy then came under the jurisdiction of the Hanoverian Crown. The Prince-Elector (*Kurfürst*) of Hanover, Georg Ludwig, had the previous year become heir to the British throne as the first monarch of the House of Hanover, becoming King George I of England. In other words, the Prince-Elector of Hanover was simultaneously the King of England! For the next 123 years, the House of Hanover was the family seat of the kings of Great Britain.

While researching our northern German ancestry, it seemed odd at first glance to find early 19th century parish registries listing one ancestor as having been born in the Kingdom of France, while another is listed as having been born in the Kingdom of Hanover. Born in the Kingdom of France? Born in the Kingdom of Hanover? The explanation is quite simple: 1803 to 1814 was the time of Napoleonic Rule. At various times during this period, French forces occupied the Electorate of Hanover, and in 1810 it was even annexed by France. Then, following Napoleon's defeat in 1814, the Congress of Vienna upgraded the Electorate of Hanover to an independent kingdom – the Kingdom of Hanover. Its Prince-Elector, George III of Great Britain, became King of Hanover. This, then, explains why several of my mother's maternal great-grandparents, born during Napoleon's occupation, were born subjects of the King of France, while a generation later, her grandparents were born subjects of the King of Hanover.

Since the succession laws in Hanover prevented a female inheriting the title, the personal union between the House of Hanover and Great Britain, in which the British monarch was simultaneously the King of Hanover, ended in 1837 on the accession of Queen Victoria. Queen Victoria's uncle then inherited the throne of Hanover, thus ending the 123-year joint rule of Hanover and Great Britain. The Kingdom of Hanover itself came to an end in 1866 when it was annexed by the much stronger nation of Prussia. The Kingdom then became the Prussian Province of Hanover. All this greatly upset the citizens of the former Kingdom, who did not feel kindly toward the war-like Prussians. They much preferred to identify themselves as Hanoverians, even well after German unification in 1871 and the founding of the German empire, when the King of Prussia, Wilhelm I, became the German Kaiser.

This brings us right up to the time when my mother's parents were born – in 1871 and 1872, respectively. Although both were born subjects of the German Kaiser, it would take many decades before they would think of themselves as "Germans" rather than as Hanoverians, or to think of Germany as a single nation in the modern sense.

Lying almost at sea level, the northern Lowlands, stretching from the Dutch border through to Hamburg, are crisscrossed by many small, peaceful rivers that flow into each other, eventually becoming navigable and draining into the North Sea and the Atlantic – the Weser River in Bremen and the Elbe River in Hamburg. One small river, the Oste, a tributary of the Elbe, flows westward through the southern end of Sittensen, just a short walk from my mother's childhood home. She would have walked across the narrow bridge over the Oste each day on her way to school.

Of course, at that point, so close to its source, the Oste is more a creek than a river – only about five meters wide, and shallow. But just forty kilometers to the northwest, after Bremervörde, it is already deep enough and wide enough to be navigable.

The landscape is flat, flat, flat! Even the slightest rise or elevation is rare. And since the terrain is invariably flat, chances are that my mother, assuming she (like most people in those days) never travelled any further than a 20-mile radius from home, had never seen a hill, much less a mountain!

When my mother was a child, the countryside surrounding Sittensen was scattered with moors, and a vast brown heath stretched from the north right down to the edge of town. The farms and villages dotting the landscape were like islands surrounded by heath *(Heide)* and boggy moors.

Today, the large heath north of town is long gone, converted into agricultural use, but the moors remain. In fact, up until the 1960's, residents were still digging peat from the nearby bogs which they, like their ancestors, used for fuel, in place of wood or coal.

Just southeast of Sittensen lies a huge expanse of moorland, the Tiste Bauernmoor, which until recently was used for industrial peat-cutting. The moor was drained to allow for large-scale mechanical peat extraction, and an industrial plant then converted the peaty humus into garden compost, bales of which were shipped as far as the United States. Today, however, in keeping with Germany's environmental consciousness, the Tiste Bauernmoor has been re-naturalized, the drains previously dug blocked in order to rehabilitate the moor and return it to its waterlogged state. In 2002, the Tiste Bauernmoor was declared a nature preserve, a breeding ground and resting place for many species of migratory birds, including cranes. Nature lovers now come from far and wide to enjoy the flight of migrating cranes as well as the beauty of the restored moor.

Tourists also enjoy visiting the Lüneburger Heide, a vast stretch of heath to the south of Sittensen which is now a national park and wildlife preserve. It is especially nice to visit the heath when the purple heather is in bloom.

Sittensen was what is known as a *Straßendorf*, a town built around one main street. Houses and small shops lined both sides of the single main street, with strips of farmland extending out behind.

Sittensen was also a *Kirchdorf*, large enough to support its own church. Sittensen had been Lutheran since the time of the Reformation. On Sundays, people from the surrounding farms and villages came on foot, in horse drawn carts and on farm wagons to attend Lutheran church services there.

Built on a rounded mound above the Oste, the church in Sittensen is very old, its origins dating back to the time of Charlemagne. It is said that the Emperor himself ordered that a small chapel be built beside the river, on an ancient Saxon cult site, a sacred tribal gathering place. The present church, named after Charlemagne's patron saint, Sankt Dionysius, was constructed between 1606 and 1613, financed by the Schultes, a wealthy local aristocratic family with large landholdings. A steeple was added in 1679.

In 1906, the year of my mother's birth, the townspeople of Sittensen held a festival commemorating their church's 300th anniversary! Two other significant events in the church's history also occurred within a few years of my mother's birth. A plaque at the entrance reads:

797 A.D.	Erected by decree of Charlemagne
1606-1613	Newly constructed
1898	Addition of south wing
1907	Steeple destroyed by fire
1909	Steeple rebuilt

Being a *Kirchdorf*, Sittensen was the center of social and economic life. Eleven outlying villages also belonged to the St. Dionysius parish, and the people in these villages came to Sittensen to attend church, to be baptized, confirmed, married, and buried. Some came great distances, so they often combined attending church on Sunday with running errands, both before and after the service.

In fact, Sittensen became such a thriving economic hub, known for the goods and services it could provide, that even people from more distant villages – up to a 15-kilometer radius – would come to shop and to conduct business. The town's favorable location, at the intersection of two main roads, one leading north-south and the other east-west, made all the difference. Since goods in those days were still transported by horse and wagon (picked up from the nearest railway station and then transported on mostly unpaved roads), being at the intersection of commerce, with ready access to goods, was significant to the town's growth.

St.-Dionysius-Kirche zu Sittensen

St. Dionysius Kirche, Sittensen

Nowadays, the Autobahn, constructed in 1937, connects Sittensen with Hamburg and Bremen, and it takes less than an hour by car to reach either city. But when my mother was a child, a trip to Hamburg or Bremen would have taken more than a day by horse and wagon. Most likely she made the trip only once – on her way to America.

My mother's father, Jacob Bredehöft, was a *Schmied,* or blacksmith, by trade. (The English word "smith" comes from the German *"Schmied"*.) A blacksmith was an important member of the community; his skill was a much valued and needed one, much like a mechanic today, but even more so.

Not many men could or would take up the job of blacksmithing. Blacksmith's work required physical strength and endurance; it was not easy to hammer a piece of red hot iron into shape or to manage large and heavy iron pieces, such as wagon axles or wheel rims, or to shoe sometimes unruly horses.

Local farmers depended on the blacksmith for their survival, as he kept their horses and farm tools in quality condition, but blacksmiths were also needed for the horse-based commerce from far away. In fact, in the early decades of the 20th century, there was enough work to keep four blacksmiths busy: My grandfather, Jacob Bredehöft was known as "Jacob-Schmied." Just up the street was another blacksmith known as "Wahlers-Schmied." There was also a "Voss-Schmied," and directly across from the old, water-powered grain mill was "Meyer-Schmied."

My grandfather's blacksmith shop was located at the "upper" edge of the marketplace, right at the curve where the main street branches off, heading west towards Zeven. Since, in an otherwise flat landscape, even the slightest elevation was referred to as a *"Berg"* (hill or mountain), and since the street leading north through town, away from the river, was on a slight incline, my grandfather, Jacob-Schmied as he was known, was often referred to as "Jacob-Schmied *auf dem Berg"* since his smithy was located "atop the hill!"

The reason why all four blacksmiths were located so close to each other was to be within walking distance of the mill. When farmers brought their grain to the mill to have it ground into flour, they usually had to anticipate a wait, so during that time they would take care of other errands. Often they would stop by a smithy to have their horses shod, a broken wagon wheel mended, or they would bring in some other tool or piece of machinery whose metal part needed to be repaired. There was no shortage of work.

My aunt once explained to me how my grandfather worked hand in hand with the *Stellmacher* (cartwright). The *Stellmacher,* who made and repaired wagons, carts and wheels, would bring the finished wooden parts to my grandfather who would then affix the corresponding metal reinforcements to the wood.

Although shoeing horses was just a part of a blacksmith's work, it seems that horseshoeing made up the greater part of Jacob Bredehöft's day. People preferred bringing their horses to him, and he soon gained a reputation for being the best smithy in town for shoeing horses.

Sittensen was home to many skilled craftsmen. You could choose between four *Schuhmacher* (works with leather) to repair your worn shoes or measure you for a new pair. You could have an article of furniture made or repaired (a bedstead, chest, kitchen cabinet, a table and chairs) by one of two *Tischler*. You might want to pick up a loaf of freshly baked bread from the *Bäcker*. A man could replace his old work jacket, be fitted for a new suit of clothes, or a young man be fitted for his first communion suit by going to a *Schneider* (Sittensen had three tailors!). Ladies had their dresses made and altered by a *Schneiderin*. There were also two carpenters *(Zimmermann)* in town, a bicycle maker *(Fahrradmacher)*, and a *Sattler* who made and repaired harnesses. At the *Postamt* you could post a letter or send a telegram. If you were ill, you would consult Dr. Ludewig, the town's doctor, who also made house calls, or you could pick up a remedy from the *Apotheker.*

Since roads were largely unpaved, getting around was not easy; a trip into town by horse and farm wagon could mean a journey of an hour, two hours, or more, so there were four taverns or inns with livery stables in town where people could rest and take some refreshment before their return trip home, as well as have their horses fed and looked after.

Sittensen had four general merchandise shops, *Gemischtwarenläden* – small mom-and-pop stores that sold everything from foodstuffs to household and hardware items. Herr Wilhelm Burgdorf, who lived just around the corner from the Bredehöfts, operated just such a *Gemischtwarenladen* out of the front room of his house. In floor-to-ceiling shelves on one side he sold dress material (ready-made dresses were not yet available), sewing supplies, linen goods, ribbons and notions, and any other items you could think of that one might need for daily household use – from matches to mousetraps. On the other side were grocery staples – pickled herring and *Sauerkraut* in barrels, tea and coffee, sugar, salt, flour and other bulk items in bins. Often the Bredehöft children had to run and purchase some last-minute item for their mother, and then Herr Burgdorf might give them a piece of candy!

The world into which my mother was born is often referred to as Germany's Golden Age. The Kaiser's portrait hung at the front of her classroom, next to that of Chancellor Otto von Bismarck, the great statesman responsible for Germany's unification in 1871. It was a time of peace and prosperity and of great promise for the future of mankind, with all sorts of scientific inventions and advancements being talked about. The German people would later look back on this era full of longing and nostalgia, as a time when all was right with the world, the Kaiser was still on the throne, and everything was as it should be.

The *Kaiserzeit* was a time of huge economic growth as well, and the economic boom at the turn of the 20th century was felt even in rural Sittensen. New industrial centers brought rapid population growth to Hamburg and Bremen, which in turn lead to increased demand for meat, butter, grain, potatoes and other farm products. New chemical fertilizers made it possible to open up the surrounding heath to cultivation, which in turn meant that local farmers were not only able to raise sufficient food to meet their own needs, but now had surplus to sell, via the newly constructed railroads, to the growing urban centers. With the local economy now flourishing, more and more skilled craftsmen, like Jacob Bredehöft, came to town and established businesses all up and down the main street. When word spread that the railroad was coming to Sittensen, the town began to expand northwards, shifting away from the old town center, towards where the railway station would be located. In 1917, the railway line to Sittensen was completed and lots of commercial enterprises took hold around the train station. The southern edge of town, however, with the church, the marketplace, and the old watermill (built alongside the Oste and dating from the 16th century) was the historical core.

Sittensen's rapid development created a need for new housing. Until the beginning of the 20th century, most of the houses were of *Fachwerk*, or half-timbered construction. But after a brick-making business started up just outside of town, more "modern," brick homes were built. By 1915, there were over a hundred houses in town, and Sittensen had grown to a population of over 900.

Social change, however, was slow in coming. In tradition-bound German society, the social class into which you were born still very much determined your future life, including your choice of future mate, since love seldom crossed the great divide of social class. Just as nobility married befitting their rank and station in life, so too were professionals, farmers, tradesmen and laborers also expected to marry according to their social status. There was nothing unusual, then, about my grandfather's choice of wife: As a skilled craftsman, Jacob Bredehöft proposed marriage to Meta Adelheid Bartels, a cooper's daughter from Zeven, the next town over.

But Meta Bartels herself **was** unusual – a single woman in her late twenties, who, at a young age, had left home to make her way in the world. Even her children later on would sense that she was special, was "different" from the other mothers, because she had lived in America! Indeed, Meta Bartels had spent thirteen years living abroad, quite independently, and since she had seen something of the world, we can assume that she was more knowledgeable and more open-minded than someone who had never been away. It was during the "Great Emigration," the boom period for German immigration in the 1880s, when Meta Bartels and three of her siblings had emigrated to New York to make a new life for themselves. Only Meta had returned….

In the evening, when it was time for her children to go to bed, and after Meta had listened to their prayers, she would sometimes tell them about America.

"Mama, vertell uns doch wat von Ameriko," they would plead as she tucked them into the cozy warmth of their featherbed.

Their mother, who was strict and no-nonsense, but loving and nurturing as well, would insist that there was nothing new to tell, and besides, it was *"höchste Tied"* (high time) that they were asleep! *"Wat wit ji schon woa von Ameriko hürn? Dat ward nun ober Tiet, dat je schlopt!"*

Usually, however, she would relent. The Bredehöft children enjoyed listening to their mother describe the splendid surroundings in New York where she had once been a house cook in charge of running a large kitchen in a city mansion more grand than anyone in Sittensen could ever imagine, a huge house with a grand staircase and many rooms, both upstairs and down, each with its own fireplace! How, in the evening, the chandeliers were lit in the dining room, and she would have prepared the most delicious dishes for the elegant guests....

Sometimes she would tell them about her sister Anna in New York, and Anna's children, their cousins, the twins Otto and Annie, and their uncle, Anna's husband, Otto Schmiemann, who was a very kind man. Their uncle did not work close to home like their father, but left early each morning to make a living painting and wallpapering people's homes and offices.

Occasionally, she would describe how the less fortunate families lived in the city, which was how her siblings and their young families had started out– not in nice, comfortable homes like theirs, but in dark, overcrowded tenement housing, cramped together, one on top of the other, like rabbits in their hutches.

Other times she would describe the vast city itself – the tall buildings, the busy streets below so crowded with carriages and wagons and horse-drawn streetcars and trolleys that you could hardly cross from one side to the other, or the noisy elevated trains that ran on tracks high above the city streets…

Soon the children would be fast asleep. Holding the kerosene lamp, Meta left the room, quietly closing the door behind her.

* * *

EARLY NOVEMBER 1901. In spite of the chill, a lone female passenger was pacing back and forth on the lower deck of a steamer bound from New York to Bremen. Apparently lost in thought, she paused only occasionally to wrap her heavy woolen shawl more securely about her head and shoulders to ward off the cold, wet ocean air. The unaccompanied young woman, Fräulein Meta Bartels, was returning to Zeven, the hometown in northern Germany, which she had left thirteen years earlier, presumably never to return.

Midway across the Atlantic, thirty-year-old Meta, her heart heavy with sadness, was still trying to come to grips with recent distressing family events, trying to envision a future life away from New York, while simultaneously struggling to make sense of the resultant conflicting feelings and emotions: sorrow, a profound sense of loss, intermingled with feelings of resentment and regret. And yet, – and this is what was so troubling – an odd sense of anticipation as well.

Just a few weeks earlier, her usual workaday life had been abruptly disrupted by the arrival of a letter from home. *"Komm Heim!"* her brother, Ernst, had written, ordering her to come home at once. Ernst's young wife had died suddenly in late September, and he was summoning Meta home to take care of his three small children, now motherless, the youngest but an infant. Although Meta had never even met her brother's wife, Katharina (or Trina as she was called), the two had corresponded frequently, her sister-in-law's letters filled with wonderfully outdated news from home. It was Trina who had informed her of the sudden illness and passing of her mother less than a year ago. Such warm words of comfort her sister-in-law had written to her! And now poor Trina, too, was dead. Such sad, terrible news! To die so young! How could she, Meta, hope to fill the awful vacuum left by her sister-in-law's untimely death? How could she take the place of the children's mother?

Not once did it occur to Meta to question her eldest brother's directive. *Er gab das Kommando!* He gave the orders, and it was her place to obey. Obedience took precedence over all other considerations; defying a parent would have been totally unacceptable. Meta, a product of her time and culture, would follow the values she had been taught as a child, to respect her elders and to obey. If your father, or in this case your eldest brother, said to come home, you went home!

So Meta had left her position in the household of the Upper East Side brownstone, reluctantly saying goodbye to the family of the *Brauerfürst*, the wealthy beer baron with whom she had been *"in Stellung"* since coming to New York – initially as a lowly scullery maid, lighting and tending the fires and scouring the copper pots and pans. In the kitchen, however, the young immigrant girl's interest in food preparation had not gone unnoticed. The elderly German cook, recognizing her talent, had taken her under her wing, grooming her to be her assistant. When the old woman retired, Meta was subsequently promoted to cook.

No, Meta was not thrilled at the idea of returning to Germany. Although her workload was demanding, her free time limited to just one afternoon and one evening per week, Meta was rightfully proud of what she had achieved. From her cook's wages she had diligently put money aside towards her dowry. Naturally, she had pictured herself eventually married and living in America the rest of her life.

She would especially miss her sister, Anna! There was no one to whom she was closer than to her married sister. She had followed Anna to New York in the 1880's, when she and three of her siblings had gone to America. So many young people had left Germany during that time…

Born in Zeven on July 14, 1871, Meta Bartels had spent the first sixteen years of her life in that small northern town where her father, Hinrich Bartels, was a *Küpermeister* (master cooper) by trade.

Coopers, skilled cask and barrel-makers, were highly valued, and theirs was a relatively profitable trade. In fact, Hinrich Bartels had one of the busiest occupations in town. Wooden barrels were the main containers of the day, and life without them would have been difficult to imagine. Barrels came in all sizes and were used to store and ship all sorts of goods, foods and liquids. Wine, of course, was stored in wooden casks, and brewers also stored beer in wooden beer kegs. Flours and grains were stored in barrels. Butter was stored and transported in butter kegs; fragile items like eggs, packed among layers of straw, were stored in barrels; sauerkraut (a diet staple) was fermented and stored in barrels, cider was fermented in wooden casks, fish (herring) and meat were dried and salted, then stored and transported in barrels. In fact, most any item that could be stored for a length of time was stored in a wooden barrel.

As a young man, Hinrich Bartels had apprenticed with his stepfather, Ernst Sievers, *Küpermeister* in Harsefeld. Thanks to this kindly man, who had treated him like a son, Hinrich had learned a skilled trade.

Normally, a young man would have to pay someone to teach him. His parents (if they could afford it!) would sign a contract binding him to a *"Meister"* for a set amount of time – from three to five years. During this apprenticeship period, the young man would learn from the Meister, but he would also have to perform all types of unrelated, often menial work as well, not receiving anything but room and board (a cot and three meals) in return. Upon successful completion of his apprenticeship, he would be promoted to journeyman. Then, like the journeymen of every trade, he would "hit the road", go on an obligatory *Wanderschaft* – a three-year journey to find work and develop his skills, walking from town to town, looking for work in different shops and under different masters, before settling down.

Once a journeyman reached the age of twenty-five, he could advance to a master by taking an examination, the so-called *"Meisterprüfung"*, which included submitting a "masterpiece" to qualify as a master craftsman. Becoming a *Meister* would then allow him to train apprentices and open a shop of his own. Many journeymen, however, did not have the means to set up shop. They would continue working for a *Meister*, usually for the rest of their lives.

In 1862, after Hinrich Bartels earned his master's certificate, he married Metta Viebrock (1838-1901), whose father, Conrad Viebrock (1796-1884), a *Halbhöfner*, also served as *Gemeindediener* (parish clerk), assisting the chief magistrate. Conrad Viebrock's father, Christian Viebrock (1766-1833), also a *Halbhöfner*, had served as a *Kirchenvorsteher* (church elder), a position of considerable respect The Viebrocks thus represent the "academic" line in my mother's ancestral tree; their descendants would later become teachers, and one even a university professor.

Hinrich and Metta Bartels went on to have seven children, six of whom survived infancy: <u>Ernst</u> Conrad Johann (1863-1938) eldest son and heir; <u>Catharina</u> Anna (born 1864); <u>Hinrich</u> August (1867-1950); <u>Anna</u> Catharina (1869-1940), <u>Meta</u> Adelheit (1871-1926), and lastly <u>Johann</u> Christian, a latecomer born twelve years later, in 1883.

Hinrich Bartels was conceivably better off than some of the other skilled craftsmen in Zeven, prosperous enough to keep horses, since a team and wagon for the transport of barrels would have been essential in his business. We know that he eventually came into ownership of several acres of land, along with his barrel-making workshop and the large residence adjacent thereto, the fine house at Nr. 14 which the Hinrich Bartels family called home.

A rare portrait of the Hinrich Bartels family of Zeven, dated 1876. Ernst, eldest son and heir, is positioned to the right of his father, his hand placed on his father's shoulder. Hinrich and Catharina are standing on a raised platform in back. Anna is on the right, and five-year-old Meta, then the youngest, is in front. [Johann was born eight years after this portrait was made.] Having a portrait taken was a rare luxury, and in order to get clear images, people had to keep still, which helps to explain why the family members appear posed – stiff and unsmiling. But take a closer look, and perhaps the 19th century won't feel quite so distant.

ALTHOUGH OUR ANCESTORS in northern Germany all were farmers and agrarians, they would not have been referred to as *Bauern*. The term *"Bauer"* may have denoted the occupation of "farmer" elsewhere in Germany, but in northern Germany, where land holdings were substantially larger, the term was rarely used, as it was not adequately representative. Instead, there were different designations for men who farmed. Just as a skilled craftsman was identified by his occupation or line of work (blacksmith, cooper, etc.), so too were those men who worked the land given various designations which served to denote the size of their land holdings, while simultaneously indicating their standing in society, as follows:

Hausmann or **Baumann,** later **Vollhöfner** (mid-19th century) was the designation given to a landholder of the highest status, the household head of a very large estate, from 75 to 100 acres in size. He relied on hired labor and farmed with four to five horses.

The system of land ownership and management dated back centuries, to the time of the Middle Ages, when ownership of the land was in the hands of either the nobility or the church (ecclesiastical property). Noble lords (landlords) owned the land and the soil, but "let" their property to tenant occupants. Gradually, a tenant occupant would come to view the leased property he "administered" as his own, which indeed it was, so long as he continued to meet his obligations – an annual rent (*Zins*) and delivery of a set amount of goods, usually in the form of grain, along with other obligatory services to the lord.

The law governing leasing was known as *Meierrecht* (Meier Law). Unlike today, where a landlord and a tenant sign a contract for a fixed number of years, under *Meierrecht*, all "let" property was hereditary in nature and the *Meier*, the farm's tenant occupant, could pass it down to his heir apparent (customarily to the eldest son). The tenant had a hereditary right to the use, and the landlord a hereditary right to be paid for the use. Once a land-lease was signed between the landlord and the tenant, it could not be altered, and as long as a property stayed within the same family, the lease, including the rent obligations, remained the same. Both the landlord and the tenant had to abide by the terms of use. For example, a tenant occupant could not be removed unless he committed some gross impropriety (unfit to farm, untrustworthy, insane) or unless he did not meet his rent obligations. In turn, he could not put his leased property up for auction or trade it. Neither could two properties be joined through marriage (meaning the heir or heiress of one estate could not marry the heir or heiress of another estate). If a tenant died without an heir, the property reverted back to the landlord.

Meierrecht remained in effect until the Agrarian Reforms of the 1840s when tenant occupants were (at last!) given the opportunity to claim full property rights; to "own" the land that some families had administered for generations. A tenant occupant could then acquire legal title by paying twenty-five years' worth of rent in advance. Of course, many could not afford to do so, and thus were forced to abandon their holdings.

Halbhöfner, Viertelhöfner, etc. These were tenant occupants or (after the 1840's) owners of lesser status, their land holdings had at one time or another been reduced to one-half or one-quarter of their original size, or even less. The owner/occupant of half of a full-size estate was referred to as *1/2 Höfner (Halbhöfner),* the owner/occupant of a quarter of a full-size estate as *1/4 Höfner (Viertelhöfner),* and so forth. A *Halbhöfner* had approximately 50 acres of land and thus farmed with fewer horses.

Knechte und Mägde. Farming back then was very labor intensive, so *Knechte* and *Mägde,* male and female farmhands/servants, usually unmarried, were hired to help with the work. Large estates could have as many as ten full-time servants! Needless to say, *Knechte* and *Mägde* were at the very bottom of the social scale.

For centuries, the North German farmer and his family, along with his *Knechte* and *Mägde* and his livestock, all were housed together in a type of farmhouse found mainly in the Northern Lowlands and known as the "Low German Hall House" or *Niederdeutsches Hallenhaus,* a style dating back to the Middle Ages and which combines living quarters, stalls, and hay and grain storage – all under one roof. It is built as a large hall, with the livestock at one end and the family's living accommodations in a smaller area at the opposite end.

The Low German Hall House was a timber-framed, elongated structure with a vast slanting roof, thatched with reed, which swept down low on two sides. A great rounded door at the stable end allowed carts to drive in and opened into a large central hall known as the "*Diele*". With its tamped clay floor, the *Diele* was the working area of the farmhouse. It was here that the harvest was gathered before being stored in the hayloft above. It also provided protection from the weather for activities such as the breaking of flax, the spinning of textiles or the threshing of grain. Celebrations, too, like weddings and confirmations, were held in the *Diele*.

To both sides of the *Diele* were the half-open stalls or stables of the cattle and horses, as well as the bed chambers for the maids and farmhands. Poultry was kept near the entrance way, but pigs were not allowed inside. They were banished to a separate shed outside the building due to their smell.

At the far end of the hall, at the back of the farmhouse, the *Diele* opened out to a small open kitchen and eating area, the so-called *Flett,* or living quarters, with a central open hearth around which meals were cooked and eaten. Originally there was no cookstove, only the open hearth. The hearth was not like a fireplace in other regions, since it didn't have a chimney. Without a chimney, the smoke from the fire in the open hearth circled around overhead, eventually finding its way upwards where it "smoked" the hams and sausages hanging from the hayloft before eventually escaping through a hole in the top corner of the roof. The biting smoke of the hearth fire, mixed with the smell of the animals, permeated the house.

As there was no dividing wall between the *Flett* and the *Diele*, you might say that the family members, their servants and their livestock all lived in one large room together. The hearth fire, plus the warmth of the animals, was the only source of heat, and since the family's living quarters were entirely open to the stalls and the hayloft above, the house was quite cold in winter – just a few degrees warmer than the outside temperature.

In the evening the family and their servants sat around the open hearth in the center of the *Flett*. At night, family members retired to a small separate area at the rear of the *Flett*, where they slept – usually four to a bed, on straw mattresses covered with a cloth and a thick, heavy featherbed for their cover – in cupboard-like alcove beds, with a sliding door in front. The male and female servants slept in the *Diele*, in a space under the eaves of the low-hanging roof, next to the livestock.

For centuries, having everything under one roof was considered an advantage, but by the end of the 19th century, the *Hallenhaus* had become outmoded and was no longer being built. The living quarters were considered too small for "modern" needs, plus farmers needed more room for additional livestock and more modern buildings to store their crops and farm machinery. Also, rising standards of living meant that the smells, breath and manure from the animals were increasingly viewed as unhygienic.

Typical Niederdeutsches Hallenhaus

Our ancestors most certainly lived in this type of farmhouse, and my mother, too, would have been very familiar with the *Hallenhaus*, since many were still in use, standing alongside the more modern houses in town, their elongated structures positioned sideways alongside the street.

Nowadays, many of the traditional thatched Low German farmhouses have been lovingly restored; others have been converted into museums, such as the *Heimathaus* (heritage house and museum) in Sittensen, a large, reconstructed thatched-roof *Hallenhaus* located near the old water mill. If you travel through northern Germany today, you will notice that the style of this type of farmhouse still characterizes the appearance of many north German towns and villages.

Köthner or **Kötner**. A *Köthner*, or cottager, was a smallholder of lower status. Since only the eldest son could inherit, a younger, non-inheriting son might become a *Köthner* if a smaller holding was willed to him or if he could otherwise manage to purchase a small plot of land on which to build a small cottage. A *Köthner* always had to supplement his livelihood with some type of additional earnings, either by performing a part-time craft on the side or by hiring out as a day-laborer. A *Köthner* might keep a cow or two and some sheep, which he could let graze alongside the road or on farmland after the harvest. Usually a *Köthner* had some kind of personal relationship with his more successful neighbors, who counted on his labor and also provided him with grazing land and the use of a horse when needed.

The *Köthner* designation really caught on after the Agrarian Reforms, when those tenant occupants without sufficient means "lost" their holdings when they became available for purchase and were thus reduced to the status of *Köthner*.

Häusling. A *Häusling* was a landless laborer, usually the younger son of a farmer. In olden times, a younger brother and his wife and children might live in the same house, together with the older brother who had inherited the property. He would then be called a "*Häusling*", or "*Inhäusling*". However, around 1850, it became customary to build a separate, smaller house for the *Häusling* and his family. Aging parents and their younger children as well would often move into a small *Häusling* house to allow for the eldest son and his wife to live in the main house.

The *Häusling* house was usually large enough for the *Häusling* to keep a cow or a few goats, plus the *Häusling* would be allotted a small garden plot for his own family's use as well. The cottage he lived in, however, belonged not to him, but to the owner (usually his brother). In lieu of paying rent for cottage and garden, the *Häusling* was obligated to work for his brother every day, and usually his wife and children had to help as well.

A *Häusling* seldom could get enough money together to become independent, nor did his children have much of a future, since it was very uncommon for a *Häusling* (or the son of a *Häusling*) to marry the daughter of a large-scale farmer, especially a solo daughter and heiress. A *Häusling* was always dependent on some type of additional wage work (such as weaving, mending shoes, etc.) in order to make ends meet. His children usually ended up working as (unmarried) farmhands, day laborers or servants on neighboring farms.

Thus we see that our ancestors lived in a highly stratified society in which everyone knew exactly where they stood, either through the status of one's birth (nobility), by one's education (clergy, civil officials, doctors, teachers), by one's trade (skilled craftsman), occupation (miller, merchant, innkeeper), or by means of land ownership (*Baumann, Hausmann, Vollhöfner, Halbhöfner, Köthner*) or lack thereof (*Häusling,* and the sons of *Häuslinge* and *Köthner* who had to work as farmhands or as *Tagelöhner* for daily wages and who had practically no chance of ever improving their situation).

For generations, our direct-line Bredehöft ancestors were occupants of large farming estates passed down to the eldest son. After the Agrarian Reforms, several became actual owners, but of holdings reduced to one-half or one-quarter in size, or even smaller. Others "lost" their holdings and ended up as *Köthner,* without adequate land to sustain a family. Some were *Häusling*e, without land or means. Of these, however, several Bredehöft men were extremely lucky and managed (either through competence, good looks or charm!) to marry the heiress to a large farm. (One of the few ways to improve one's situation in life was through marriage…)

There is one more designation for "farmer":

Neubauer or **Anbauer**. A Häusling could change his status to *Neubauer* if the landowner (usually his older brother) agreed to sell him a small plot of land and the *Häusling* house was also put in his name. A *Neubauer* was thus a very small landowner whose plot of land was even smaller than that of a *Köthner*. As a rule, the land owned by a *Neubauer* or *Anbauer* was of inferior quality – heathland recovered for cultivation.

In the 19th century, there was a movement not only to cultivate the adjacent heathlands, but also to drain the surrounding moors to make them suitable for agriculture. The folks who colonized the moors were usually farmhands (*Knechte* and *Mägde*) and day-laborers (*Tagelöhner*) from the surrounding area, attracted by the prospect of owning their own land. These moor farmers were also known as *Neubauer* or *Anbauer*.

Sadly, it turned out that the moor's sandy soils, after draining, were not very fertile and unsuited to farming. Moor farmers were thus the poorest of subsistence farmers, their living conditions dismal, and life expectance in their dark, damp bog dwellings was short. It would take three generations before the wretched moor farmers were finally able to make a living. The following rhymed verse in Low German describes their plight:

"Den Eersten sien Dood, den Tweeten sien Noot, den Drüdden sien Broot."

"The first (generation) works itself to death; the second suffers want, the third (finally) has enough to eat."

* * *

HINRICH BARTELS' MOTHER, Anna Katharina Fitschen, born July 6, 1809 (my mother's great-grandmother), grew up on the moors where her father, Lütje Fitschen, died an impoverished *Anbauer* in a place called Ahrensmoor, south of the village of Harsefeld. At the age of eleven, Anna Katharina was hired out to work for a family in a nearby town where she was assigned menial tasks, but where she at least had food and lodging, plus a clean dress and a pair of shoes. Her own family's living conditions on the moors were so bad that just for her to live in a comfortable house and to be able to eat every day was enough recompense!

Fourteen years later, a chance encounter with a young man by the name of Johann Bartels (born 1804), a *Tagelöhner* from the town of Schwinge, would lead to romance. Theirs was not a fly-by–night relationship, but one of genuine affection. The young couple would like to have married, but lacked the necessary means.

In the fall of her twenty-fifth year, Anna Katharina Fitschen found herself with child, a desperate position for an unmarried woman in those days. We know that her child, Hinrich Fitschen Bartels, was born on July 4, 1835 in Weißenmoor by Stade. But what happened then, in particular, what became of the child's father is a mystery that nobody, not even local genealogists, have been able to solve. He simply vanishes. Parish records confirm Johann Bartels as father of the child, but later his name is nowhere to be found. Anna Katharina most likely left her newborn to the care of a relative on the moors and returned to town to resume her life of drudgery.

Based on what little we know, I can easily imagine a tragic love story between two young people who, like so many others, were condemned to a life of poverty and toil, with no chance at improving their situation. At age thirty-one, Johann Bartels had been on his own, surviving as an agricultural day-laborer, for some time, as both his parents were dead. His father, a *Häusling* in Schwinge, had moved to Weißenmoor, where he had died attempting to eke out a living on the moors.

Johann and Anna Katharina were head over heels in love, but love or no love, they were not allowed to marry, even with a child on the way, since as a *Tagelöhner* Johann Bartels had not the necessary means to establish a household or to support a family.

One day, with their situation becoming increasingly desperate, a leaflet fell into Johann's hands. He could barely read it:

> **Heil Dir Columbus, sey gepriesen, sey hoch geehrt in Ewigkeit, Du hast uns einen Weg gewiesen, der uns aus harter Dienstbarkeit erretten kann, wenn man es wagt, und seinem Vaterland entsagt.**

> "All praise be to You, Columbus, and be You glorified in all eternity, for You have shown us the path which will deliver us from a life of bitter servitude, if we but dare renounce our Homeland."

Trembling, young Bartels quickly hid the pamphlet, for even he understood there was something subversive about it. He later learned that the police throughout the Kingdom (of Hanover) were confiscating such incendiary writings as unpatriotic libel.

Johann Bartels had heard rumors about America, how even a common laborer could be free and could earn a good living there. He confided his plan to Anna Katharina, and she enthusiastically agreed: When her time came, Anna would go to Johann's sister in Weißenmoor to have her baby. In the meantime, Johann would go to America, find work there and a place to live, and then send for her.

Thus, at winter's end, March 1835, Johann Bartels set out on foot for Hamburg where he probably waited a week or so before he could board a sailing ship. Once on board, the ocean voyage in those days would have taken from six to eight weeks, ten at the most, depending on wind and weather conditions. The plan was for him to write as soon as he arrived in Baltimore.

Anna Katharina never saw her sweetheart again. Perhaps he never even made it onboard! Perhaps he did, but then succumbed to the miserable, overcrowded conditions on board sailing vessels in those days and was buried at sea. Perhaps he died later in America of a fever or some other illness or calamity before he could ever write to her. In any event, Johann Bartels, like so many others, was never heard from again.

Anna Katharina waited patiently for a letter to arrive. She was still waiting for word from Johann when their child was born, in July, and then she continued to wait some more. It would take a long time before she gave up hope. Little Hinrich was already six years old when Anna Katharina married Ernst Sievers, a kindly man, a cooper in the village of Harsefeld. It seems remarkable that Ernst Sievers would have chosen to marry a woman without a fortune (dowry) and with an "illegitimate" child. Anna Katherina must have been quite exceptional!

*   *   *

UNLIKE IN SOME PARTS of Germany, where farms were traditionally divided and sub-divided among all the inheriting siblings, farms in northern Germany, following the law of primogeniture, were passed down over generations to the oldest male, intact and undivided, so that the wealth and social standing of the family was maintained. The sole heir, in turn, was supposed to provide for his younger siblings – in the case of his younger brothers, either pay them off with a small sum or keep them on to help work the farm in return for food and lodging. His sisters were to be provided a dowry.

Theoretically, this was a viable system; however, in reality things were quite different. Siphoning off most of the wealth to just one sibling was deeply unfair, especially since quite often younger siblings did not receive any type of compensation at all – monetary or otherwise.

As with some of our Bredehöft ancestors, a younger brother would then try his best to marry the heiress of another farm. If such a woman could not be found, he was left with one of two choices: to be tolerated as a *Knecht*, an unmarried servant on his older brother's farm, without hope of ever improving his material status; and/or to hire himself out as a *Tagelöhner*. Either way, he would have to postpone any thoughts of marriage or establishing a family indefinitely.

A younger brother might be given the (rare) opportunity to apprentice himself out to learn one of the few skilled trades available at the time. He could then look forward to growing old as a low-paid "elder" journeyman in some small workshop, since even after working for years as a skilled journeyman, his wages would hardly be sufficient to allow him to set up shop on his own.

A younger sister, or for that matter any young, unmarried working-class woman in those days, had three options: she could either be a *Magd*, a nanny or a maid. Many a younger sister stayed behind to work as a *Magd*, or unmarried servant, on her brother's farm – helping with the housework and in the fields. Others were sent away to neighboring towns or cities to work as nannies or housemaids. Without an inheritance or a proper dowry, their chances of finding a suitable husband, a man who could support them, were definitely not good, since a man, too, would naturally try to improve his own situation through marriage.

The following is an example of the significance of marriage as a means of improving one's situation: By the late 1930s, my mother's younger sister, Adelheid, then an attractive young woman in her late twenties, had already had two eager suitors, but both times her chances at marriage fell through. In the first situation, the young man's mother was against the marriage because Adelheid came from modest circumstances (insufficient dowry). In the second situation, her handsome suitor was the sole son and heir of a wealthy landowner adamantly opposed to the marriage, since Adelheid was "not good enough" (working class). The handsome farmer's son later lost both legs as a soldier in World War II and returned home a cripple. How his devastated father then regretted his earlier disapproval of his son's marriage to Adelheid. At least Adelheid would have furnished him with an heir!

Young women of all social classes were expected to maintain their virginity and ensure their good reputation until marriage; it was a scandal to get pregnant out of wedlock. At the same time, many young men couldn't afford to marry and thus had to postpone marriage indefinitely. As a result, women were vulnerable to sexual betrayal. But a working class girl who became pregnant out of wedlock was doomed. She alone would be held responsible for her moment of weakness, becoming the subject of gossip and humiliation. More often than not, her parents, in order to ensure their respectability, would banish her for having brought shame and disgrace upon her family. In order to show the whole world that they condemned their daughter's actions, they had no choice but to do what society expected them to do. The shamed girl would then become a social outcast, most certainly destined to a life of hardship and poverty.

Thus a mother's words of warning (including my own mother's words, a half-century later) would always ring in a daughter's ears: "If you get pregnant, don't come home!"

Compared to England, Germany was late entering the Industrial Age. Not until after German unification, in 1871, did the modern, centralized German state begin to industrialize rapidly. But Germany's population had exploded during the 19th century; and before industrialization took hold, there were not enough jobs for the surplus rural population. Many people were simply stuck, with no hope at all for the future. That is why so many young people tried to get a ticket on a ship bound for America, especially in the years from 1860 to 1890. America needed an unlimited number of workers! If you could afford the passage to America, it was the only means of ever getting ahead.

So many people emigrated during this time! And in Zeven, the Bartels children were no exception: Four of them emigrated in the 1880s, the highpoint of German immigration to America – Hinrich, Catharina, Anna and Meta.

[Later on, once industrialization took hold and more employment opportunities became available, many rural Hanoverian laborers preferred migrating to Bremen and Hamburg where they could find employment in the newly created factories. Although Germany lagged at least 50 years behind England in terms of industrialization, by 1914 it was the leading industrial state in Europe.]

Hinrich August Bartels, the second eldest son, was the first to leave, in May of 1882. He was only fourteen when he booked passage on the *Elbe* out of Hamburg. Knowing that his older brother, Ernst, would be the sole heir, Hinrich must have foreseen a rather bleak future for himself. Either he could continue as an apprentice in his father's workshop and look forward to a future life in service to his elder brother, postponing marriage and family indefinitely, or he could try his luck in America!

Since Hinrich was a non-inheriting sibling, most likely his father helped finance his passage to America. In those days, an immigrant did not need a passport or a visa or even a sponsor. But he did need to be able to afford the trip! The average cost of passage in steerage class was around 25 dollars (about $700 in today's money). An additional 25 dollars was needed to enter the United States – so $50 total, or about $1,400 in today's money. But 50 dollars was more than the average German laborer or farmhand earned in six months, from which he still had to pay food and rent!

[Crossing the Atlantic in an iron steamship in those days was very rough. The crossing could take up to twelve days, and the trip was long and arduous, as immigrants were booked into the less expensive steerage class. Steerage compartments were located in the lowest decks, where the engines were also housed. Each steerage passenger was assigned a numbered metal berth, a canvas or burlap mattress stuffed with straw or seaweed, a life preserver which doubled as a pillow, and a tin pail and utensils for meals, which were usually served from a huge tank. The bunks were stacked two high and side-by-side. The steerage compartment could sleep up to 400 passengers. Without a separate dining room, and with all the crowding, conditions were very unhygienic. It was very difficult to keep clean, to follow even the most elementary rules of personal hygiene, and with everyone forced to live at such close quarters, infectious diseases could develop easily.]

After a grueling voyage, fourteen-year-old Hinrich arrived at Castle Garden (America's immigration center prior to Ellis Island) on May 22, 1882. Most likely he boarded with a family in *Kleindeutschland* on Manhattan's Lower East Side. With more than 70,000 Germans living in "Little Germany" at the time, young Hinrich would have felt right at home there, surrounded by German-speaking businesses and cultural institutions – schools, churches, newspapers and social clubs.

In the 1880s, the beer-brewing industry was in German hands, and Hinrich Bartels soon found work at one of the many German-run breweries in northern Manhattan as the driver of a horse-drawn beer delivery wagon. Young Hinrich fully embraced America – eventually changing his name to Henry, nicknamed "Harry" – and never once looked back. In 1891, at age twenty-five, less than a decade after arriving in New York young and penniless, Hinrich had done well enough for himself that he could afford to marry – a whole year ahead of his elder brother back in Germany! News of their younger son's marriage must have astounded his family back in Zeven, where, had Hinrich remained at home, as the non-inheriting younger son he would have still been a "nothing". Hinrich Bartels and young Eva Margareta Topper were married on

July 22, 1891. They moved to Brooklyn and had a total of eight children, of whom only two would survive infancy.

Henry Bartels worked his entire life for the John F. Trommer Brewery in Brooklyn – initially as a driver, later as a salesman and chauffeur – until he finally retired at age 75. As a young man, he recalled driving a beer delivery wagon all the way out to Long Island, delivering his load, picking up the empty kegs, enjoying a few beers with his customers, and then falling asleep on the way home. The horses knew the way home and would bring him safely back! Things were a bit different in New York in the 1890's...

Through his "brewery" contacts, Hinrich was able to find work for all three of his sisters, either as *Kinderfräulein* or as housemaids. Catharina, age twenty-four, arrived on the *Eider* from Bremen on March 30, 1886. Eighteen-year-old Anna followed a year later.

Young Meta was the last of the Bartels children to emigrate. She left Hamburg on the *Harmonia* on April 5, 1888 and arrived in New York Harbor twelve days later, on April 17, just a few months shy of her seventeenth birthday.

They must have been heart-wrenching scenes – the Bartels parents saying goodbye to four of their children, one by one, as they left for America. After all, working-class children who made up their minds to emigrate anticipated that their decision was final. It meant that they would probably never return, that they would most likely never see their parents and family and homeland again.

Nowadays, with radio, telephone, television, air travel and the internet, it is easy to stay connected with family and friends. For the Bartels family, however, the occasional handwritten letter was their only means of staying in touch. When someone left home in those days, they did not say *"Auf-wiedersehen"*, till we meet again, but rather *"Lebe wohl"*, meaning goodbye forever...

In New York, the Germans formed the largest immigrant group, and before long, the Bartels siblings felt quite at home among the large German community. It was easy for them to meet other young people at church or through the various German clubs, or even at the many German beer gardens and wine taverns where German-American families and the general public met for relaxation and drink.

As sisters, Anna and Meta Bartels were very close, even after Anna married in 1893, although, in Meta's opinion, John Koehler, Anna's young husband, could ill afford a wife and family. Anna was soon pregnant, but her first-born, little Henry, sickened and died when he was only nine months old, in August of 1895. Anna was devastated. But worse was still to come. In December of the following year, her young husband also fell ill and died. He was only twenty-seven!

Meta hardly knew how to console her sister. But Anna did not stay a widow for long. In September of 1897, in a union born of tragedy, she married Henry <u>Otto</u> Schmiemann, a young (he was 28 years old) widower and fellow Hanoverian who had himself suffered terrible personal loss. Within a period of three years (from 1894 to

1896) Otto had buried two children and a wife: Their firstborn, August, had died just a few days after his first birthday, in February 1894. Their daughter, eight-month-old Augusta, had died a year later, in August 1895, leaving only his grief-stricken young wife, Margaretha, who passed away the following year, in July 1986. She was only twenty-six…

To a modern-day person it all sounds a bit bizarre – that Anna and Otto's first families, five people, all died within a three-year period. Today, babies are vaccinated against all kinds of diseases, and if someone gets pneumonia, it is cured with massive doses of antibiotics like penicillin. But penicillin was not discovered until 1928 and was only introduced in the 1940s. Today, the leading causes of death are degenerative diseases – heart disease, diabetes, cancer and stroke, but the primary causes of death at the end of the 19th century were infectious diseases (pneumonia, tuberculosis, and diarrhea) and epidemics (measles, diphtheria, whooping cough, and typhoid). Before penicillin, things as common as strep throat or even a child's scratched knee could kill.

Anna's second husband, Otto, a housepainter by trade, gradually built up a successful business. He and Anna were able to move to a middle-class section of Brooklyn and into the front apartment of the four-flat apartment house they owned.

Meta was glad for her sister, and Otto and Anna Schmiemann were happy in their marriage, so happy, that in 1899, when Anna gave birth to twins, the thrilled parents named the twins after themselves – Otto and Annie.

*   *   *

L ATE NOVEMBER 1901. Back in Zeven, the Bartels family, still deep in mourning, welcomed Meta home, greeting her warmly – her elderly father, much aged; her younger brother, eighteen-year old Johann (whom she hadn't seen since he was five!), and of course, her older brother Ernst, grave and reserved as always, and whose two little children, *"die zwei Lütten"*, peeked shyly from behind their grandfather's chair. It didn't take long, however, for them to warm to her, especially when Meta unlocked her steamer trunk and pulled out a toy for each *aus Ameriko*!

From that day on, Meta Bartels determined to put New York behind her. In the following weeks and months, she employed every skill she had into managing the household for her father and brothers, and in bringing comfort to her brother's children, so that by summer she had succeeded in restoring a semblance of normal life to the bereaved family. All the while, however, that strange sense of anticipation never left her...

Their neighbor across the way was a blacksmith. Meta walked by his shop each day on her errands – usually with the infant supported upright in the baby carriage, and the other two *Lütten* in tow. Soon she caught the eye of the handsome journeyman working there; he seemed always to be out in front of the forge whenever she and the children passed by.

"Moin!" he would call out in greeting, nodding in her direction and politely tipping his cap. Meta soon found herself smiling, looking forward to, and even anticipating the journeyman's friendly greeting. One summer day, feeling bold and daring, she stopped in passing to exchange a few polite words with him. She learned his name was Jacob Bredehöft.

Meta was astonished to find herself fancying the strapping journeyman blacksmith with his quiet, courteous and respectful demeanor. She could see herself as a blacksmith's wife. So this, she suddenly realized, was what she had been 'anticipating'!

For his part, her journeyman admirer could not quite believe his good fortune. Initially he had not dared approach the fashionable, worldly-wise Bartels daughter who had lived so many years abroad…

Jacob Bredehöft, along with his identical twin, Johann, and their two older half-sisters, Anna and Marie, had grown up in Hesedorf, a village near Bremervörde. Their elderly father, Jakob Bredehöft (1824-1891), a *Neubauer*, in an effort to ensure his twin sons' economic future, had supported them both in learning a skilled trade – apprenticing Johann to a *Tischlermeister*, master cabinet-maker , and Jacob to a *Schmiedemeister*, master blacksmith.

Traditionally, it took ten or more years to become a full-fledged master blacksmith. During his initial years of apprenticeship, Jacob had lived in his master's home as a member of the household, performing all kinds of menial work, for which he received no compensation, only room and board. But he was lucky; the *Meister* treated him well, and Jacob learned quickly, so that after only four years of apprenticeship, he had already acquired sufficient knowledge to pass the examination to become a journeyman. He had then travelled the countryside for several years, working under different masters, before coming to Zeven, where he had been content with his journeyman status until he began harboring thoughts of marriage. Indeed, it was the prospect of marrying Meta Bartels that had given him the impetus to become a master blacksmith.

The Bartels family was highly respected in town. Without the prospect of a *Meisterbrief* (master's certificate), Jacob Bredehöft would not have dared approach the elderly Hinrich Bartels for his daughter's hand in marriage. Several months earlier, he had submitted pieces of his work to the guild for evaluation. Only recently had he received word that the guild had judged his work and found it of sufficient quality and his knowledge base strong enough to qualify as a *Meister Schmied*. As a *Schmiedemeister*, Jacob could theoretically set up shop on his own, could employ and train others.

Meta Bartels and Jacob Bredehöft were married the following spring, on March 29, 1903. Both thirty-one, they were anxious to get started with their lives. As luck would have it, they saw in the newspaper that in the neighboring town of Sittensen, Frau Catharina Pape was advertising for a smithy to take over her late husband's forge. The small cottage adjacent to the forge was also available. *Köthner* Christian Pape had died quite suddenly, and his widow was anxious to get the forge up and running again.

So the newly-weds hired a horse and buggy to drive over to Sittensen, seventeen kilometers (10 miles) to the east, where the widow was expecting them.

Jacob Bredehöft (in the next several paragraphs referred to as "JB") was born and raised in Hesedorf, a village south of Bremervörde, a good day's journey to the north. His father had been a *Neubauer* in Hesedorf, but JB was descended from a long line of Bredehöfts who, over the centuries, had put down deep roots in the villages and hamlets east of Zeven. We can trace these ancestors back to the early 17th century, to the time of the Thirty Years' War, beginning with *Baumann* Marten Bredehövet/Hövet (also known as Marten zum Borstel), who died in 1670 in Boitzenbostel. *Baumann* Bredehövet and his descendants were occupants of large farming estates situated in the countryside just east of Zeven and to the west of Sittensen.

Marten Bredehövet's son, Hinrich Bredehöft (1640-1699) was *Hausmann* in Boitzenbostel. Hinrich's son, Paul Bredehöft (1673-1754) was *Baumann* in Klein Meckelnsen. Paul's son, Jacob Bredehöft (1708-1778), was *Hausmann* in Volkensen.

In 1781, Jacob's son, JB's great-grandfather, also named Jacob (1760-1820), a non-inheriting sibling, got extremely lucky and was able to marry Wübke Catharina Margaretha Danckers, heiress to the estate of *"zu Adiek"* located midway between Zeven and Sittensen. Their eldest son, Jochen Bredehöft, became heir to the estate in 1819.

Meta Adelheit Bartels

Jacob Bredehöf

Zu der am Sonntag, den 29. März ds. Js.
stattfindenden Hochzeitsfeier beehren sich er-
gebenst einzuladen

Meta Bartels,
Jacob Bredehöft.

Zeven.

Hesedorf
b. Bremervörde.

Die Hochzeit findet im Hause der Braut statt

[Note: In 1848, true to custom, Jochen Bredehöft's first-born son then inherited the ancestral estate from his father. A few years later, however, the estate fell upon hard times, possibly through no fault of the occupants, but most likely due to recurring years of bad weather resulting in back-to-back bad harvests and crop failures. Unable to pay the taxes owed, they were forced to declare bankruptcy. Thus, the estate of zu Adiek, after three generations, passed out of Bredehöft hands.]

Of course, JB knew nothing of this. Plus, having been born much later and having grown up some 25 miles to the north, I wonder how he could even have known about the ancestral estate. And yet, when the young couple on their way to Sittensen approached the turn-off leading to zu Adiek (several kilometers outside of Zeven), JB could not help but boast to his wife that his Bredehöft ancestors had once been the occupants there – for three generations! This information, of course, sparked Meta's curiosity, but JB could furnish her with few or no details. In fact, he could recall only a few bits and scraps he had overheard as a child...

JB's grandfather, Jacob Bredehöft (1787-1837), was a younger brother to Jochen Bredehöft. As a non-inheriting sibling, he had to leave zu Adiek. He spent the rest of his life in the nearby village of Meinstedt, where, as *Köthner*, he barely managed to eke out a living. He eventually married, in 1821, but his children grew up poor, so very poor, in fact, that his eldest son, JB's father, Jacob Bredehöft (1824-1891), was a *Tagelöhner* most of his life, unable to marry until the age of forty-three, when he, too, got lucky and gained the affections of a young widow, Maria Buddelmann, née Wille, of Bremervörde (1836-1888), whose husband, Johann Buddelmann, had passed away less than three years into their marriage, leaving her a widow with two baby girls. It was the widow's inheritance that ultimately secured the financial situation of JB's father, enabling him to marry and start a family, as a *Neubauer* in Hesedorf.

JB's mother passed away when he and his twin brother Johann were only sixteen. Their elderly father died three years later. But by then, JB and Johann were already starting out as journeymen, able to survive on their own. Most likely a relative was appointed guardian to their half-sisters, Anna and Marie.

*   *   *

I N SITTENSEN, Frau Catharina Pape took an immediate liking to the newly married couple. The tall, broad-shouldered Jacob Bredehöft looked every inch the strong, capable blacksmith, and Frau Pape was especially pleased that his fashionable wife did not turn up her nose at the lowly cottage adjacent to the forge, but rather seemed delighted with its old-fashioned "charm". A close and lasting relationship would develop between Frau Pape and the Bredehöfts. The widow's fourteen-year old son, Diedrich, was Jacob-Schmied's first apprentice, plus parish records list Frau Pape as one of three godparents of their first born.

On May 14, 1903, the following announcement appeared in the *Zevener Zeitung*:

Geschäftsempfehlung

Den geehrten Einwohnern von Sittensen und Umgebung
zur Nachricht, daß ich hierselbst die Papesche Schmiede
übernommen habe. Ich gebe die Zusicherung, daß jede
in mein Fach schlagende Arbeit schnell und reell ausgeführt
wird und bitte um freundliches Wohlwollen.

Sittensen im Mai 1903

Jacob Bredehöft, Schmiedemeister

Forge Reopening

This is to notify the esteemed townsfolk of Sittensen and surrounding area that I have taken on the local Pape forge. I pledge to perform all blacksmithing work promptly and faithfully, and I ask for your favorable patronage.

Sittensen, May 1903

Jacob Bredehöft, Master Blacksmith

Adjacent and to the left of the forge, sheltered beneath a giant linden tree, stood an old, half-timbered *Häusling* cottage whose front door opened directly out onto the street. This is where the blacksmith would reside.

A thick, thatched roof covered the four low-ceilinged rooms inside. Four worn sandstone steps led from the street up to the front door, which opened into the kitchen, a warm and cozy place where the family came together for meals and where they gathered in the evening around the heavy wooden table positioned in front of a sturdy, L-shaped bench that fit into the corner by the window. The large iron cookstove in the opposite corner was the only source of warmth. Beside the stove was a crate filled with kindling and blocks of dried peat, used for fuel. This was the warmest corner of the kitchen and a favorite place for their father to sit. A long, high shelf, lined with decorative plates and jars, ran the length of one wall, while most of the opposite wall was taken up by a solid wood kitchen cupboard, its upper part displaying shelves filled with crockery and china, while assorted cookware was stored out of sight in the lower part. A bread box, along with ceramic containers for storing flour, salt, sugar, coffee and tea, rested on the cupboard's worktop, while drawers below held kitchen utensils, cutlery, dishtowels and the like. The floor was of unfinished, bare wood. The lace curtains at the window were starched and ironed.

Bredehöft forge (at right) with a view to the south. The sign reads Scheeßel 14 km.

Old postcard showing the Bredehöft forge (at left) with a view looking west onto the Zevenerstrasse (now Lindenstrasse). The forge was located on the main street leading north through town, close to the marketplace, and stood directly on the corner where the street curved off west towards Zeven, 17 kilometers to the west. The forge's thatched roof was later replaced with slate.

Although meals were cooked atop the large iron cookstove in the kitchen, most of the actual food preparation took place in the adjacent room at the rear of the kitchen, the so-called "*Wirtschaftsküche*" (scullery), which opened to the backyard. The scullery floor was stone and it was a step lower than the rest of the downstairs. With its stone floor, the scullery was almost always damp and cold, but even so, this "back kitchen" was the actual center of daily activity, the busiest room in the house. It was used for basic food preparation, for washing up afterwards, and for doing anything else that required water. The sink was a glazed stone trough which drained directly to the outside. A hand pump was installed next to it, which pumped cold water from the well to the house. In order to heat water, buckets of pumped water were added to a copper, a type of water heater/boiler set over a fire grate and which was fired up from the bottom using dried peat. The copper was the only means of obtaining hot water in significant amounts – for cleaning, for bathing, for washday, etc.

On washdays, the scullery served as the laundry room where twice monthly *die große Wäsche* took place – the dirty laundry first boiled in the wash copper before being scrubbed clean on a washboard, then rinsed and hung out to dry.

Parents and children washed themselves at the scullery sink – sponge baths, in a basin of cold water, and sometimes adding a little hot water to the cold if the copper was lit or if someone had bothered to boil a kettle on the stove. There was a curtain you could draw across to provide some privacy…

The scullery was also the "mudroom" where the men washed up when they came in from the forge, rolling up their sleeves to wash away the grime in a basin of hot water set out for them.

Washing one's hair was always a big production. Twice a month or so, women helped each other to wash their long hair in a wash basin, using rainwater from barrels collected outside. Rinsing their long hair in rainwater got rid of any soapy residue (shampoo was not yet available) and left their long hair soft and silky.

Hot water was always a scarce commodity. Once a week, on Saturday evenings, the copper in the scullery was fired up to heat water for the family bath. Then pots of hot water were emptied into a zinc wash tub that doubled as a bathtub and the whole family would get in, one after the other. The children sat with their knees scrunched together while their mother gave them a thorough scrubbing with a soapy sponge, then rinsed them by pouring several pitchers full of warm water over them. Later, the scullery door was closed and the children were told to keep out while their mother scrubbed their father's back, and vice versa. There was a lot of embarrassment involved with undressing…

To the left of the front door was a sparsely furnished *Stube*, a small sitting room used mainly on holidays or to sit quietly on a Sunday afternoon to read the Bible. At its rear was a space divided into two rooms: a larger room containing a wardrobe, a storage trunk and their parents' bed, and a small alcove where the children had their bed. From the back door of the scullery a path lead to an outhouse attached to a shed. The outhouse was used in all kinds of weather, rain or shine, but chamber pots were also often used inside the house, particularly at night.

In the evening, after supper, the oil lamp in the center of the kitchen table was lit and the family sat together around the table and played board games or the mother taught the girls how to embroider and crochet while their father read the newspaper, sometimes out loud. Around eight o'clock they started getting ready for bed, and by the time the church bell struck nine, everyone was asleep, the apprentice(s) and the journeyman having already retired to a separate corner of the blacksmith shop where each had a cot and a small chest to store his belongings. Since the fire in the forge was never extinguished, the shop, even in winter, was not unbearably cold.

Befriended by Frau Pape, and welcomed by the parish, Jacob and Meta Bredehöft settled down to their new life together. According to tradition, they had ordered handmade bedroom and kitchen furniture, while Meta's ample dowry, including her fine, embroidered table and bed linens, provided for everything else. With hard work and thrift, the young couple had a reasonable expectation of a successful future.

Three children were born to Jacob and Meta Bredehöft in rapid succession:

JACOB HINRICH (JONNY) was born January 5, 1904. As firstborn, he was named "Jacob" after his father, his grandfather, his great-grandfather, and his great-great-grandfather, reflecting the importance of family lineage. His second name was that of his mother's father, Hinrich Bartels of Zeven. Little Jacob, however, was never actually called by his real name. To everyone, he was known simply as "Jonny".

META MARIA SOPHIA was born the following year on May 2, 1905. [In northern Germany, it was not uncommon to give three baptismal names.] She was given her mother's name, which was also the name of her maternal grandmother, Metta Viebrock. Her other two names were those of her godparents: Maria Bartels née Maria von Bargen (the second wife of Onkel Ernst Bartels of Zeven, her mother's eldest brother), and Sophia Baden, a friend of her mother in Sittensen.

AGNES ANNA ERNESTINE, born a year and one month later, exactly, on June 4, 1906, was also given three baptismal names. She was named after two of her godparents: Agnes Vogel, her mother's (Viebrock) aunt, and Anna Tietjen, her father's married sister in Büsum. She was named Ernestine in honor of Onkel Ernst Bartels of Zeven, her mother's eldest brother.

It would seem that Jacob and Meta Bredehöft were making up for lost time – having three babies in roughly three years.

"Tsk, tsk, tsk," went the aunts, shaking their heads disapprovingly…

Three and five years then passed before two more children were born:

ERNST JOHANN, born May 29, 1909. Named after his mother's eldest brother and his father's twin brother, little Ernst Johann died when he was only one year old (due to pneumonia?) on June 29, 1910.

ADELHEID MARGARETA KATHARINA, born October 14, 1911. She was named after her aunt and godmother, Adelheid Bredehöft, Onkel Johann's wife. (Adelheid was also her mother's second name.) She was named Margareta Katharina specially after Onkel Ernst Bartel's first wife, Catharina Margaretha (Trina), whose premature death, leaving three children motherless, had resulted in Meta Bartels' returning to Germany in 1901.

Agnes' childhood was a happy one. The Jacob Bredehöft family of Sittensen, ca. 1908, with Jonny (seated), Meta (standing), and Agnes (seated on her mother's lap)

Agnes, my mother, never really talked about her growing-up years. Why, I do not know. Perhaps in their "un-eventfulness" she thought there was nothing much to tell. Or was it because she could not reconcile the simplicity and ordinariness of her growing up years with the difficulties and challenges she would encounter later in life? Perhaps her childhood, like the illusory era in which it took place, was too removed from the reality of what was to follow. Maybe she simply would not allow herself to return to that peaceful, faraway world…

My mother's childhood was a happy one, exceptional only in its ordinariness. Her mother was kind and warm-hearted; her father worked hard to provide for his family. Although discipline was strict, with the customary respect and obedience demanded by German parents, we know that there was love and affection in the home, and that between the first three siblings especially there was a very close bond.

Growing up, the Bredehöft children had no awareness of being either rich or poor, since everyone they knew lived similarly to the way their family lived and had a lifestyle that was basically the same. Although never "well off", there was always enough food on the table. Even during the meager years following World War I, they were not too deprived, since as soon as she could (once the British blockade was lifted, in July 1919), Tante Anna (in New York) sent packages with materials and goods that were in short supply, such as shoe leather and sewing fabric.

The Bredehöft children were lucky; their mother was an excellent cook. With potatoes, greens and a few vegetables from her garden, flavored with a bit of salted pork or *Speck*, she created nourishing and delicious meals.

Cooking in those days was an arduous process; preparing even a simple meal took considerable time and required constant attention. Their mother, like all housewives, would spend many hours of her day going back and forth between the scullery and the kitchen – preparing meals from scratch, firing up the iron stove in the kitchen, keeping an eye on the stove's temperature the whole time… Then, after the food was served and everyone had finished eating, heating water for the clean-up – the pots and pans scrubbed in the stone trough in the scullery, the dishes washed in an enamel dishpan on top of the kitchen table, then hand dried and put away. In-between, the iron stove had to be rubbed down with wax to keep it from rusting…

Then there was the garden… The Bredehöft children were vaguely aware of the fact that their mother had a green thumb. Something grew in every inch of space in the family's allotted garden plot, where, in addition to the indispensable vegetables she cultivated – potatoes, turnips, cabbage, kale, onions, and beans – their mother also managed to reserve a space for growing flowers. Neighbors and townswomen would often stop by to admire Frau Bredehöft's flowers, especially her gorgeous dahlias, which flowered along the fence in the late summer and into the fall.

With her superb housekeeping skills, Meta Bredehöft succeeded in transforming a humble blacksmith's abode into a pleasant and cozy place where neighbors and friends alike enjoyed stopping by for a chat in a kitchen made even more inviting by a clean cloth and a few fresh-cut flowers in a glass on the table. In fact, the blacksmith's cottage was known for its cleanliness, for always being sparkling clean, neat and tidy.

Their mother disliked clutter. *Ein jedes Ding an seinem Ort,* she would say. "A place for everything, and everything in its place!" This expression might be applied to the class system under which they lived as well, where everyone knew their place and their role in society and had expectations accordingly. Perhaps people were happier, because they didn't focus on what they didn't have, since no one in their social circle had it either. An ordinary craftsman never thought of one day owning a large business, for example, or of having his children go on to higher education, because these were things for people of another class.

Indeed, it never would have occurred to Agnes' parents to "educate" their children beyond grade school. Working-class children terminated their education at age fourteen, even sooner. Since there was no secondary school in Sittensen, upper-class children had to be sent away to attend *Mittelschule* in Bremervörde, where they had to pay room and board, plus tuition fees, books, etc. There was no way a blacksmith could afford to send a child to secondary school. Only the children of professionals – teachers, clergymen, physicians – went to secondary school.

Sittensen was a small town where everyone knew everyone, and where the children played outside and could roam freely. As their parents were far too busy to watch over them, the children entertained themselves. The unpaved road in front of their houses was not a busy or dangerous place – passersby mostly on foot, an occasional horse drawn vehicle, and only rarely an automobile. So the street was their playground.

There weren't many toys – mainly building blocks and a few other handmade wooden toys. Agnes and Meta each had a doll, and they also made "rag" dolls out of remnants of fabric. Since there were so few toys, the children used their imagination. A few of their favorite outdoor games were hoops (played with a stick and an old wagon wheel), marbles, tops, hopscotch, rope skipping and tag, as well as games passed down from child to child over generations: Blind man's bluff, hide-and-seek, *Hinkebock*, *Der Kaiser schickt Soldaten aus* (catch the flag), and *Der Pott is fott* (kick the can!). "Kick the can" would later become my favorite childhood game.

The children also enjoyed playing pretend, or make-believe, where they would act out in great detail such grown-up events as weddings, funerals, etc. When there was a funeral, the church bell would toll as the funeral procession approached. School children from the upper grades had to sing for the funeral. They stood outside the church, alongside the pastor, to await the funeral procession. They then sang in church for the funeral and also again at the gravesite for the burial. The schoolmaster, who also taught them Bible verses and hymns, was the organist at church, and on Sundays the children in the upper grades had to stand next to him at the organ and sing along at the top of their voices.

All the town children and those from the immediate surrounding villages walked to school. Although the more distant villages had their own school, once a week, the older children throughout the far-flung parish still had to come to Sittensen to attend confirmation class in the evening. Usually these "older" children would then stay overnight with a family in town.

At school, Agnes had to learn to speak, read and write *Hochdeutsch*. The schoolteacher was very strict. Discipline was a part of the culture, and physical punishment was considered a tool to build character as well as to enforce obedience. For example, if you hadn't done your homework or didn't pay attention, the teacher would say: *"So zeig mal die Hände her!"* You had to hold out your hands, and he would hit you on the fingers a few times with a stick! That was, if you were a girl. If you were a boy, you were thrashed.

All children in those days were brought up to be well behaved and respectful to their elders. The Commandment "Honor thy father and thy mother!" *[Exodus 20:12]* was taught from an early age. Children were raised not to talk back; it would have been unheard of for a child in those days to contradict a parent, to disagree, or even to question.

In short, children were to be seen and not heard and were to behave in a way that would maintain dignity within the family. The home atmosphere, therefore, was usually one of peace and harmony, with little discord. My mother sometimes mentioned how peaceful their homelife had been…

Crime was practically non-existent; there was no crime to speak of in Sittensen. Now and then a tramp would enter the town and the constable would keep his eye on him, sometimes locking him up for a few nights. On occasion men would get drunk at the *Wirtshaus* and be lying in the ditch in the morning.

On New Year's Eve, some of the town boys might sneak into the church and ring the church bells at midnight, climbing up the dark steps leading to the bell tower and pulling on the thick ropes attached to the bells. Then all the dogs in town would begin barking and yowling and the roosters would start crowing!

Things were usually quiet in town, although every now and then something exciting happened, like when gypsies came through town in their gypsy wagons. One time, Agnes was with her mother in the kitchen when they heard the wagons stop outside. Her mother peeked out the window. "Agnes, go lock the door," she ordered in a low voice.

But too late! Two gypsy women, with ragged children clinging to their skirts, were already making their way up the front steps. Before you knew it, one of them was already in the kitchen. There she stood, begging for food.

"Agnes, run and get your father", her mother instructed, placing herself firmly in front of the kitchen cupboard.

But Agnes could not move, so terrified was she of the scene unfolding before her, and of leaving her mother alone with the woman, who was now frantically begging for food, gesturing towards her stomach, then towards her hungry children, who were covered in filth.

The gypsy woman would not be put off. Agnes' mother gave her a few coins and the loaf of bread from the breadbox, and then she left.

"Where is the second gypsy woman that came towards the house?" Agnes, recovering from her fright, wanted to know.

"I suppose she returned to the wagon," her mother answered.

But later that afternoon, when Frau Pape went to gather eggs from the hen house, the hen's nests were all empty! Clearly, the second gypsy woman had made her way into the henhouse while her accomplice was in the kitchen.

Then their journeyman spoke up and told the story of how a gypsy woman had once stolen a chicken from a farmer and was about to twist its neck off when a *Knecht came* around the corner and caught her red-handed.

"You see, Gypsy women are obligated to provide food for their lazy husbands," he explained.

"*Zigeuner! Lumpenpack!*" her father said in disgust. "They're a dirty lot, those gypsies!"

The town constable would make certain that the gypsies and their wagons didn't remain for long...

Agnes' little sister was not fair complexioned like the rest of the Bredehöft children. Adelheid's skin would turn dark after playing outdoors all summer long. She also had long, black hair and dark eyes (not exactly "Nordic" features), so the other children would tease her, claiming that she was really a gypsy child who had fallen out of a gypsy wagon!

Since Sittensen was supposedly so peaceful, I once asked if there was anything the townspeople did fear in those days. The reply came quickly and without hesitation: "Fire!" Many of the older, timber-framed houses had thatched roofs. If lightning struck, they would burn quickly. Thus, fire was the one thing that was feared. .

Not even the church was safe from fire. In 1907, during the worst thunderstorm anyone could recall, lightning struck the church steeple around nine o'clock in the evening, igniting the uppermost shingles. The flames ate their way slowly downward, slowed by the heavy downpour. When the rain finally stopped, around eleven o'clock, only half the steeple remained. All the townspeople gathered round to watch the painful scene now unfolding before them – the church's steeple, their town's beloved ornament, being consumed by bright flames silhouetted against the pitch black darkness. There was nothing the volunteer firefighters could do. Overcome by feelings of helplessness, stillness fell over the crowd, a silence interrupted only by the terrible sound of crashing beams from above. Over the hushed conversations of the onlookers, someone was overheard saying: "I wonder how long before the bell tower with the clock comes falling down?"

Then, as the old striking clock began to sound the hours of midnight, the onlookers began to count along silently, until, at the stroke of nine, the dying clock was silenced forever as it, along with the church bells, came crashing down in a huge ball of fire.

Usually the storms came in from the North Sea, at night. So great was the fear of fire that parents would awaken their children in the middle of the night, make them get dressed and lace up their shoes, so that in case lightning struck they wouldn't have to flee the burning house in their nightclothes. Family members would then sit quietly together until the worst of the storm had passed.

"Don't go near the windows", Agnes' mother cautioned; while their father took comfort in the fact that the giant linden tree would (hopefully) protect the cottage from a lightning strike.

Childhood, though generally carefree, was not a time of doing nothing. From an early age, Agnes and her siblings were taught responsibility and the value of work. Since school was only in session during the morning hours, schoolchildren were always home for the noon meal. The smell of their mother's cooking, signaling *Mittagessen,* would greet them at the door. Agnes and Meta would hurriedly set the table while their father and the journeyman and apprentice(s) were washing up in the scullery. At 12 o'clock sharp everyone would sit down for the main meal of the day. Afterwards, Agnes and Meta took turns – either helping their mother with the dishes, the housework and the gardening, or spending the afternoon looking after the only animals they kept – goats! Every afternoon after school and all summer long, someone was stuck with the daily chore of tending the goats! In those days, everyone kept a cow or two and even a pig, but since the Bredehöfts didn't own any land, and thus could ill afford to keep a cow (one cow would eat the same amount of feed as six goats!), their mother, determined that her children should grow up strong and healthy, kept four or five nanny goats in the shed attached to their cottage. The Bredehöft children always had a plentiful supply of rich, delicious goat's milk.

Confined in a small pen, the hungry goats had to be let out each day to graze. But unlike sheep, which tend to flock together, goats have to be actively herded while they are foraging for food, or else they skip off on their own. Thus, during the warmer months (from May through October), Agnes' daily afternoon chore, from one o'clock until suppertime, was herding goats. Most of the time it was not a lonely pastime; she shared the chore with other neighborhood children, some tending geese, so that herding goats (at least during pleasant weather) could be enjoyable.

Since goats are very curious animals and never stand still for a minute, the children got lots of fresh air and exercise keeping up with the goats while they browsed, foraged and grazed on the grass that grew alongside the half-paved road leading through town and on the various plants and shrubs that grew in the ditches on either side of country lanes and alongside the river bank. During the winter, the goats were kept mostly inside and were fed hay (expensive!) along with turnip greens, potato peels and other kitchen scraps, plus dried leaves and brush that the children gathered in the woods, as well as fresh-cut birch tree branches to gnaw on. The goats also had to be watered and otherwise tended to, and, of course, once a day they were milked.

Agnes, too, had to learn to milk the goats. When she initially protested, her wise mother firmly admonished her: "A woman must learn everything. You never know when you might need it!" The never-ending daily chore of tending goats was the one thing that my mother often mentioned about her childhood!

Tending the goats (Adelheid, at right, with friends)

Around the end of May, after the crops had been planted and there was a brief respite from the fieldwork, it was time for everyone, farmers, villagers and townspeople alike, to head out to the nearby peat bogs just a few kilometers outside of town, for the annual peat-digging. Peat, or turf, was hand cut and then dried out for use as fuel. Each family would purchase the right to cut a section of peat, digging a deep trench through the hard layers of dead organic matter that had accumulated over thousands of years. Peat was the main source of fuel, so the head of each family had to be able to calculate just how many peat blocks he needed to cut and store for the coming year in order to meet his family's cooking and heating needs.

Hopefully, by the end of May, the warm spring sun would have dried the earth somewhat, making the peat bogs, watered by rain and snow, a bit less water-filled. Then their father would borrow a horse and wagon, and after loading picks, shovels and a wheelbarrow, he and the apprentice, often the journeyman as well, along with the children, would set out for the nearby peat-moors. There the men would spend the whole day hard at work cutting out blocks of peat, while the apprentice and the older children were kept busy loading the soggy, cut-out blocks of black muck into the wheelbarrow, hauling the chunks of earth, heavy and dripping wet, to dry ground and, following their father's strict instructions, carefully stacking them on top of each other in a circular fashion, forming neat round mounds in such a manner as to allow air to circulate through, so that the peat could dry over the summer.

In the fall, the mounds would be dismantled; the now (hopefully) dried, hardened blocks of peat were loaded onto a wagon, transported home and then stacked in the shed adjacent to the forge. For the winter, the shed had to be filled to the top, as there was not only the kitchen stove to heat, but also the fire in the forge had to be kept going. Peat had to be thoroughly dry, or else it wouldn't burn properly. But of course, you couldn't always help it if the peat was damp, especially if it had rained too much during the summer and it hadn't been able to dry out properly.

Peat was an efficient fuel that burned by various degrees, depending on the density of its composition. Towards the surface, peat was looser, like densely packed moss. But the deeper one dug, the more solid and dense it became. Their mother would use a loose clump of peat to quickly boil a pot of potatoes, while a more solid block, almost like coal, would provide long-term heat. Loose peat was also used instead of straw as bedding for the goats.

Agnes' father fashioned special shoes for the horses so they could more easily tread upon the soggy paths that crisscrossed the bogs – a type of wooden platform beneath their hooves, secured by leather "booties" fitted around the legs. Without them, a horse's hooves would sink too deeply into the soggy muck. Then the terrified, struggling animal would have to be hauled out of the sucking pool of stagnant water by strong men with ropes.

Digging peat was hard work, wet and messy, but even so, going to the peat-moors was something the children looked forward to. Their father always chose a warm, dry and sunny day, and their mother took special care to prepare a plentiful picnic lunch. But what really made the outing so special for the children was the sense of danger and adventure that came with being out on the moor – the creepy-crawlies, the need to heed their father's constant warning to stay on the path and to watch out for the "*Kreuzotter*", the poisonous snake that hid behind the clumps of tall grass and bushes – but above all the sense of adventure, limited only by the children's' imagination, derived from all those scary stories they had heard, stories of people who had simply disappeared in the moors, and how every so often a dead man would be discovered in the bogs – his long-dead body perfectly preserved!

In those days, almost everyone in town was by necessity also a "farmer". Everyone knew something about farming, as every family either owned or rented a plot of land on which to grow vegetables and potatoes for its own consumption. Most townspeople didn't have the space, nor could they afford to keep a horse, so whenever they needed to "prepare" their plots for planting, they would have to borrow a horse along with the necessary implements.

The Bredehöfts also had a plot of garden ground, allotted to them by Frau Pape, on which they grew vegetables and potatoes – especially potatoes!

It was common knowledge that from as little as one acre of potatoes, you could feed six people for a year! Harvested in the fall, they stored their potatoes in special storage clamps – mounds of built-up earth with the potatoes embedded in straw – where they would keep throughout the winter. There were other clamps for storing root vegetables. Since their cottage did not have a cellar, they also stored some of the harvested potatoes under their beds. The potatoes kept well in the cold, unheated rooms.

Frau Pape also let them raise a pig alongside her own. When winter came, along with colder weather, the butcher came to help slaughter the family's pig. The meat from the butchered pig, preserved in the form of *Wurst, Speck* and *Schinken*, would have to last the entire year.

"Die Mutter hat immer aus grossen Töpfen gekocht," my aunts liked to tell me. "Mother always cooked in large pots!" For, in addition to her husband and four children, there was always a journeyman and one or two hungry young apprentices at the table. Potatoes were a staple in their diet; hardly a day went by without eating potatoes. Agnes learned from an early age how to peel potatoes with a paring knife – dirt-encrusted potatoes, rough and uneven, their peels not as tender and thin as today. Agnes' father would get extremely upset if he caught anyone peeling the potatoes too deep. (I doubt my grandfather knew that the vitamins are very close to the skin, but all food was precious, and not to be wasted!)

I still remember my mother sitting at our kitchen table, a bowl in her lap, and peeling potatoes with a paring knife. I thought it was an art, how she created such thin peelings curling off the potato....

Sunday mornings the family attended church, and on Sunday afternoons Agnes' mother liked nothing more than to visit family in Zeven. When she was newly married and planning to move to Sittensen, one of Meta's chief concerns had been to find someone to replace her in her brother's household, as she had become very attached to her nephew and nieces, especially little Meta, her namesake, who, not yet three years old at the time, had never known any other "mother". Knowing how difficult the separation would be for the children, she very much wanted to find just the right person to whom she could entrust the nurturing of her brother's children. Maria von Bargen (Tante Marie) had proved to be such a person. In fact, less than a year after officially assuming her duties as housekeeper, the 34-year-old spinster gladly accepted Ernst Bartel's proposal of marriage, becoming his second wife and stepmother to his children.

My mother never knew her grandparents (her last living grandparent, her *Großvater* Hinrich Bartels of Zeven, died in 1908 when she was only two). But Agnes did know her aunts and uncles. For the Bredehöft children, it was always an adventure to visit Onkel Ernst and Tante Marie in Zeven and their three older Bartels cousins – Hinrich, Anna and Meta, their older cousins, whom their mother had cared for before she was married and had children of her own. Agnes also knew her father's twin brother, Onkel Johann, and his half-sister, Tante Maria (Gütsch) who lived too far away (south of Bremervörde) for them to visit, but with whom their mother corresponded frequently, along with their father's other married half-sister, Tante Anna (Tietjen) who lived in Büsum on the North Sea.

Usually people walked everywhere, but Zeven, nine miles away, was too far to walk, so for Sunday visits to Zeven, their father would have to rent a horse and wagon. Then the whole family would pile in, leaving behind the apprentice to tend the goats!

On Sundays the children also looked forward to eating *Kuchen* – usually *Butterkuchen,* a "sheet cake" with a yeast dough base and a simple topping of butter and sugar, baked the day before. Around four o'clock in the afternoon, their mother would spread a fresh, clean, hand-embroidered tablecloth, starched and ironed, over the kitchen table, take down china plates, cups and saucers from the cupboard and set the table nicely while she brewed a pot of coffee and prepared hot cocoa for the children.

In a German household, the tradition of *"Kaffee und Kuchen"*, Sunday afternoon coffee time, was taken very seriously and is still very much alive today, a non-negotiable cultural ritual enjoyed by people of all ages, classes, and social groups throughout Germany and Austria.

Besides summer, the most favorite time of the year was Christmas. In those days, Christmas was celebrated quite differently than today; it had less to do with receiving lots of presents and more to do with the coming of the *Christkind* – Christmas carols, special holiday food (and plenty of it!), and last but not least - the Christmas tree itself, its candles all aglow!

Christmas trees were always freshly felled and were not set up and decorated until December 24. In the afternoon on Christmas Eve, the church would be packed for the Christmas service, with a dramatization of the Christmas story and the whole congregation joining in singing the ancient and beloved Christmas carols: *"Macht hoch die Tür"*; *"Vom Himmel hoch, da komm ich her"*; *"Es Ist Ein Ros Entsprungen"*; *"Nun singet und seid froh"*; *"O du fröhliche, o du selige"*, and *"Stille Nacht, Heilige Nacht"*.

The traditional meal on Christmas Eve was potato salad and *Würstchen* (sausages). Afterwards, the door would be opened to the *Stube* which was lit only by the (real) candles on the tree their mother had decorated with homemade ornaments of straw, pine cones, small red apples, strings of nuts, and baked and decorated figures. In those days before electricity, how the children's eyes lit up as they stood in amazement in front of the burning tree, while everyone joined in singing *"O Tannenbaum"*. Then their father would open the family Bible and read from the Christmas story of *Luke, Chapter 2*: "And it came to pass in those days, that there went out a decree from Caesar Augustus that all the world…" Although everyone knew the story of Jesus' birth by heart, yet it was always new and fresh. It would not have been Christmas without the reading of the Christmas story.…

All the while, the children would be peeking at the side table, where a *Bunter Teller*, "colorful plate" was awaiting each child, filled with a colorful assortment of traditional Christmas goodies – nuts, *Lebkuchen* (gingerbread), sweets wrapped in bright-colored paper, a shiny red apple, and maybe even an orange (considered a rare, exotic treat in those days)! Each child would also receive a small gift, but nothing extravagant; it was always something practical: warm woolen stockings; a new pinafore (apron); linen handkerchiefs or a new piece to embroider; hair ribbons – a ball for Jonny. Their doll always got a new dress, hand crocheted by their mother.

Afterwards everyone joined in singing more of the beloved Christmas carols: *"Alle Jahre wieder"*; *"Leise rieselt der Schnee"*; *"Ihr Kinderlein kommet"*; *"Süßer die Glocken nie klingen"*, and again at the end, *"Stille Nacht"*!

Why all the singing? Well, because in those days, that's what people did when they got together. People made their own music and entertained themselves by singing. Children learned the songs at school, at church, and from the grown-ups. Their repertoire was huge – from folksongs to hymns to more popular songs – and they could sing all the verses!

Back then, it seemed, people were always singing: Women sang as they went about their housework and sang their babies with lullabies to sleep. Men also sang or whistled while they went about their work – men with horses and carts sang on the road, and it was not at all unusual to hear someone singing or whistling in the street as they went by. One of my fondest recollections as a youngster is of listening to our relatives singing the beautiful German folksongs whenever they got together. Their nostalgic singing was always spontaneous and from the heart.

On Christmas Day, their mother cooked a goose. The side dishes were always red cabbage with apples, boiled potatoes, and the gravy from the roast goose. And for dessert: *Rote Grütze*, compote of stewed red fruits, served with vanilla sauce. Later in the afternoon, the table would be set one more time for *Kaffee und Kuchen*, and their mother would bring out the Christmas cookies, baked weeks in advance, and kept hidden…

The second day of Christmas, December 26 (in Germany, Christmas lasts for three days, beginning with Christmas Eve) was spent visiting relatives. Going anywhere required a great deal of planning. Their father would have to borrow a horse, and as long as the children were small, it was too cold for them to travel in an open cart. It was easier for their relatives to come to Sittensen. But once the children were older, the Bredehöfts would spend the second Christmas day visiting the Bartels family in their large house in Zeven where there was much more room.

When Europe went to war in 1914, Agnes was just eight years old. By the time the Great War ended, she was twelve. At school, she learned that their beloved Kaiser was surrounded by enemies: the Franzmann, the Tommy, and the Iwan – the French, the English and the Russians. (Since U.S. forces only entered World War I at the tail end of the conflict, I'm not certain what they were called, but by that time, it didn't matter. By then, the German people just wanted desperately for the fighting to end.)

At the start of the conflict, August 1914, nobody thought it would last very long. The young boys leaving to fight in 'the war to end all wars" were sent off with brass bands and cheers. Everyone was certain of victory and that the fighting would be over by Christmas. But the soldiers did not come home for Christmas. Instead, the war would drag on for four long years...

Two years into the war, conditions were already rapidly deteriorating on the home front, with severe food shortages reported in all the urban areas. Since the German government had not made any preparations for a long, drawn-out conflict, there weren't any food supplies in reserve, and due to the British sea blockade, any supplies arriving by sea were cut off. Also, since many farmers had been recruited into the army, their horses requisitioned by the military, there were not enough farm workers or horses left to work the fields or bring in the harvests.

Then came the *Hungerwinter* of 1916/17. That year, not only the potato crop failed, but an abnormally cold winter would lead to a shortage of coal for fuel. The overburdened railway system, also short on coal, was unable to transport potatoes to urban areas in a timely manner, so that many potatoes rotted during transport. Plus feeding the troops took priority, which also resulted in food shortages for the civilian population. Before long, people in the cities were going hungry. That is when the government, in order to prevent mass starvation, turned to the lowly rutabaga (*Steckrübe* or field turnip) and began distributing this root vegetable (usually fed to livestock) as a substitute for potatoes and meat.

And so it was that large parts of the German population were kept alive on a diet consisting of rutabaga and little else. People had no other choice than to eat rutabaga fixed every way they could think of for breakfast, dinner and supper. During the *Hungerwinter*, or so-called "turnip winter" of 1916/17 (and the following year as well), the townspeople of Sittensen held mass action days for the collection and transport of wagonloads of field turnips to the starving populations of Bremen and Hamburg.

The war dragged on, with newspapers reporting horrendous casualties. The "Great War" would cause death and suffering on an industrial scale.

[Out of a population of 65 million, Germany would suffer the loss of 2 million young men, with another 4.3 million men being wounded (crippled, blinded, etc.) during the conflict. The total casualties, including the death of 800,000 German civilians (from malnutrition and starvation!) amounted to almost four percent of the population.]

To compensate for the heavy combat losses, ever more civilians were called up to serve. In 1916, Agnes' father (forty-four years old and father of four, all under the age of twelve!) was conscripted into the *Landsturm*, a reserve or support militia. Although the *Landsturm* rarely went into combat, Agnes' family would be without its main provider for the remainder of the war. Their apprentice, too, had to be let go. Only the old journeyman stayed on to work the forge.

Jakob Bredehöft with his reserve unit in World War I

Their mother was an excellent cook, but especially during the final winter of the war, she was limited to the few ingredients available: Fresh meat was no longer available, but potatoes and rutabagas together made a tasty stew, mashed with *Schmalz* (lard). *Braunkohl*, or kale, which could be harvested throughout the winter, was also flavored with *Speck*. Sometimes there was nothing to eat but *Brotsuppe*, "bread soup" made from the remnant of a loaf of rye bread. Their mother would soak the old, hard bread in hot water, then press it through a sieve and cook it in goat's milk until it was thickened, then sweeten it with honey or beet sugar. She often

The Bredehöft sisters Agnes (left), Adelheid and Meta during World War I. Here they are dressed in their Sunday best, the white sailor-suit inspired cotton dresses fashionable at the time. For everyday they wore "pinafore" dresses, covered with an apron, with thick black stockings, tightly-buttoned or lace-up boots, and woolen undergarments. How thin they were!

made milk soup with potatoes. A really good meal was hand-made noodles mixed with breadcrumbs that had been fried in butter. Supper usually consisted of *Bratkartoffeln*, fried potatoes served up in a large skillet with *Speck* (diced bacon) and onions. Pickled herring served with boiled potatoes had always been a favorite dish, but with the British blockade in force, and with fishermen unable to put out to sea, even herring, considered poor people's fish, was unavailable.

The increasing food shortages eventually lead to hunger protests and massive strikes in the cities. The German people began to demand an end to the senseless war; they began demanding peace. In the end, the German Navy itself mutinied, and by early November 1918, when it appeared that a revolution was breaking out, Kaiser Wilhelm II was forced to abdicate and fled to safety in Holland. With the signing of an Armistice on November 11, 1918, the Great War was finally over!

Breathless from running, Meta and Agnes came home from school one day with the shocking news that the Kaiser's portrait had been removed from their classroom! Their teacher had explained that Germany was no longer a constitutional monarchy, but a Republic with a democratic constitution.

Germany had lost the war. Its economy was in shambles. In cities like Hamburg and Bremen, there was hunger, lawlessness and chaos, with communist, radical right-wing and leftist political groups battling it out in the streets. But unlike in the large urban areas, small, rural towns did not experience much hunger, unemployment or street fighting after the war. In fact, in Sittensen, life quickly returned to normal. Agnes' father returned home, and the farmers and townspeople once again went about their business and tried their best to pick up where they had left off four years earlier.

The photo below shows my grandfather preparing a horseshoe for shoeing a horse. He has lifted the searing-hot horseshoe from the blazing forge and is hammering it into shape, fitting it to the horse's hoof. The apprentice, meanwhile, is plunging the other horseshoe into the fiery pit, which explains the cloud of smoke arising next to the horse.

The man holding the splendid horse is Köthner Diedrich Pape, Frau Pape's now grownup son.

The large gear-wheel next to the door is a type of horse-drawn winch powered by a horizontal shaft to which horses were yoked and driven round in a circle. It was used to power the early threshing machines.

At the far right, Agnes' brother, Jonny, is working on an old ammunition wagon (left over from the war) which has been converted into a lime spreader for agricultural use.

The sign above the door reads: "Jacob Bredehöft, Schmiedemeister – Fahrrad-Reparatur".

Jacob Bredehöft blacksmith shop, ca. 1924

*Agnes' father,
Jacob Bredehöft,
hard at work
(ca. 1924)*

Agnes was now thirteen years old, and with just one more year of school to go, she was also attending evening catechism classes in preparation for her confirmation the following spring. Meta, one year ahead of Agnes, had been confirmed the previous Easter.

Fourteen was usually the age when children were confirmed as members of the church. It was also the age when formal schooling came to an end. Only a very small minority of children belonging to the professional or upper classes went on to higher education. Working class boys would either become apprentices to a trade or would go to work as rural farm laborers or as urban factory workers. For girls, there were hardly any occupational choices. Most would seek work as maids or servants, but were paid very little for their services, as there were so many young girls looking for work. It was always assumed that Jonny would learn the blacksmith trade from his father, while Meta and Agnes were taught domestic skills by their mother. At the time, it was common practice for a young girl just out of school to earn some pocket money as a *Haustochter,* a young (female) live-in servant usually regarded as one of the family. As *Haustochter,* she would look after the younger children and assist the housewife in whatever chores she was assigned. Once a young girl had gained experience as a *Haustochter,* she could enter into service (*"in Stellung gehen"*) as a housemaid, usually for a well-off family in a larger town. She could then begin saving for a dowry in the hope of eventually marrying and becoming a housewife.

In June of 1920 Agnes turned fourteen. Since Meta had already been away, working as a *Haustochter* the previous year, it was now Agnes' turn. (Only one of the sisters could leave home at a time, since the other was needed to help at home.)

With so many of her schoolmates eager to find work, Agnes was fortunate to find a position as *Haustochter* at the parsonage. Her mother had assured the pastor's wife that Agnes had always been good at looking after her younger sister, Adelheid, that Agnes already knew a great deal about housekeeping, that she had a serious attitude toward work and was sure to be diligent in her duties. So Agnes went to live with Pastor Willenbrock and his family in the large, newly-built parsonage where she was kept busy from morning to night looking after the

Meta (second from left) with her confirmation class – Easter, 1919

Picture postcard of Meta posing with Jonny at her confirmation

The reverse side of the postcard is dated April 21, 1919. Written by Agnes' mother and addressed to Herrn Johann Tietje, husband of Anna Tietje, her sister-in-law. The Tietjes resided in the distant town of Büsum near Osterdeichstrich on the North Sea.

In her exquisite handwriting, Agnes' mother writes: "Fröhliche Ostern senden Familie Bredehöft. Das sind nun unsere beiden konfirmierten Kinder." ("Easter Greetings from the Bredehöft family, with a photo of our two confirmed children.")

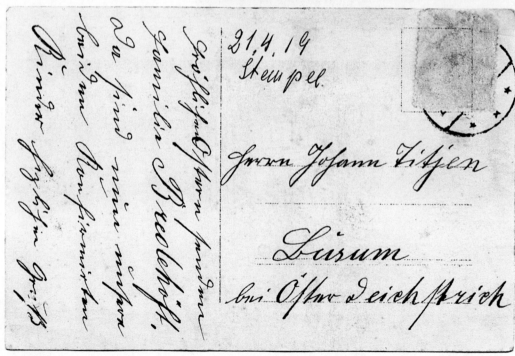

children plus helping with the housework. She could visit her family only on Sunday afternoons and the occasional evening. Also on holidays she could go home.

The following two years were spent in the same manner – Meta and Agnes taking turns working as *Haustöchter* outside the home.

In June of 1922 Agnes turned sixteen. That year, her birthday on June 4th coincided with the official holiday of *Pfingsten,* the church holiday celebrated fifty days after Easter. In Germany, *Pfingsten*, like Christmas and Easter, is celebrated two days – *Pfingstsonntag* and *Pfingstmontag.*

Pfingsten was one of Agnes' favorite holidays. Since it took place either at the end of May or the beginning of June, it meant the coming of warm weather. The whole town would be decorated with fresh greens and birch branches to symbolize nature's reawakening. The festivities were geared towards young people, with a maypole, sports contests, and in the evening – dancing! There was also a procession through town. Agnes rode alongside Meta atop a float decorated with garlands of fresh greens.

As sisters, Meta and Agnes were very close, but Meta could also be unkind, teasing Agnes, calling her *"Spitzbart"* (pointed beard) because she had inherited their father's prominent chin. Meta, who resembled their mother, had a pretty, rounded face. But although perhaps not as good-looking as Meta, Agnes had a distinctive beauty of her own. Tall and slender, what really set her apart, not only from her older sister, but from every other young girl in town, was her bearing – the elegant way she carried herself, so that even the townswomen would comment on her erect, upright posture. Agnes, with her light walk and straight posture, exuded confidence. (I never noticed my mother slouched or stooped over. Even when she was exhausted or defeated, she never revealed it in her posture.)

Meta and Agnes atop a decorated "Pfingstwagen" featuring the young maidens of Sittensen, all dressed in white (1922)

Agnes at age sixteen

The next year, 1923, was Agnes' turn to remain at home. Meta was now *"in Stellung"* some distance away, in Stade, a port city some forty kilometers to the north. For the working classes, time off or leisure time as we know it was unheard of. Meta would only have every other Sunday afternoon off, and since Stade was so distant, she would not return home until after her full year of service was up.

Economically, it was a very bad time in Germany. Under the crushing terms of the Treaty of Versailles (Article 231), Germany had been forced to accept all blame for the War and to pay huge reparations to the Allies. Faced with reparation payments it could

Meta at age seventeen

Adelheid at age eleven

Agnes with friends (1923)

not afford, the German Government began printing exaggerated amounts of money, which resulted in inflation. By the spring of 1923, inflation was out of control; prices had increased by millions of times their previous level! The Germans, who believed in the values of hard work and decency, were dazed and inflation-shocked. How was it that their money had become worthless?

As a result of runaway inflation, many people had to give up their lifetime plans. For example, it was the custom for the bride to bring some money (dowry) to a marriage; thus, many marriages were called off. People who had worked a lifetime found that their pensions would not even buy a cup of coffee; those who had put money aside lost all their savings. They would receive a letter from the bank stating that their savings account was being closed. The bank would then enclose a 1-Million mark banknote, as that was the smallest denomination they had. But the postage alone was 2 million marks!

Much to her dismay, Agnes discovered that her earnings from the previous year were now worthless. She had worked an entire year and couldn't even afford to buy a pair of stockings!

"Pity the wage earners who have a family to support!" her mother tried to console her. "By the time they get paid at the end of the week, there's not enough money to buy bread to feed their families."

Agnes' mother kept her weekly household money in an old tea canister. One day Agnes watched as her father took out a handful of banknotes, spread them out and counted them.

"Look here, Agnes, millions and billions worth of cash! Never did we have so much money! What do you think, one day we'll be rich? Wouldn't that be nice!" he uttered sarcastically, as he added a brand new 1-Billion!! mark banknote to the container and then returned to the forge, where a farmer was waiting to have his horses shod.

Agnes walked over to the container, lifted the lid, and then stared at the worthless money inside. She still couldn't grasp the idea that she had worked a whole year and yet had nothing to show for it. For a long time, she just stood there, listening to the sounds of the forge, the familiar sound of hammer striking anvil.

"How hard father works!" she thought. "And for what!?"

Agnes knew that her father had long since set up bartering arrangements with the local farmers and tradesmen like himself whereby they would pay each other in produce, labor or skills instead of in valueless currency. Now, perhaps for the first time in her young life, she realized how poor they were, and that in future, her parents would never be able to provide for her. Her father, though highly respected, was only a blacksmith who didn't even own his own shop. And now, on top of everything, like millions of others, his modest lifetime savings had been wiped out, lost to inflation.

No wonder that Agnes began to conceive the idea of going to America! Or was it her mother's bedtime stories, her mother's own America experience, which fueled her desire. After all, her mother had done the exact same thing when she was her age, although things had been quite different in her mother's time. Back then, you didn't even need a sponsor to go to America. But Agnes was hopeful that her aunt in New York, Tante Anna, might agree to sponsor her....

The neighbor's son, twenty-year old Heinrich (Heini) Burgdorf, a druggist's clerk by trade, was very keen on emigrating. Heini Burgdorf was totally convinced that in America he could get rich. There was just one drawback: He didn't have any money, and he didn't know anyone in America who could sponsor him. But Agnes, he knew, had relatives in New York...

Agnes, tired of being poor, thought she would replicate what her mother had done. She would go to New York, work hard for a few years, earn good wages, and then return home.

To her surprise, her parents were not entirely against the idea. Given the dire economic situation at home, emigration would at least provide one of their children with a chance to get ahead. But at the same time, Agnes' mother was wise enough to know that her young daughter was clueless, that she didn't really understand the full implication of what it meant to emigrate – the very real possibility that she might never return, might never see her family again. Nor did her daughter have a grasp of the loneliness and homesickness that awaited her. Agnes was so youthful, so naively confident. Obviously, the Burgdorf's son had done a good job of convincing her that they could both "get rich" in America.

Agnes' mother thought long and hard. It was obvious that the Burgdorfs were counting on her to find a sponsor for their son, and she sincerely wanted to help, as the Burgdorfs had been their neighbors and friends these many years. Wilhelm Burgdorf was even a godfather to her oldest daughter! Still, she hesitated to write to her sister in New York. Most likely Anna would agree to sponsor Agnes and (hopefully) pay for her ship's passage, but she couldn't possibly ask her sister to sponsor the neighbor's boy as well!

What to do....

And then it occurred to her: She would ask her brother Ernst in Zeven for the address of the Tobabens!

Agnes' mother could barely remember the Tobabens. Her aunt, Käthe Tobaben, née Sievers, was her father's half-sister; they shared the same mother, Anna Katharina Fitschen! Aunt Käthe's son, Henri, had gone to America some thirty years earlier to homestead in a place called Nebraska, where his parents and sister had later joined him. It was rumored among their relatives in Germany that the Tobabens had done very well in America, that Cousin Henri owned a lot of land...

She would write to these "forgotten" relatives in America. Surely Aunt Käthe, if she was still alive, could use some household help, and one always heard that farm laborers were very much in demand in America. And even though Heini Burgdorf had apprenticed as a druggist, surely he wouldn't mind working as a farm laborer for a few years… If only Cousin Henri would agree to sponsor both children! Besides, it would be such a comfort to her if Agnes and the Burgdorf boy could make the long trip to Nebraska together.

And that is exactly what happened. Six weeks later, Agnes' mother received a reply from her cousin, Henri Tobaben, stating that he and his elderly mother (Tante Käthe) would be willing to take young Agnes into their home, and that they had already found a place for the young Burgdorf boy where he could work off his passage. In short, Henri Tobaben had agreed to sponsor both young people and to pay their ship's passage to New York plus their train fare to Nebraska! Agnes and Heini were scheduled to sail from Bremen on September 29th aboard the brand new trans-Atlantic liner, the *S.S. München*.

Agnes was simply bursting with excitement, filled with anticipation of her new life in America. She was seventeen years old – a young, working-class girl who had never been anywhere in her life. With everything she owned packed inside a small cardboard case, she said goodbye to her family and friends, gave her mother one last hug, and then, gaily waving to their neighbors and friends who had gathered to see them off, she and Heini Burgdorf climbed onto the horse drawn wagon that would take them as far as Zeven. From there they would continue by train to Bremen where they would board the ship for America.

In her old age, Agnes' then twelve-year-old sister, Adelheid, could still vividly recall the parting scene: Agnes in an open farm wagon, gaily waving and calling out in farewell: "I'm going to America! I'm going to get rich!"

November 1923 was the height of the German inflation, with one U.S. dollar worth 4.200,000,000,000 German marks – **that's 4.2 trillion!**

But Agnes was gone; she had left the whole mess behind her.

Sixty-eight thousand people emigrated from Germany to America in 1923. My mother was one of them.

A&A

CHAPTER 4

Sei allem Abschied voran, als wäre er hinter Dir.
[Anticipate each goodbye, as if it were already behind you.]
– Rainer Maria Rilke, Sonnet #13:2

NEARLY ALL the passengers were on deck that bright, clear morning of October 9, 1923 as the stately SS München slowly steamed its way toward New York Harbor. As the skyline came ever nearer, eager immigrants crowding the railings of the lower decks looked with wonder and then began waving enthusiastically, many crying with emotion, as the great ocean liner passed by the Statue of Liberty – that lovely lady who lifted her lamp to welcome them and who seemed to represent all of their hopes and dreams for the future!

But the exhilaration and anticipation Agnes shared with her fellow passengers soon gave way to a combination of confusion and anxiety as she and the other 557 people in steerage disembarked and were immediately directed onto ferries that shuttled them to Ellis Island, the immigrant receiving and processing station for third-class/steerage passengers entering the United States.

The anxious immigrants already had a vague idea of what awaited them. On Ellis Island they would have to undergo a legal and medical evaluation. Pinned with their name and number from the ship's manifest, the 558 third-class passengers were herded up the stairway to the Registry Room where they were made to file past a line of health inspectors.

Agnes nervously awaited her turn. The first medical examiner inspected her ears and scalp, her neck and hands. In his fingers he held a piece of white chalk. Agnes held her breath. Although she was certain that she was healthy and free of disease, she knew that if she did not pass this initial inspection she would be marked with the chalk and be led out of line for further medical evaluation.

Next was the dreaded eye exam. On board the ship, rumors of this particular inspection had terrified her. But it was over in a few seconds, as the doctor tilted her head back and swiftly flipped her eyelids inside out with a button hook, looking for symptoms of trachoma. The discovery of this disease, God forbid, meant certain deportation!

A quick legal evaluation followed. An immigration inspector, assisted by an interpreter, quickly reviewed the twenty-nine items of information contained on the ship manifest questionnaire pertaining to her person: five-foot-six, fair complexion, dark blond hair and green eyes; her legality, including name and place of origin; whether she was a polygamist or an anarchist; occupation (none), whether in possession of fifty dollars, or less (Agnes had the requisite $25 in her pocket), a pre-paid rail ticket (yes) and/or sufficient funds to pay the railroad fare to her final destination; whether she had a sponsor (yes), sponsor's name, address and relationship. Having a sponsor was a must; without one, most unskilled would-be immigrants were rejected outright because they were considered "likely to become a public charge." Since everyone had already practiced answering these questions on board the ship, the long line moved quickly. When it came her turn, the inspector quickly checked the manifest, and glancing at young Agnes, gave her a brief nod of approval and her landing card.

She had made it! Five hours later, Agnes and Heini Burgdorf found themselves again being ferried on a barge to the main railway terminal where they would board one of the many steam-engine trains en route from New York to Chicago. Traveler's Aid, an immigrant aid society, came to their assistance, helping them board the right train, and handing them each a box lunch. And so, with their admittance cards, their railway tickets and their box lunches in hand, they were on their way in America!

The passenger arrival list had noted their final destination as Eustis, Frontier County, Nebraska. Since they spoke no English, Traveler's Aid tagged their coats with a destination card to alert the train conductor where they should change trains and where to get off.

The journey from New York to Nebraska would prove long and exhausting. As immigrants, they traveled the most cheaply, "second class" – meaning, by "day-coach" – sitting upright all day and all night, as coaches back then did not have reclining seats. Air conditioning in the coal-burning, steam-powered train was via open windows. The sun was hot in the late afternoon; the air inside the coach soon became warm, the musty smell of steam and coal dust overwhelming. But when the unwitting passengers opened the windows to let in fresh air, they were soon covered in smoke and cinders.

Agnes and Heini could not afford to eat in the dining car (which anyway was used almost exclusively by those traveling in the Pullman sleeping cars). They tried to make their box lunches last; Heini shared the apples he bought from one of the 'newsboys' that boarded the train selling newspapers, candy and other food items.

The 800-mile train ride to Chicago would take twenty-four hours. Since they had left New York in the late afternoon, there was no way they could make their connection in Chicago – the Chicago, Burlington & Quincy Railroad's daily 9:30 a.m. departure. Once in Chicago, they would have to spend their second night in America on a station bench at Union Station. After a restless night, they splashed cold water on their faces, purchased some sandwiches for the trip west, and at 9:30 a.m. caught the Chicago Burlington, due to arrive at Holdrege, Nebraska at 6:51 a.m. the following day. There they waited for the local "milk-run" that left Holdrege at 8:30 a.m. and arrived in Eustis at 10:20 a.m.

Thus it was that Agnes, wearing high-top leather shoes, a long, heavy skirt and a shirtwaist wrinkled and no longer fresh, her braided hair untidy and her face smudged with soot, arrived in Eustis on the morning of Friday, October 12, 1923 – three days after arriving in America.

The state of Nebraska was sparsely populated in the early 1920s. Even today it is still very rural, especially the Holdrege-Eustis area. From her seat by the train window, Agnes watched the rugged Nebraskan countryside pass by – a brown, nearly treeless, prairie landscape totally unlike the lush green landscape of fields, meadows, streams and scattered forests of her low-lying homeland. Instead of compact, well-tended fields, she looked out on wild, unfenced grazing land and rough, hilly terrain. Deep canyons came into view; cattle appeared, grazing on dry, bare hillsides. From his seat opposite, Heini, who in his youth had read a great many adventure stories about the "Wild West", was secretly hoping to catch sight of a herd of buffalo or even a red-faced *Indianer* on horseback, while Agnes, for her part, was inwardly relieved when farmland fields gradually appeared – not the compact, tidy, familiar looking fields of home, but long, wide stretches of dry wheat stubble and tall, pale yellow corn stalks – fields that appeared to go on forever. Nebraska, by its sheer size, seemed to her a very deserted country, empty of all but the occasional isolated farmstead and a scattering of small towns where their slow "milk train" regularly halted to pick up and deliver milk cans, mail, freight and a handful of local passengers along the way.

Agnes did not yet know the history of this place. She did not know that until quite recently, this land had been home to the Plains Indians who had roamed the territory for thousands of years, hunting buffalo. Only in the middle of the last century had the white, professional buffalo hunters arrived. Armed with powerful long-range rifles, they had killed off the buffalo by the millions, thus destroying the Natives' traditional way of life. When the buffalo were all but gone, the Indians could no longer survive and were 'removed', forced onto reservations. Then the cattlemen had come, followed by the first white settlers in the 1870s.

The Homestead Act, signed into law by President Lincoln in 1862, offered free land to anyone willing to brave the frontier, which at that time meant west of the Mississippi River. Beginning January 1, 1863, any U.S. citizen – or *intended* citizen – could claim up to 160 acres (a quarter-section, or a half-mile on each side) and take title by simply living on and farming the land for five years. Those brave early settlers found a vast prairie awaiting them, with hardly any trees except a few cottonwoods and willows along the creeks and river bottoms. Since timber and stone were scarce, the settlers plowed up chunks of the rich, heavy prairie soil and then constructed houses made from the dense sod, praying that their sod homes would withstand the hostile weather – rain and drought, extreme heat and cold, prairie fires, blizzards and the strong winds of the Nebraska plains that constantly threatened to lift off their roofs. Due to fear of flooding, the early settlers avoided the river bottoms, settling first along creek land and then in the hills and the uplands, where access to water, however, was a problem. Since water was scarce, in addition to collecting rainwater, they had either to haul it for long distances or dig for it (although they had not the means to dig deep wells). For many of the settlers, the venture was "a dream come true." But life on the prairie was not a paradise, and others did not succeed. Some of the settlers had no familiarity with farming; some nearly starved, and after years of hard work, simply gave up and abandoned their claims to the land.

To encourage the planting of trees, the Law was later modified. Homesteaders could obtain an additional eighty acres if they planted four or five acres of trees for vegetation and shade. The settlers planted ash and elm and box elders, and rows of red cedars to serve as a windbreak around their farmsteads.

In time, the settlers would dig wells powered by windmills to pump water from deep underground and constructed cisterns to store the water. Eventually, farming became profitable, and in a decade or two, the sod homes were replaced by frame structures using lumber shipped in by rail.

The thought of free land not only enticed folks living in the eastern United States to settle in the West; it also lured millions of Europeans to America. To working class

Sod home with windmill (1902). George Johnson (husband of cousin Dorothy Heller Johnson) and his twelve siblings grew up in this three-room sod house, nine miles south of Brady, Nebraska.

people in Europe, where land ownership was severely limited and where people had been forced for generations to "stay put," the idea of being able to move out and stake their claims to free land must have seemed unimaginable. German settlers were the first to arrive in Nebraska in great numbers toward the end of the 19th century. Known for their diligence, hard work, and respect for the law, German immigrants were welcomed, and by the 1920s, Germans were the most populous ethnic group in Nebraska.

Until World War I, the German language was often heard throughout the United States: Church services were held in German, German was taught in schools, and German was the language of many local newspapers. But all this was forbidden during the 1914-1918 anti-German hysteria, when fear or hatred of Germany reached new heights, thanks to the propaganda put out by the American government in which Germans were depicted as "brutal barbarians who reveled in nailing babies to fences and gouging out their eyes!" From 1917, when the United States joined the War, German was forbidden in schools, churches, in meetings and in public places. German music was neither played nor sold. Restaurants changed the names of German dishes: *Sauerkraut* was given the name "liberty cabbage" or "pickled vegetable", frankfurters were renamed "hot dogs", and even hamburger was renamed "Salisbury steak" because its name was considered to be too German! German measles were called "liberty measles".

In cities and towns with telephone service, German was even forbidden over the telephone; if a telephone operator overheard you speaking German, she had instructions to immediately disconnect the call! Newspapers printed reports of people in cities being arrested on the street for speaking German! In fact, German language and culture in the United States was dealt such a severe blow during and after World War I that it never really recovered. In rural communities, however, especially where Germans were in the majority, such open hostility toward German-Americans was rare. In Eustis, the German language was still alive and well.

Incorporated in 1888, the thriving town of Eustis was a pure German farm community. Located in Frontier County in the southwestern part of the state, the town, with a population of 450, supported many prosperous businesses that provided for the needs of the townspeople as well as those of the surrounding farms.

Two hours out of Holdrege, the slow-moving train with Agnes and Heini onboard finally pulled into Eustis. Their sponsor, Henri Tobaben, was waiting at the busy train depot, dressed as always when he came to town, in a suit and hat.

"Herzlich Willkommen!" Henri greeted them warmly, as he politely picked up Agnes' flimsy cardboard suitcase (carrying all her worldly belongings) and carried it over to where a motorized vehicle was standing. Agnes could hardly believe her eyes.

"Ist das etwa Dein Motorwagon?" she asked incredulously. She had never ridden in an automobile. Indeed, back home, only two people in town owned a *Motorwagon* – Herr Pastor Willenbrock und Herr Doktor Ludewig! But sure enough, Henri was

soon stooping to crank up his Ford Model T, ordering them to climb in, and before long, Agnes and Heini were being transported by motorcar along Middle Canyon Road, the narrow dirt road leading directly south from town.

On this dusty gravel road there were two very deep canyons to navigate. At the base of the first steep incline, Agnes was first astonished, and then quickly panicked when Henri Tobaben suddenly stopped, turned the motorcar around, and then proceeded to slowly climb up the long, steep hill backwards!

"That way it won't stall," Henri explained to his bewildered passengers. [The car could not climb a steep hill going forwards, as the Model T, having no fuel pump, relied on gravity to feed gas to the carburetor.]

Agnes sat wide-eyed, white-knuckled and speechless. She had never even seen a hill before, much less such a steep canyon!

Thus the little party of three made its way south, motoring along the narrow gravel road at the exhilarating speed of ten miles per hour. After a good nine miles, and after negotiating some very steep hills indeed, they arrived at the Christ Naumann farm shortly after noon. Here they stopped to drop off Heini, who in the coming weeks would be working for Henri and the Naumanns as a farmhand, at least until the corn-husking season was over. As a trained druggist's clerk, a tentative job then awaited him in Eustis at Taborsky Pharmacy where Heini hoped to work off his debt to Henri Tobaben in no time.

The Naumanns were expecting them, and all were invited to join the family for noon dinner – boiled potatoes and stuffed cabbage – Agnes' first hot meal since arriving in America.

Mrs. Anna Naumann (Agnes already knew) was Henri Tobaben's sister, and during dinner Agnes was told the story of how Henri had come to Nebraska as a young man in 1892. After acquiring a quarter-section under the Homestead Act, he had sent for his parents and his sister the following year. Henri had never married; his sister had married Christ Naumann in 1901.

Agnes found the Naumanns and their three children, Otto, Gertrude and young Raymond, warm and welcoming. Their two-story frame farmhouse, with its wrap-around porch and surrounded by a white picket fence, seemed to Agnes such a pleasant, homey place. She was especially delighted to meet Gertrude, who was only a few years older. She hoped the two of them would become friends.

Later that afternoon, Henri Tobaben again fired up his Model T, and turning eastward, he and Agnes rattled on for another bumpy two miles toward their final destination – the Tobaben farm, where Henri lived with his elderly widowed mother. The wind had picked up, and Agnes began to shiver. In spite of her excitement, she suddenly felt chilled and very tired. Her long journey was finally over. On an isolated homestead eleven miles southeast of Eustis, her life in America could begin.

* * *

HENRI'S MOTHER, wrinkled, worn and stooped, welcomed the young girl warmly. Agnes would have her own bed, in an alcove off the kitchen, and since the following day was Saturday, in the morning she could have a nice bath. Totally exhausted, Agnes went to sleep early. Lying in the dark, before drifting into sleep, she could still feel the rhythm of the train as it clacked endlessly along the tracks.

Agnes awoke early to find Mrs. Tobaben already heating water in a large boiler on the kitchen stove. Agnes quickly helped fill the round, galvanized tub that Mrs. Tobaben had placed next to the stove, alternating pails of cold water carried in from the outside pump with boiling hot water from the stove. Then, crouched in the metal tub, first she, then the old woman, took turns bathing in front of the warm stove. At last, she felt clean again!

Later that morning, they drove over to the Naumanns from where Henri, together with Heini and the two Naumann boys, continued into Eustis by motorcar, while Agnes and Henri's mother were content to ride into town alongside Gertrude and her parents atop their farm wagon laden with eggs, cream and butter. They would not return until late, as going to town was an all-day affair. With a team and wagon, the trip into Eustis took almost two hours. It was a lovely fall day, however, and Agnes and Gertrude chatted the whole time, Gertrude acquainting Agnes with the other three families whose farmsteads they passed along the way, explaining how on Saturdays all the farmers drove into town to sell their fresh eggs, cream and home-churned butter, to run errands and pick up supplies, and to socialize. Gertrude assured Agnes that on the following day, Sunday, she would introduce Agnes to everyone at church.

Henri Tobaben and his mother

Henri Tobaben, in the driver's seat of his 1919 Ford Model T Center Door Sedan. Christ Naumann is in the back seat; young Raymond Naumann is perched on the running board.

The Naumanns and the Tobabens attended Salem Lutheran, a small pioneer church located three miles east of Henri's farm. Christ and Anna Naumann were very active in worship services there and were faithful workers in the little country church. Services were held in German, so Agnes felt comfortable right away, although in the beginning she couldn't understand a word during Sunday school, where the instruction was in English. Agnes soon looked forward to attending both Sunday church and Wednesday evening prayer services, as well as the many other social activities the small congregation afforded. She also looked forward to Sunday afternoons, which were often spent visiting the Naumanns, since the two families were so close. Other times they would take turns visiting with neighbors and friends.

Agnes had anticipated that there would be additional workers beside herself (*Knechte* and *Mägde*) on Henri's farm. And in fact, Henri Tobaben did occasionally hire a man or two to help out. However, most of the time Agnes was alone with Henri and his elderly mother, especially in the winter when there was very little fieldwork.

Anna Katharina (Katie) Tobaben, seventy-seven years old and widowed for over twenty years, had emigrated from Germany in 1893. At that time, she explained to her attentive young listener, the long ocean voyage, followed by an arduous overland journey (first by train, and then with a team and wagon from Omaha), had taken over four weeks! Mrs. Tobaben went on to explain to Agnes how she, her husband Otto and their two children, Hinrich (Henri) and Anna, had homesteaded in a small, two-room sod house, or 'soddie'. She described to Agnes how sod houses, built of dirt and grass, were not only difficult to keep clean, but they were also notorious for attracting insects, mice, and even snakes. Mrs. Tobaben especially enjoyed telling the story of how one morning, when she went to fetch her Sunday bonnet for church, she discovered a bull snake coiled up inside!

After homesteading nearly a decade in a primitive soddie, Mrs. Tobaben now took justifiable pride in her "real" home. A wood-frame house, it had been custom ordered from the Sears-Roebuck mail-order catalog. The entire wooden structure had arrived by railroad car in the form of pre-cut lumber, numbered and ready to be assembled like a giant puzzle. Henri, together with ten men from the surrounding farms, had gone into Eustis with their farm wagons and teams to collect it. Of course, the house had no electricity or indoor plumbing, but it was a fine structure nevertheless, quite roomy for a one-story dwelling, with a large, sunny kitchen, a dining room, and a seldom used front room or parlor, its windows lovingly hung with white lace curtains. Three smaller rooms – two bedrooms and a tiny alcove off the kitchen pantry – all faced the rear of the house.

With a thick row of cedars planted along the north and west sides of the farmhouse to shelter it from the wind, and with the ever-present windmill standing guard, Henri's farm was a typical Nebraska farmstead – a simple frame house surrounded by a large fenced-in vegetable garden, and a farmyard that sloped downward towards the barn and outbuildings that housed the livestock. There was also a corncrib, a grain bin, and a shed for farm implements and tools.

Unlike the mono-crop farming methods of today, Nebraska farms in the 1920's included a variety of plants and animals, a diversity that allowed the farmers to feed both themselves and their livestock. To preserve soil nutrients, farmers rotated what they planted. For example, in one field, a farmer planted oats one year, wheat next, and corn the next. Then, for two years, the farmer let clover or alfalfa grow to put nitrogen back in the soil. The alfalfa would also provide hay to feed the horses and cattle.

Cows supplied the farmer and his family with milk and cream. An average farm in those days had three or four milk cows and their calves, along with some heifers and a bull. Almost everyone kept a few hogs as well. Although the main cash crops were wheat and corn, an additional source of income came from the sale of a hog or a calf. A flock of several dozen chickens, scratching around the farmyard, provided the family with eggs as well as fresh meat.

In addition, each farmer had to keep from six to eight horses that required constant care and attention. Horses were the working animals about the farm, absolutely indispensable to tend the land. They required lots of oats and pasture hay.

In the fall, when the weather turned cold, it was time to butcher a hog to provide meat for the family through the winter. Men who had learned the butchering trade in Germany went around and helped others to butcher. Butchering was done during the cold months of the year so that the meat would not spoil. Since there was no electricity for refrigeration, the meat had to be preserved. The blood, intestines and meat scraps were turned into sausage. Larger cuts were salted and preserved as hams and bacon, but mainly meat was fried down and then stored in crocks, in between layers of lard. On butchering day, the housewife would fry the fresh meat all up at one time, layer it piece by piece in a large crock, and then pour melted pork grease (lard) over it to seal it. During the winter, she would then simply remove a layer of meat and lard as needed to cook with. The meat would stay good as long as the lard was cold and firm.

Everyone kept a vegetable garden for raising vegetables of all kinds. Most of the food was homegrown; very little was store-bought. In addition to a large potato patch, Mrs. Tobaben also grew beans, beets, turnips, carrots, onions and cabbage. Garden vegetables needed plenty of water and it was a lot of hard work irrigating the garden by hand. But Agnes enjoyed tending the garden; gardening reminded her of her mother, although the two vegetable gardens couldn't have been more different. The garden in Nebraska, where summers were dry and scorching hot, needed frequent watering, while back home in northern Germany, where rain fell in abundance all the year round, Agnes' mother had often fretted over the soil being too wet.

For nourishment during the winter, people relied heavily on the potatoes kept in the root cellar, where the canned goods preserved during the summer were also stored. Piled in a bin and covered with straw or burlap, the potatoes would keep well for months in the cold root cellar. Carrots and beets, layered in boxes of moist sand, would also keep for months in the dark dampness of the root cellar.

In October, *"The Eustis News"* would give notice when a railroad freight car was heading into town containing bushel baskets of apples. The apples would last for months if stored in a cool, airy place, but you would have to check them frequently, because it only took one rotten apple to spoil the whole bunch.

And then there was the cabbage. Preserved as *Sauerkraut* in a large crock, sauerkraut would also "keep" for a long time in the root cellar. Eating raw, fermented cabbage was sure to keep you healthy during the long winter months…

Besides canning vegetables, Mrs. Tobaben also made jam, from strawberries and other berries. In late summer, she sent Agnes along with Gertrude out to the hills to pick buckets full of wild grapes, wild plums, chokecherries and orange-colored buffalo berries that grew on bushes along the sloping sides of the canyons up in the pasture hills. Ever on the lookout for poison ivy, not to mention bull snakes and rattlers, these wild berry picking excursions reminded Agnes of outings to the moors, but when she tried to tell Gertrude about peat-cutting, Gertrude could not grasp the idea of treading on wet, soggy ground.

Later, Agnes and Mrs. Tobaben would spend hours in the sweltering kitchen in front of the hot stove, making preserves from the wild berries she had gathered.

To suddenly find herself living on an isolated Nebraska farm, eleven miles from the nearest town, must have been somewhat of a culture shock for young Agnes, who was used to living in a bustling town, surrounded by friends and neighbors, shopkeepers and craftsmen, in a predictable, orderly atmosphere, and all within easy walking distance.

She was also accustomed to certain "creature comforts" that did not exist in rural Nebraska. For one thing, Sittensen was also already wired for electric lighting. Even her parents' humble cottage had been wired for electricity the year before. But although by the late 1920s the town of Eustis itself had electricity, the surrounding farms would not have access to rural electrification until the late 1940s. Agnes carried a coal oil lamp when she went out to milk the cows at dawn and at dusk, and in the kitchen a kerosene lamp supplied light for reading, sewing or mending in the evening.

For another thing, her family's cottage back home was plumbed for water (it had a hand pump installed in the back kitchen), and used water from the scullery drained directly to the outside. But Henri Tobaben, in his extreme frugality, had not yet "modernized" the kitchen (by laying down a pipe connecting the cistern to the kitchen and installing a hand pump at the kitchen sink). Instead of having "piped", running water, all the water used in the house for cooking, washing or bathing had to be hauled in, bucket by overflowing bucket, from the cistern by the windmill. Just the mere job of bringing water into the house was exhausting. Then, since the kitchen "sink" was not fitted with a drainage pipe to direct the water outside, all the used water had to be collected and carried out of the house again – all by hand!

Monday was washday. On that day, Agnes hauled lots of water. After carrying it to the kitchen, the water had to be heated in a big wash kettle on the stove before the dirty clothes could be washed clean, scrubbed by hand on a washboard, using homemade lye soap. The rinse water also had to be carried in, but usually was not heated.

Since the Tobabens did not have a scullery for washing up dishes and laundering clothes, Mrs. Tobaben did the weekly washing in the kitchen. In summer, to avoid building such a big fire in the stove and making the kitchen even hotter than it was, she would heat the water outside in a big, black iron kettle and do the washing outside.

Back home, doing the family laundry had been a communal effort, with Frau Pape or one of the neighbor women sharing the laborious chore. Agnes wondered how Mrs. Tobaben had managed by herself all these years…

While the water on the stove was heating, two washtubs were brought into the kitchen and placed on a bench – one for rubbing the clothes on a washboard, and the other for rinsing them.

When the water in the large wash kettle came to a boil, soap shavings (using the bar of homemade lye soap) were added and the water was stirred until the soap dissolved. In the meantime, the clothes had been sorted according to color and degree of soiling. First the whites – bed sheets, linens, underwear – were dumped into the wash kettle and boiled for ten minutes, after which they were lifted out with a stick into the first washtub, where they were scrubbed first, rubbed on a washboard with more soap, followed by the darks (colored items), and lastly Henri's work pants. The colored clothes were never boiled, but were added to the soapy water in the first washtub after the whites had been scrubbed, lifted out, wrung out by hand, and then transferred to the second washtub to be rinsed.

After rinsing (more hauling of water!), the sheets, and then the remaining clothes, were wrung out by hand, loaded into a wash basket, and then taken to the clothesline and hung to dry, winter or summer.

When done with the washing, the soapy wash water was used to scrub the porch and the outdoor toilet. The rinse water was used to give the rough board kitchen floor its weekly mopping. Water was never wasted!

Washday was hard work, and I can only imagine what a woman's hands must have looked like after all that scrubbing in lye soap and rubbing her knuckles off on the scrub board…

When the wash was dry, it was taken down, laid on the kitchen table, sprinkled with water, and then rolled up until ready to be ironed – usually the following day. There were no synthetic fabrics in those days, so everything – from the unbleached muslin sheets, the linen towels and tablecloths to the cotton dresses, aprons, handkerchiefs, pants, shirts and underwear – had to be ironed.

But ironing, again, was no easy job. Just like Nurse Laura in the film "Dr. Zhivago", women ironed their family's clothes and linens using flatirons heated on the stove. Placed atop the stove to heat up, each hot iron would retain heat for only a few minutes before it would have to be replaced by another iron, and so on. It was quite a trick not to singe the clothes…

Doing the weekly washing (washing, drying and ironing) normally took two full days.

Since there was no electricity, just the windmill to draw up water, Henri Tobaben, like his neighbors, always had to keep one eye on the windmill, making certain that the underground cistern was kept filled. Usually the prairie wind blew constant, pumping water from the well into the cistern, but if the wind didn't blow for two days, there wouldn't be enough water in the cistern. Sometimes the cattle drank all the water out of the tank; then the cistern would be empty. Thus, water in the farmhouse was always used sparingly. For example, dishes were washed using two large dishpans, one for washing and one for rinsing. Then, the rinse water was used to water the garden; the dirty dishwater itself went into a slop bucket for the hogs. Believe it or not, the hogs liked the soapy water from the homemade soap made from lard, lye and cracklings! People made their own soap. When a hog was butchered, they would trim off the fat from the meat and then boil it down. The rendered fat was then strained, poured into a crock, and stored. This pure, rendered pig fat (lard) was used to bake with (piecrusts) and also to cook with. In fact, farm women cooked and baked mostly with lard, as their homemade butter was meant to be sold in town for badly needed cash. The leftover cracklings were saved for another day when they would be used to make soap.

Only the kitchen was heated; in the winter the bedrooms were icy cold, the windows frozen over with ice crystals. Agnes, having grown up in the mild maritime climate of the North Sea, had never experienced such frigid temperatures! It seemed to her that their cottage back home, with its thick thatched roof, was much warmer than the Tobaben's wooden-frame house. Agnes would often awaken in the morning to find a thin layer of snow (frost?) atop her quilt! Often during a Nebraska blizzard, the Tobabens would be snow-bound for days. They wore long underwear to keep warm, and often in the extreme cold they would forego the weekly bath. Just to wash and dry one's hair was a big production, so farmwomen didn't wash their long hair very often in winter; often during a long cold spell, they would apply rubbing alcohol to their hair and scalp instead, to stop the itching.

The toilet, a two-seater outhouse, was located at the end of a path some distance from the house. In the extreme cold, Agnes would dash out in the morning, during the day, and just before going to bed, dreading putting her bare bottom on the icy bench. In the middle of a dark winter night, she would, of course, use the chamber pot under the bed. But the chamber pot was used exclusively for #1, and not #2. If you had to do "that", you still needed to run to the outhouse.

Agnes soon learned that in place of peat, Nebraskans used corncobs to fire their cookstoves. The box in the kitchen next to the stove had to be kept filled with corncobs. Agnes would gather up the corncobs left over from shelling corn to feed the chickens, or from the pigpen. During the winter, Henri would augment their supply of corncobs with coal hauled in from Eustis. A big chunk of coal would keep a slow fire going in the cookstove through the night…

Mrs. Tobaben was very proud of her cob-fired cookstove. When baking bread or a cake, she knew just how to test the temperature of the oven by briefly holding her hand in the oven. She also knew just how many corncobs she would need to complete the baking process. Agnes observed the old woman closely; all these things and more she would need to learn.

Already familiar with milking goats, Agnes now learned to milk cows, as handling the milk became her daily chore, mornings and evenings, a chore the old woman gladly relinquished to the young girl. Agnes got up by daylight every morning. While

Henri fed and watered the livestock and tended to the horses, Agnes milked the cows. After she was finished milking, before breakfast and while the milk was still warm, she would separate it using a hand cranked cream separator. The separated milk (skim milk) was fed to the calves, and if there was any left over, to the pigs and the chickens. The cream was poured into two- or five-gallon cans to be stored until it could be taken into town and sold to the creamery. In the summertime, the cream was kept cold by hanging the cans down the cistern.

Finished with their morning chores, she and Henri would then go in for breakfast. Henri's mother always had a hot breakfast waiting for them. After breakfast, Agnes would wash the cream separator and rinse it well. In the evening, the milking process would be repeated.

Some of the cream was saved up for the wooden butter churn. Every two or three days, Agnes would churn the cream and help Mrs. Tobaben in preparing the butter, a tiring and time-consuming process. When finally completed, they would wrap the molded butter in butter paper and then lower it down into the cistern until it too could be taken into town and sold. In summer they would wrap the butter in wet sacks or blankets to keep it cold and hard during the long trip into town.

There was a German bakery in town, but Mrs. Tobaben preferred to make her own bread, and for Sunday breakfast, *Hefekuchen,* sweet braided yeast bread served with fresh butter and jam, and, of course, Agnes' own favorite – *Butterkuchen*, the same sheet cake her mother made with sweet yeast dough, dotted with butter and sprinkled with cinnamon and sugar (sometimes topped with sliced plums or apples and sweet cream custard) to be enjoyed with Sunday afternoon *Kaffee und Kuchen.*

Agnes had arrived in Nebraska in early October, shortly before corn-husking season. In those days, crops were harvested by hand, and during both the summer grain harvest and the corn harvest in the fall, farmwomen were kept busy for days on end, cooking for the neighbor men plus the extra hired men who came to help. Soon, she too was asked to help on the neighboring farms. She was needed to help butcher chickens early in the morning or to attend to the small children while the farmer's wife, and any other women who came to help, baked fresh pies and then prepared mounds of fried chicken, along with mashed potatoes and gravy, peas, onions, and green beans. From the windmill cistern they brought out bowls of homemade butter to eat with the homemade bread, and from the root cellar jars of homemade jellies and jams.

When the men in the fields heard the dinner gong at noon, they hurried to the house, first washing their hands and faces at the outside pump before sitting down at the kitchen table (which had all its extensions inserted!). While the men ate, the women replenished the serving dishes from the pots on the cob-fired cookstove. When the men had eaten and had returned to the fields, the women washed the dishes and then set the table again, so that they and the children could sit down to eat.

Agnes never forgot what one farmwoman told her: If a wife served good food and plenty of it, her husband would always find it easy to round up enough help during the threshing and corn husking seasons.

Cheerful, enthusiastic, quick to learn and conscientious in her work, people readily took to her. Although slender, she was strong and agile, and very soon young Agnes gained a reputation among the farmwomen as a good and reliable worker, eager to help out whenever and wherever help was needed.

Youthful and venturesome, Agnes eagerly adapted to her new surroundings. In her frequent letters home she related her many new experiences. She wrote that she liked Nebraska. She liked the friendly and open people, their can-do pioneer spirit, and the sense of community. She learned that in America the social class into which you were born need not necessarily determine your future life. Agnes as a young girl had always had some idea of her capabilities, and mentally she had never entirely accepted the prevailing system – the social classes, the inequality. Having grown up under the restraints of a rigid, class-conscious social order, Agnes would come to love her adopted country both for its wonderful informality and for its wonderfully classless society. "*Hier sind alle Menschen gleich,*" she would later write home. ("Everyone is equal here.")

In the mid-1920s, the Tobabens and their neighbors did not yet have a radio. In fact, up until the late 1930s it was mostly townspeople who had radios, since the batteries needed to operate a radio were large, cumbersome, and expensive. The Tobabens got their news when they went into town, or from the local weekly newspaper.

Ever keen on learning more about her adoptive country and adapting to its ways, Agnes determined to learn English. Soon she had taught herself the English alphabet and used every opportunity to practice the language. There were no books other than the German Bible in the Tobaben household, but she diligently studied her weekly Sunday school lesson and made every effort to decipher the weekly newspaper. Of course, in the outhouse she could always study the old Sears Roebuck catalog, the torn, crumpled up pages of which served as toilet paper.

Gradually, her elegant penmanship, the German handwriting style (*Kurrentschrift*) she had learned at school, yielded to her clumsy attempts at forming the letters of the English alphabet. Agnes never totally lost her German accent. She pronounced her R's the German way, and she never learned, for example, to push her tongue forward in the *th* sound – she said *ze* instead of *the,* for example, and *zank you* instead of *thank you.* But like so many German immigrants, she would in time teach herself the spoken and written language of her adopted country without any formal instruction.

In her then elegant handwriting, Agnes wrote on the reverse side: "Das Bild habe ich abnehmen lassen. Ich hab da noch meine langen Haare. Das kleine Mädchen ist Coleen Kiesel."

Agnes, here still with long hair, enjoyed caring for children. (May 1924)

Her sponsor, Henri Tobaben, was a fifty-year-old bachelor farmer. In Agnes' young eyes he seemed very old indeed. Not only was Henri Tobaben hard-of-hearing, but he also walked with a limp, the result of a badly healed broken leg caused by a runaway team of horses. Although by no means poor, Henri was known near and far as being extremely stingy and as someone who always managed to get the better end of a deal.

Agnes soon came to understand why no woman had ever consented to marry him – Henri had a problem with alcohol! When he was sober, he could be a nice guy, but when he was drunk, he became moody and aggressive. Henri mostly drank his homebrewed beer in moderation, but occasionally he would get very drunk on whiskey purchased illegally from a bootlegger, which he would hide and drink when he was alone. A neighbor once found his whiskey bottle hidden in the haystack!

It seems that Agnes had arrived in the United States during the time of Prohibition – that 13-year period after World War I (starting in 1920) when alcoholic beverages were totally banned. Needless to say, German-Americans did not much like Prohibition. It made them feel like aliens in their own country. First the government had tried to take away their language; now it was trying to destroy their culture! It certainly seemed that the Eighteenth Amendment, outlawing the manufacture, transport, and sale of alcoholic beverages, was aimed especially against them. Not only would Prohibition put an end to the German brewing industry in America, but the very idea of prohibiting alcohol ran contrary to the core cultural values of German-American immigrants. Why, there was even a German proverb: *"Wer nicht liebt Wein, Weib und Gesang, der bleibt ein Narr sein Leben lang!"* ("He who loves not wine, woman and song will remain a fool his whole life long!"). Prohibition meant that German immigrants would no longer be able to enjoy German camaraderie over a glass of wine or a stein of beer in a German tavern or beer garden. And how could German picnics and festivals such as *Schützenfeste, Sängerfeste, Oktoberfeste, Maifeste und Bierfeste*, or any other type of traditional German celebration or social gathering, take place without beer and wine?

Prohibition reached into every town and village. In Eustis, prior to Prohibition, it had been customary for one farm family in the neighborhood to operate a still. But federal agents soon came and shut them down, so that the only way to get hold of hard liquor was by prescription (for medicinal purposes!) or illegally, from a bootlegger. But even though taverns and cafés in town could no longer serve alcoholic beverages, locals continued to brew decent homemade beer from malted barley, hops, yeast and water, and even townspeople cultivated grapes and made their own wine. Red beet wine, deep red in color, was also very popular; it was often given as medicine to sweat out a cold or the flu.

If Agnes had known what awaited her in the Tobaben household, she would never have accepted Henri's sponsorship. But unbeknownst to either her or her mother,

Henri's real motive in paying her passage was not primarily because his aging mother needed a girl to help with the chores. His intention all along had been to marry Agnes! By sponsoring Agnes, he would have a young girl hostage in his own house! He didn't see why Agnes' youth should eliminate her as possible marriage material.

Agnes, of course, wanted no part of it, and whenever Henri made unwanted advances, she let him know it in no uncertain terms. For example, when Agnes was alone with him in the barn, while milking, she would threaten him with her milk stool.

"*Kein Esel ist so doof wie das Alter!*" she would mock him, disgustedly. ("There's no fool like an old fool!")

Henri's attempts to be charming were clumsy at best, often downright laughable, but it wasn't always easy for Agnes to fend him off, to outwit or discourage him. When Henri was drunk, he would become ever more persistent, then annoyed and enraged. Agnes' scornful remarks or the scolding of his mother could no longer keep him in check. Agnes would then have to flee and lock herself in Mrs. Tobaben's bedroom, often together with the old woman, terrified, and pray that Henri would not break down the door. These were new and terrible experiences for her.

As was her way, Agnes determined to make the best of the situation. Henri Tobaben had paid her ship's passage and train fare. She would stay until she had worked off her debt. With weekly wages for young servant girls averaging from two to three dollars, Agnes figured it would take her two or three years…

During that first winter away from home and as the novelty of her new life began to wear off and the wind blew fierce and cold over the Nebraska plains, Agnes felt the isolation of the farm closing in around her. Back home in Sittensen, her father's blacksmith's shop had been a hub of activity; just about everyone in town required her father's services at one time or another. His shop had been a gathering place. Men would stand around and gossip and debate and solve the problems and politics of the day while they watched him work. Women passing by their cottage often called out in greeting or stopped by for a chat. Alone with Henri and his mother during that first long winter, often snowbound for days, Agnes would sometimes catch herself listening for the sounds of the forge, the ringing sound of hammer against anvil…

Living on an isolated farm, alone with Henri and his mother, separated from her family, friends and familiar environment, it was inevitable that Agnes would become homesick, although in her pride she tried not to mention it in her letters home. Agnes had no idea when she would be reunited with her family again, and she missed them terribly, especially her mother.

Like many when they are disheartened and lonely, Agnes turned to her childhood faith for solace. After awhile, her letters home took on a religious overtone and she would frequently refer to a time when she and her family would one day all be together again in heaven.

As a young girl, the idea of becoming a Lutheran parish nurse, a *Diakonissen Schwester*, had often appealed to her and her sister, Meta. It was the only "career" choice available to a young, working-class woman with no formal education, and it was also a means to secure one's financial security in case you were unable to find a husband to provide for you. These church-sponsored nurses were the Protestant equivalent of the Catholic nun. A nurse deaconess did not marry, but dedicated herself completely to the care of the parish poor, sick and the aged. Now, in her terrible homesickness, Agnes wrote to Meta instructing her to take the necessary steps to prepare the way for her to join a *Diakonissen-Orden* (Order of Deaconesses). Later she apparently reconsidered and had a change of heart. But the idea of becoming a nurse professional always appealed to her, even if she herself, an uneducated immigrant, could never hope to aspire to any such lofty career.

Spring finally arrived and the garden and field work began. Having already gained a solid reputation as "hard-working", Agnes was often hired to provide extra help on the neighboring farms.

It was during her first summer in Nebraska, while helping out at the Leon Hermann farm that she made the acquaintance of Gottlob Betz, a nice young man, two years older than her, who was also working there. Of course, she had already been noticed by other young men at church, but if any of them was curious about the new German girl and dared to stop by the Tobaben farm to pay her a visit, Henri, in his controlling jealousy, would assign Agnes to her bedroom or otherwise make it very difficult for the young men to visit.

Agnes would usually just laugh and shrug it off. With the Betz boy, however, it was different. She really cared for him, and the young man apparently tried to court her seriously, with Agnes even attempting to escape through her bedroom window. Her sponsor was not amused. Getting out his shotgun, Henri managed to frighten off the young suitor for good, with Agnes all the while protesting and weeping with impotent rage and humiliation.

Twenty-year-old Gottlob Betz, had he had the means, would have paid off Agnes' debt to Henri Tobaben, as other men had been known to pay off their future wives' passage. But neither Gottlob nor Agnes had the financial means to purchase her freedom.

Why didn't Agnes and Gottlob simply run off together? Their situation is difficult for us to appreciate, as it was the year 1924. Bound to the consciousness of their own time, they would have perceived things differently. Agnes especially, having grown up in a society of rigid traditions and morality, was a child of her times. For her to elope would not only have been morally wrong, but it would have been an act of disrespect for parental authority, and she had not been brought up to be disrespectful, to disobey her elders, or (God forbid!) to bring shame to her family.

As she had hoped, Agnes did become good friends with Gertrude, and she enjoyed visiting the Naumanns and riding along with Gertrude and her family whenever they drove to town. Gertrude, who had taken piano lessons and could play quite well, often entertained family and friends at the piano, and Agnes, who loved to sing and who filled the Tobaben's home with song as she went about her work, was soon singing in English, not only the beautiful old hymns she learned at church, but American folksongs as well, along with the lyrics for the latest "Roaring Twenties" hit tunes that Gertrude taught her on their long trips into town.

Life in rural Nebraska was, of course, in stark contrast to the life of city dwellers. The Jazz Age glamour of the 1920's was far removed from the everyday life of the hardworking people in Frontier County, Nebraska. But rural folks did get to view the flapper fashions and glamorous lifestyles in the movies...

Agnes and Gertrude loved going to the picture shows – the silent movies of that era! After seeing one silent comedy film, Agnes was introduced to a new English word. The film, "Never Weaken!" was a 1921 thriller starring Harold Lloyd.

"What does it mean, 'never weaken'?" Agnes wanted to know.

"To weaken," explained Gertrude, who spoke German quite well, means "*schwach werden.*"

"*Ach so,*" replied Agnes, who readily understood. "*Nur nicht schwach werden*"!

She liked that expression, which she thought she could apply to her own situation as well: "Never weaken!"

Farmwomen in those days generally had three sets of dresses: one good dress to wear to church, and two 'everyday' dresses so they could change off every Monday washday. During the week, they wore long cotton aprons over their everyday dresses to keep them from getting dirty. Since there was seldom enough money for store-bought dresses, their 'everyday' dresses were often sewn from flour sacks or chicken feed sacks. Chicken feed, for example, came in 100-pound printed cloth bags. Farmwomen would recycle these sacks, which came in various patterns, using the fabric cloth not only to make dresses, but also towels, sheets and quilts – even shirts and underclothes.

Friendly and vivacious Gertrude, pleasantly plump and lovely with her cropped, curly hair, stayed up on the latest fashion trends. Influenced by the fashion of the '20s, she and Agnes were soon dreaming of selecting fabrics and patterns for the plain flapper dresses then in style.

Deciding to have one's hair cut was serious business in those days, but after her second winter in Nebraska, Agnes finally dared to rid herself of her long, thick braids, to have her hair cut after the fashion of the day. With her hair snipped into a bob, and wearing a short (knee-length), drop-waisted dress and silk stockings, Agnes morphed into a fashionable young lady. Back in Sittensen, however, short hair was still considered scandalous, and her tradition-minded family was shocked and dismayed by the photo Agnes sent of her short, modern haircut, her "*Bubikopf*". Her mother bemoaned the loss of her daughter's thick braids – Agnes' lush, beautiful hair!

A fashionable young Agnes, her hair cut and bobbed. (Spring, 1925)

Agnes enjoyed taking care of children. Dirt roads meant muddy wheels. The car on the right, I believe, is a 1925 Durant.

On Sunday afternoons, folks went visiting. Agnes here wearing an ill-fitting, home-sewn, flour-sack dress

Heini Burgdorf, having apprenticed as a pharmacy clerk, was not content in rural Nebraska. In just one year he had worked off his debt to Henri and had then hopped a train to New York where, he was quite certain, he would get rich. [Apparently he was successful, as in 1932 he returned to Germany and became the owner of a drugstore in the Frickestrasse in Hamburg!]

Agnes, two years later, was tempted to do the same, even though it would mean leaving all her newfound friends behind. After all, her whole reason for coming to America was to earn enough money so that she could return to Germany. Accordingly, once she felt her debt to the Tobabens had more than been repaid, and after putting aside enough to pay for a one-way rail ticket, she bravely set out for New York, determined to make money. Her mother had written ahead to her sister in Brooklyn with the idea that Tante Anna's husband, a self-employed housepainter and decorator by trade, could place Agnes with one of his well-heeled customers.

Thus Agnes, full of youthful energy and expectation, left rural Nebraska in early 1926 and joined the thousands of other young immigrant women who went into service as housemaids and/or nannies in New York City.

She was delighted to meet her Tante Anna, a warm, pleasant person who very much reminded Agnes of her mother. Tante Anna and Onkel Otto Schmiemann resided in a middle-class section of Brooklyn. They lived in the front first-floor unit of the four-flat apartment building they owned. Their two children, the twins Otto and Annie, born in 1899, were seven years older than Agnes. The Schmiemanns were a close-knit and harmonious family. Cousin Annie and her husband, Joseph McGuinness, rented one of the top-floor apartments in the four-flat. Married in 1919, the young couple had already experienced great sorrow: the death of their son and only child, Bernard Josef, who had died just shy of his second birthday, in July 1922, of whooping cough which developed into pneumonia.

Cousin Annie's twin brother, Otto, was still single and living at home with his parents. Cousin Otto had followed in his dad's footsteps, working alongside his father in the family paint business. He and his fiancé, Winifred (Winnie) Adolph, were planning to marry the following year.

Agnes was stunned that neither one of her cousins spoke a word of German. Then, when it came time to attend church on Sunday morning, she was even more shocked to learn that Cousin Annie's husband, Joe, and Cousin Otto's fiancée, Winnie, were both Roman Catholic! Agnes was totally bewildered. She was not at all certain that a proper Lutheran should even consider marrying a Catholic. Of course, there hadn't been much opportunity for socializing with Catholics back home; in the northern German Protestant stronghold where she had grown up, there simply weren't any! Germany was not only divided between its regions and classes, but also by its religious denominations. In fact, before coming to New York, she had never known anyone of a non-Protestant religious background.

Tante Anna, knowing exactly where Agnes was coming from, lightly dismissed her niece's concerns.

"Here in America, things are different," she reassured Agnes. "And besides", she continued, "Joe is not a strict Catholic; he rarely attends Mass, so Annie still goes with us to Lutheran church services. And Otto's fiancée, Winnie (Agnes had to agree), is a really nice girl. *Hauptsache, dass sie glücklich sind!*" ("The main thing is they are happy!")

Agnes' uncle, Hinrich (Harry) Bartels, was also in Brooklyn. Onkel Harry worked as a driver for the Trommer brewery, which in spite of Prohibition was managing to stay afloat. Onkel Harry's wife, Eva Margareta, had given birth to eight children, but only two had survived: Cousin Louis Henry (born 1892) and Cousin Mildred (born 1901). I am sure Agnes was pleased to meet her mother's brother and his family, although I do not recall any mention of her Onkel Harry in later years…

A well-off Jewish family in the Bronx agreed to employ Agnes as a live-in nanny/housemaid. In return for her services, she would be paid wages significantly higher than she could ever have imagined in Nebraska. Agnes was elated, but nervous. She had never met anyone Jewish before and did not want to make any mistakes due to being unaware of unfamiliar customs….

The family employed a cook, a heavy-set, African-American woman who lived out and only came in during the day. Agnes was stunned her first morning to find a Negro woman in the kitchen. It was her first exposure to another race.

At first, she felt very insecure working in an urban, upper-class household. But conscientious, hard-working Agnes soon met her employer's expectations. Warm and nurturing by nature, she enjoyed looking after the family's two small children. But caring for them, plus completing the various household chores assigned to her, took all her energy. By evening, after bathing the children and putting them to bed, she would be bone-tired. Sitting alone in her tiny room, she might do some crocheting or embroidering, or write a letter to her family back in Germany or to Gertrude in Nebraska, before collapsing into bed.

Agnes had been in New York less than a year when news of her mother's illness reached her. Her mother, at age fifty-five, was terminally ill with liver cancer. Apparently surgical intervention was attempted, but she succumbed to the disease a few weeks later. Meta's letter bearing the news of their mother's death reached Agnes in late November, 1926. Now, at age twenty, Agnes was alone with her awful grief and the unbearable realization that she would never see her beloved mother again.

Not long afterwards, Agnes received a letter from Meta asking if Agnes couldn't help out financially. Times were so bad in Germany – the burial expenses yet to be paid, their father unable to earn as much as before, and they, her family, all the while under the assumption that Agnes was well-off in New York…

Agnes wired 250 dollars – every penny of her savings! Now she wouldn't be able to buy the warm winter coat she so desperately needed. But Agnes was glad she could help; she loved her family, and they would never learn the extent of her sacrifice…

She would remain in New York for another two years. All in all, it was a period in her life that she rarely, if ever, spoke of, and yet, during that time she became an independent young woman. Her exposure to the urban environment, as well as living in the homes of non-Lutherans, gave her a new perspective on life. Agnes made friends with another domestic, Mary. On Agnes' one afternoon off, she would normally visit Tante Anna and her cousins in Brooklyn, but occasionally she and Mary would venture abroad, the two young girls becoming acquainted with the city, the hustle and bustle of its crowded streets, and where the doors to the subway closed quickly…

Agnes' parents pose with her sister, 14-year-old Adelheid. The jacket worn by Agnes' father shows him a member of the local "Schützenverein", a popular social club in Germany.

But Agnes never really acclimated to city life, and so, two years after her mother's death, and along with the sad news that her father was now also ill and unable to work, it began to dawn on her that no matter how much she earned in New York or was able to save for her dowry, there would be no returning home for her, ever, as she no longer had a home to return to. With this painful realization, and feeling increasingly alone in the urban environment, she found herself thinking more and more of the country folk among whom she had felt such a strong sense of kinship and belonging. In the end, she decided to return to Nebraska – to Eustis, the place she had begun to think of as home. Gertrude had written to assure her that she would have no difficulty finding work as a "hired girl."

Agnes bade a sad farewell to the Schmiemanns, not knowing if she would ever see them again. As a farewell gift, Tante Anna gave her a hand-embroidered sheet-and-pillow-case set with Agnes' initials. Cousin Annie wiped sad tears from her eyes, while Winnie held up her baby, Henry Otto, for Agnes to admire and kiss goodbye. Born just a few months earlier, in September 1928, little Henry was the Schmiemann family's pride and joy.

Gertrude and her fiancé, Albert, met Agnes at the train depot in Eustis. She and Agnes were happy to see each other again, and the Naumanns and Tobabens were waiting at home to welcome her.

The following spring, in April 1929, Agnes' father died (of stomach cancer). Agnes was brokenhearted, for, along with her father's passing, a whole world had now died for her as well. In her grief and longing for her family, she wrote pleadingly to her siblings, urging them to join her, assuring them that Tante Anna was willing to act as sponsor.

But the decision to emigrate, a decision that would change one's entire life, required courage and a sense of adventure, and neither Meta nor Adelheid, cautious and hesitant, could be persuaded to join her. Brother Jonny, however, did have the necessary fortitude and ambition.

Handsome, athletic, and known for his good looks, Jonny had learned the blacksmith trade from his father and was himself a *Schmiedemeister*. But he was no longer happy in his line of work

Agnes' brother, Jonny

and was eager to try his luck in America, "the land of unlimited opportunity." Jonny at once set about making the necessary preparations, applying for a visa and getting his things in order. But alas, in the end, his visa application was denied! The United States had severely restricted its immigration quota, and fewer visas were being granted. In New York, the stock market had crashed; it was the beginning of the Great Depression.

Unable to secure a visa, Jonny's hopes of coming to America were dashed. We can only imagine both his and Agnes' terrible disappointment. For Jonny, it meant giving up his dream for a better future. For Agnes, it meant that she would remain alone, separated from her family.

The 1930 U.S. Census, conducted on April 1 of that year, lists Agnes residing with the Tobabens in the capacity of housekeeper, but Agnes knew better than to stay long under Henri's roof. Using the Tobabens as a home base, she initially hired out to work for the elderly Mrs. Margaret (Maggie) Hueftle, one of the earliest homesteaders in the Eustis area. Later she went to work for Mrs. Blanche Kiesel, a young farmwoman with two older stepchildren, plus four small children of her own.

The Naumanns and the Tobabens. (Spring, 1930) On the right: Agnes, Henri Tobaben and his mother. On the left: Anna Naumann (Henri's sister), her husband and their two sons, Raymond and Otto

In time, Agnes came to idolize Blanche Kiesel, and although employed by Gust and Blanche Kiesel in the capacity of 'hired girl', she was always treated as part of the family. She and Blanche Kiesel would remain friends the remainder of their lives.

Sewing Class. Agnes, wearing the latest cocoon wrap style coat, stands next to Martha Kuepler and Rose Bosh. At rear, instructor Mrs. Malomi (left), and Blanche Kiesel.

Gertrude and Agnes (Spring, 1930)

Agnes with friends Martha Kuepler and Rose Bosh.

Maggie Hueftle was a strict Methodist. Blanche Kiesel was also a devout Methodist, and it was through their church affiliations that Agnes began attending the Methodist Church in Eustis. Agnes shared their strong Christian faith, her own belief having been strengthened during the years in New York when she had been on her own. Having long ago accepted Jesus as her Lord and Savior, it was without a doubt her strong and simple faith that sustained her, that gave her the strength to perform her work, and to face each new day without fear of the future, to accept life as it comes. Agnes knew that there was someone looking after her, someone she could turn to, and who would comfort and sustain.

Her simple faith gave her that wonderful trait of self-reliance that she possessed, along with her ability to distinguish between those worries that were important and had to be immediately addressed and those that were better left to a future date. "The Lord helps those who help themselves!", "Live one day at a time!", and "Don't worry about tomorrow until it gets here!" were not empty phrases to her; they expressed the very foundation of what she believed. Agnes walked closely with her Lord. She knew His words; they were in her mind, for she needed to know that she could always turn to Him, and that He would take care of all her worldly needs. ("Behold the lilies of the field…" *Matthew 6: 25-34*)

She was skeptical, however, of some of the strict Methodist teachings. For example, she knew that Methodists were absolutely dead set against drinking, but to Agnes, having been raised in the German-Lutheran tradition, the idea of abstaining from all types of alcoholic beverages seemed ludicrous to her. Plus, she knew from her own experience of living among them that even the most devout members of the Methodist congregation would secretly indulge, hiding a bottle in the kitchen pantry or underneath the bed "for medicinal purposes!" Her common sense and open-mindedness were reflected in her later church affiliations. She would simply attend whichever church was closest, regardless of its denomination!

Agnes became fast friends with the Methodist pastor, Reverend John Schaum, and his two daughters, Lydia and Amelia. She especially admired Lydia, who later joined the foreign missions. Over the years, Agnes would continue to receive letters and postcards from Lydia from various exotic, far away places.

In June of 1931, Agnes turned twenty-five. It was now going on eight years since she had come to America as a young girl of seventeen. She had been on her own ever since, working as a nanny and live-in domestic in New York and as a hired girl in Nebraska. How keenly she felt the need for family, the desire for a home and children of her own. How weary she was of working for others, of looking after other people's children!

There had recently been one young fellow, John Toberer, who had asked for her hand in marriage, but Agnes had refused his marriage proposal. Why had she turned him down? Was it because he was two years younger? Or was she perhaps waiting for just the right young man to come along?

As children growing up, we would sometimes ask her why she had married Papa.

Her reply was invariably the same – very matter-of-fact and utterly unromantic: "Papa needed a cook."

The answer was somehow never satisfying. The truth, if truth were told, can sometimes be disappointing…

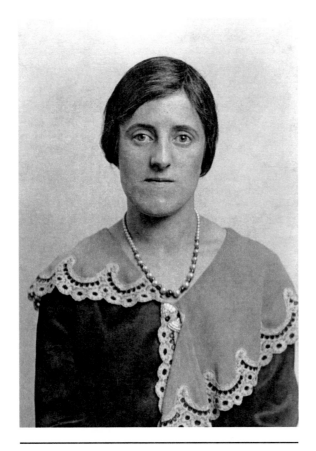

Agnes at age twenty-five (1931)

CHAPTER 5

"For this cause shall a man leave his father and mother and
cleave to his wife, and they twain shall be one flesh.
Wherefore they are no more twain, but one flesh.
What therefore God has joined together, let not man put asunder."
– Mark 10: 7-9

WHILE WORKING for Blanche Kiesel, Agnes would occasionally hire out to help at the Otto Bartruff farm. Mrs. Bartruff had eight small children, so she could certainly use the extra help. And so it happened that during the wheat harvest in July, Agnes was staying at the Bartruff farm, helping Mrs. Bartruff cook for the threshing crew, and by coincidence a young man by the name of Alfred was one of the extra men hired to help with the threshing that year. Apparently he cut quite an impressive figure that morning as he rode into the Bartruff's farmyard astride a handsome white horse…

Although short in stature (only 5'4"), Alfred was well built and quite handsome. Perhaps what stayed with Agnes were his piercing blue eyes? In any event, with his good looks, reserved demeanor and perhaps a compliment on her cooking in his strong *Schwäbisch* dialect, he must have made a favorable impression on Agnes, and given that Alfred Fritz was a very eligible bachelor indeed, with a reputation for being an especially ambitious and industrious young tenant farmer, and since Agnes was so very weary of being a hired girl, she apparently decided that he was the one.

They were married three months later. With just two witnesses and a thin, plain silver wedding band, Agnes and Alfred were wed in a private ceremony conducted by Pastor Schrein in the parsonage of Salem Lutheran, the little country church east of the Tobaben farm where Agnes had first attended services as a young immigrant girl. Sadly, no wedding photo exists. In those Depression times, two years after the Crash of 1929, a studio photo may have been deemed an unnecessary expense.

The following announcement appeared in *"The Eustis News"*:

BREDEHOEFT--FRITZ

On Saturday, October 10th, 1931, at the residence of Rev. C. F. Schrein south of Eustis, occurred the marriage of Miss Agnes Bredehoeft to Mr. Alfred Fritz. Rev. Schrein read the marriage lines and Miss Gertrude Naumann was bridesmaid. Mr. Albert Naumann was best man.

The bride was charming in a gown of pale pink georgette made after the latest style, and the bridesmaid wore printed crepe with green the predominating color. The bridgroom and best man wore the conventional dark colors

Mrs. Fritz, who received her education in Germany, came to this partof America, eight years ago. Mr. Fritz who also came to Nebraska from Germany in recent years, is an industrious farmer, located at the present time on the John Gruber farm on the Valley, where the newly married couple will make their home.

Mr. and Mrs. Fritz have the best wishes of their many friends for success and happiness in their new venture.

It is uncertain who else may have attended the wedding ceremony. What is certain is that none of Alfred's brothers and sisters was present. True to form, Alfred never once mentioned his upcoming marriage to anyone. In fact, Theo could not recall meeting his brother's wife until months later.

After the ceremony, the wedding party may have stopped off at the Tobabens or the Naumanns for noon dinner or for afternoon *Kaffee und Kuchen*. Any distance was considered far in those days; the young couple most likely set out for home early, well before dusk. Driving back to Eustis and on through town, the newlyweds would then have continued north towards Cozad to the Gruber farmstead where Alfred tenant farmed. There the evening chores awaited them, and there they would begin their married life together – two young German immigrants, totally on their own, determined to succeed.

Prior to their marriage, it is doubtful that Alfred and Agnes had a chance to get to know each other well. Since they both lived on separate farms located some distance apart, during their brief period of courtship they probably met up only once a week, on Sunday

Agnes' wedding dress   *Newlyweds Agnes and Alfred (March 1932).*

afternoons, and were never alone for any length of time. In fact, it was not really a courtship at all. They did not have a chance to become 'friends', but had moved quickly to deciding to get married without really getting to know each other on a deeper level.

In any event, romantic love did not play a role in their decision to marry. As Agnes would confide, decades later, to her eldest daughter, romance didn't really enter into the equation. She simply wanted to get married; she was tired of being a servant.

After all, what choice did she have? Marriage was a woman's only means of achieving a respectable status within society. A woman looked for security, for a man who could support her and her children. She did not necessarily look for romantic love, much less personal fulfillment in marriage. Whether or not you were 'in love' was not so important. If two people "loved" each other, that was wonderful. If not, love would perhaps come with time, and in the meantime, you approached marriage as a pragmatic union.

Nor were people that obsessed with happiness; they did not make a point of all the time questioning whether or not they were happy! A married farm couple, working together, was too busy making a go of it to afford the luxury of constantly examining their relationship, questioning whether they were happy or fulfilled. Alfred needed a wife who was young, strong, willing to work hard, and a good cook. Agnes needed a husband, a man who could provide her with a home and children of her own. It was as simple as that.

Thus began their married life together, a marriage that would last almost forty years, not unhappier than many, perhaps just as good as most. It was essentially a bonding of two people to ensure their mutual survival, and in that sense the marriage worked.

If you asked anyone in Eustis who knew them, you would get the same response: Alfred was a very industrious tenant farmer; both he and Agnes were known to be very hard workers.

Agnes, quick and agile, took work seriously. She took life seriously as well, but she knew how to enjoy life. She was happy, outgoing and liked to laugh. Pleasant and sociable, she thrived on her friendships and loved company.

Alfred was her opposite. Like Agnes, he was hardworking and industrious, having known little else but hard work all his life. But he was a loner – uncommunicative, stubborn, short-tempered and moody. He rarely, if ever, laughed, nor did he like company, as he was unable to relate to other people. Lacking everyday social and communication skills that most people take for granted, he found conversation difficult and often came across as rough and insensitive.

Once married, a naïve Agnes would have had a difficult time adjusting to her husband's ways, trying to understand and to please him. It must have become clear to her immediately that she had bound herself to a difficult and troubled man. Not one to lose heart, she resolved, as was her way, to make the best of it. Marriage, after all, was a commitment through good times and bad. And, as a person of faith who lived her convictions, she would choose commitment again and again in her life.

Busy with her own household, Agnes had little time to be concerned with her feelings. She had to learn to be even more organized and clever than before, to the degree that she could juggle her housework (cooking and baking, gardening and preserving, laundering and cleaning, sewing and mending) and later, caring for her babies, plus helping with the chores. For quite often Alfred would be out working in the fields with the horses from dawn to dusk, or he would have hired out to help on another farm, and Agnes would then be responsible for the care of the livestock – milking the cows and looking after the pigs and the chickens. Nor did she, as a farmwife, have much time to be concerned with her looks. There was no time for pampering herself, and Alfred, like every other man, expected his dinner on the table at noon, no matter what!

Was she perhaps disillusioned? Had she simply exchanged one strenuous job for another – from 'hired girl' to tenant farmer's wife, with a workload even more exhausting than before?

The Kiesel family had subscribed to the Cozad Local, in which a regularly featured popular comic strip always ended in the philosophical statement: *"It's a great life if you don't weaken!"* There was that word "weaken" again that Gertrude had taught her so long ago....

"ITS A GREAT LIFE IF YOU DON'T WEAKEN" — By Jack Rabbit

"What a life, if you don't weaken!" Agnes whispered to herself. She decided to make the saying her own, repeating it often.

In those days, women gave birth at home – often it could be hours before the family doctor arrived. Agnes' first baby, a male child, was stillborn. Nobody could explain to her why her baby had died. Confused, utterly devastated and heartbroken, in her pain and grief she poured out her heart in a letter to her sister, Meta: *"...und Kinder mag ich doch so gern!"* ("...and I am so very fond of children!")

Then, on the last day of December 1933, she bore her husband a son. They named him Rudolf Alfred. It is interesting to note that even though Alfred's father, Christian, had passed away in June that same year, they chose not to name their son after him, but rather after Alfred's oldest brother, Rudolf. Ten months later, Agnes invited Pastor Schaum,to Sunday dinner to celebrate little Rudy's baptism.

A year and four months later, on April 6, 1935, a daughter was born – Nancy Meta. Agnes had always liked the name Nancy. It was the name of the little girl she had cared for in New York. And Meta was her sister's name and that of her mother as well.

In the meantime, Alfred and Agnes had moved. They were no longer farming "on the Valley" between Eustis and Cozad, as they had had to relinquish that farm to the owner's son. Instead, they now farmed a quarter-section, 160 acres (a good-sized farm in those days) just east of Eustis. The farm belonged to Phil Schweizer, who also owned the butcher shop in town. In those days, every German community had a German butcher who made specialty sausages of all kinds. Even today, the small town of Eustis is known as the "Sausage Capital of Nebraska."

Phil Schweizer did his twice weekly butchering at the farm, and Alfred assisted him, thereby earning much needed cash. He also got the benefit of feeding the slaughtered remains to his hogs. Thus Alfred honed his skills in the art of butchery and learned the secrets of the fine art of sausage making.

On Saturday afternoons they drove the short distance into town. Ruth Kugler, the shopkeeper's daughter, remembered waiting on Agnes at Hugo's, the grocery store where Agnes brought her fresh eggs for sale. She remembered her as being quite reserved, her babies always neat and clean.

Sunday mornings they attended the Methodist church in town. Sunday afternoons Agnes spread a clean tablecloth and invited their friends and neighbors to *Kaffee und Kuchen* – the Bartruffs (Louis and Marie), the Geigers, the Lederers – all second generation German-Americans, children of the original settlers who had homesteaded in the late 1880s and early 1990s, many originally from the Stuttgart area. Everyone spoke German; many spoke *Schwäbisch*. Often guests would stay on for supper, a simple meal of rye bread and a selection of fresh sausages – *Blutwurst, Leberwurst, Mettwurst*. How Agnes looked forward to Sundays!

All things considered, I believe that the early years of their marriage was basically a happy period in their lives. I imagine Agnes, busy running her own household, and Alfred, rightfully proud of what he had thus far achieved and living up to his reputation as a very industrious farmer – two hard-working and frugal people, determined to make a go of it, to one day be in a position to own their own farm.

At the time of their marriage in the fall of 1931, they could not have foreseen that the coming years would turn out to be very bad for Nebraska farmers. Not only would market prices for corn and wheat plunge as a result of the economic turmoil of the Great Depression, but they would also have to endure the disastrous drought years that followed – devastating, demoralizing years in which their crops would often fail completely.

Drought and economic struggle would soon be upon them – years of dust, heat, poverty and despair.

INTERLUDE
Henri Tobaben's Marriage

ON OCTOBER 3, 1932, Henri Tobaben married Emma Wenck in Hamburg, Germany.

Henri was by then a wealthy landowner. His frugality and business acumen had paid off; through subsequent purchases of Nebraskan farmland in the 1920s, he could now claim ownership of an entire section – 640 acres! In addition to collecting rent from three farm tenants, he also profited from raising beef cattle. Thus we find him in the summer of 1932, one year after Agnes' marriage, aboard an ocean liner bound for Hamburg in the company of his young friend, Heini Burgdorf. Heini, having made his fortune in New York, was returning home, while Henri Tobaben was on his way to Germany to meet his future wife!

He was to marry Heini Burgdorf's first cousin, Emma Wenck (Emma's mother was a Burgdorf). Emma, alas, was a "fallen woman" – *"ein gefallenes Mädchen."* She had given birth out of wedlock, and in those days, no one would marry a fallen woman. Henri Tobaben, however, was willing to marry Emma and to adopt her two-year-old son, Horst. Emma herself had little choice in the matter; her little boy was in need of a father, a man who would provide for him and give him his name.

Henri was fifty-nine years old; Emma was thirty-three. Poor Emma! She was so embarrassed even to be seen with Henri in public. From behind their lace curtains, she knew the villagers were scrutinizing the odd couple as they strolled by. Mortified, she could feel their stares, could sense their ridicule of the supposedly well-to-do American's ridiculously old-fashioned and shabby attire. *"Geiziger Dussel, alter Trottel!"* they mocked! "Stingy old fool!"

The village children would follow after Henri, aping his clumsy limp. They also made fun of his huge ear trumpet. Holding an imaginary instrument to their ears, they would mimic Henri's frequent "Eh? Eh?"

Emma suspected Henri's drinking problem, and of course she had heard the story of how Henri had tried to pester Agnes Bredehöft into marrying him – young Agnes, the blacksmith's daughter, whom Henri had sponsored and who had gone to live with Henri and his mother in America. Emma recalled how Agnes' mother had scoffed at the very idea of her seventeen-year-old daughter marrying such an old man! Now, a decade later, that same ridiculous old guy was courting her, and she knew she must accept…

Emma, an attractive, polished young woman, had been working in Hamburg as a server at an elegant café bordering the banks of the Elbe. But the handsome young foreigner who had seduced her had vanished, disgracing her and putting her family to shame. Now a "fallen woman," she had little choice but to wed Henri Tobaben and to accept whatever fate he offered.

It was all too much for Emma, and yet, in her shame and humiliation, she put on a brave front and courageously faced a future life in America – caring for Henri and his elderly mother on a distant farm in Nebraska, far away from the world she knew...

*   *   *

[Henri's elderly mother, Katie Tobaben, died four years later, in 1936, at the age of ninety. Henri died in 1941, leaving Emma a wealthy widow. In 1945, Emma married Otto Naumann, Gertrude Naumann's bachelor brother. They lived on the Tobaben farm until Emma's untimely death in 1951.]

CHAPTER 6

"My field of corn is but a crop of tears."
– W.G. Sebald, Die Ausgewanderten

TO OWN LAND…to become a landholder, a "somebody!"… It was every immigrant's dream, especially for those coming from Europe, where land ownership was concentrated in the hands of a few, since most land exchanged hands only through inheritance or marriage, and when land did sell, it sold for a very high price

So, too, for Alfred, who had come to Nebraska a penniless immigrant, it was his dream – to own land, to one day have his own farm. And it was to that end he had worked his way up from hired man to tenant farmer, all the while placing his faith in that great American dream, the belief that if he worked hard, if he sacrificed, scrimped and saved, he would one day be able to scrape together enough money to put a down payment on a farm. His older brother, Theo, was able to do just that – purchasing an 80-acre farm six miles northwest of Lexington in 1937. That was Alfred's goal as well. As fate would have it, however, it was not to be.

The Great Depression, the effects of which would last until the start of World War II, was triggered by the crash of the New York stock market in October 1929. By the time Alfred and Agnes were married, two years later, in October 1931, the decline in the economy was already well underway, and by 1934, the country was in the midst of the Great Depression.

Corn was (and still is) the major cash crop in Nebraska. More so than wheat, everything depended to a great extent on this one crop. The 1920s had been very good years for Nebraska farmers, with ample rainfall and good prices for corn and wheat. In fact, 1929 had been the best crop year ever!

In 1930, farmers were still getting eighty cents for a bushel of corn. Four years into the Depression, however, the price of corn was falling to twenty-five cents, nineteen cents and twelve cents a bushel; the price for hogs dropped to ten cents a pound! But it was not so much the collapse of the stock market or the low commodity prices that would devastate Nebraska's farmers, but rather the record drought years that followed.

1933 was still a good year weather-wise, although the farmers' financial condition was precarious. But then came the drought years of 1934, 35, 36 and 37. With large-scale irrigation systems like the ones employed today (powerful diesel and electric pumps pumping water from the large underground Ogallala aquifer) still unheard of, only small-scale watering via a network of irrigation ditches, tended to by hand, was carried out, and then only on flatland. Eventually, even this primitive method of irrigation – watering "down the row" – no longer functioned, as irrigation ditches ran dry.

In 1934, it never rained a drop all spring. Although Alfred enjoyed a reputation as being a first-rate farmer, the land he now rented was hilly, suitable only for "dry land" (rain-fed) farming. That year, the stalks of corn did not stand tall and close together, and there were fewer corn ears to harvest. Alfred followed the long cornrows up and down, walking from stalk to stalk, having to lean and bend over for each precious ear. Instead of seventy or eighty bushels, he was lucky if he could pick twenty bushels a day.

In 1935, there was no harvest at all. The ground was parched; the hot winds burned up the crops in the fields. Farmers watched helplessly as their crops dried up in the heat; housewives watched as the hot winds killed even the vegetables in their watered gardens, vegetables that the family depended on. Struggling to feed their livestock and their families, many farmers were eventually forced to sell off their starving animals, at dirt-cheap prices. Without their livestock, and with no crops to sell, farmers could no longer make payment on their mortgages; tenant farmers could not pay the rent.

The drought was made even worse by the powerful dust storms that followed. Known as "black blizzards," instead of swirling white snow, the dust storms carried dirt – tons of fine, powdery topsoil that blew up from Oklahoma and Kansas.

The approach of a dust storm was an awesome sight. The sky would become dark and scary, and then a huge, swirling black cloud, like a mountain approaching, would roll across the land, encompassing everything in its way, shutting out the sun, making it pitch dark at noon. Townspeople and farmers would run to take shelter in their homes, where they huddled in the eerie darkness and waited for the howling wind to stop. The storms could last for hours. Afterwards, a thick layer of dust would cover everything. Regardless of how much the women tried to keep out the dirt by stuffing wet rags into the cracks of doors and windows, the fine silt still seeped in and settled onto everything – the windowsills, floors, beds, the baby's crib, the dishes on the table, even on the food – everything in the house!

When the wind finally died down, people would emerge to find that the dust had piled up in front of the door and settled outside around the fences like snowdrifts. Even when the wind subsided, the air was still gritty, as the dirt would continue to sift down. Agnes tied a cloth on top of the milk bucket to keep out the dust. At the watering trough, the horses blew through their nostrils to clear the dust from the water's surface.

Although summertime days in Nebraska are hot, temperatures usually fall to tolerable limits at night. But during the mid-1930s, there were days with temperatures of 118 degrees! And as long as the dust was blowing, you couldn't open a window for air. Often at midnight it was as hot as during the day. Farm families didn't have electricity and so couldn't run fans at night. When the dust wasn't blowing, people went outdoors to sleep on porches, in back yards, wherever they could find a slight breeze to cool them off, to escape the unbearable heat trapped in their houses. Housewives learned that an old sheet, dripping with water and placed where the wind could reach it, would cool the house a little, but the sheet had to be changed often because it would trap some of the gritty dust and soon become mud.

Sometimes, at infrequent intervals, there was rain – just a shower falling with enough dust that it was mud by the time it hit the ground; other times a thunderstorm would bring a downpour which did little good to the parched farmland or came too late to benefit the crops.

In July of 1935, Elise came out from New York to visit. The last of the Fritz children to immigrate, Elise decided to make the train trip out west to visit her brothers and sisters in Nebraska whom she had not seen these many years. Now a young woman of twenty-five, married and living in Brooklyn, she brought along her five-year old son, Henry. Elise had been a young girl of fifteen at the time her older brother, Theo, left home. They had not seen each other since.

When Elise, stylish and smartly dressed, arrived at Theo and Dora's house, Frieda and Berta quizzed their brother if he knew the young woman who they had brought with them, since Elise's visit had been kept a surprise. Theo replied in all earnestness that the lady looked strangely familiar, yet he could not recall when or where he might have seen her before. Was he ever surprised when they told him she was his sister!

Elise spent a week at the home of each of her sisters and brothers. Later, she would recall how poor they were, struggling to stay on the land, trying to hold on until conditions improved.

It seems that the severe drought of the previous year (1934) had been followed by weeks of dust storms in April (the worst occurring on Palm Sunday, April 14, 1935, which would later become known as "Black Sunday"), and then a torrential rainstorm in May, with the result that they had to redo all the corn planting in June, late in the season, as all the seed had been washed away.

Fritz Reunion in Nebraska (July 1935)
Left to right: Dora and <u>Theo</u>, Elise, <u>Frieda</u>
and Paul Kleinknecht, <u>Alfred</u> and Agnes (with
children), Gottlob and Fredricka Heller and
daughter Dorothy, and Emil and <u>Berta</u> Heller
Children in front: Betty and young Ted Fritz,
Dorothy Heller, Henry Wagner

Many of their neighbors were struggling to feed their families, since they had been forced to borrow heavily from the bank to carry them through, to buy more seed, and thus they had no cash on hand to buy food or other basic necessities. Elise's worried siblings explained how the bank would suddenly show up without warning to claim a heavily mortgaged farm, and that even farms that were clear of debt often went on the auction block for non-payment of taxes. [Between 1930 and 1935, a total of 750,000 farms in the United States were lost through foreclosure and bankruptcy sales.]

Elise also spent a week with Alfred and Agnes. Agnes had given birth to baby Nancy only a few months earlier, on April 6th, just eight days before "Black Sunday." Worried about "dust pneumonia", she was careful to drape wet kitchen towels over the baby's bassinet and wet sheets over Rudy's crib.

Agnes was looking forward to her sister-in-law's visit and invited Reverend Schaum to Sunday dinner in her honor. Elise would later recall how Agnes served a layered Jell-O dish for dessert and how, without a refrigerator, she had placed the Jell-O at the bottom of the cistern to chill and set.

Elise also recalled attending a quilting party at someone's home and how all the ladies had suddenly rushed to get into their cars and drive home as the sky had turned black with the approach of a dust storm.

Agnes told Elise about tornadoes, scaring her with warnings about how they would have to run and take shelter in the root cellar if they saw a twister approaching!

Five weeks later, Elise boarded the train back to New York where she reported to her husband that her siblings in Nebraska lived a very poor and hard life indeed, and that there was dust everywhere.

One day, in the midst of all the drought and despair, an important looking envelope arrived in the mail. Bearing a German postmark, it was addressed simply to Karl Alfred Fritz, Eustis, Nebraska. Inside was a letter bearing an official notice from a court of law.

The fateful letter was to change their lives forever. Had it not been for the letter, Alfred and Agnes would have remained in Nebraska where they would surely have weathered the economic storms of the 1930s, and where, like Alfred's brother, Theo, they too would have prospered. But that was not how it was meant to be.

And this is how it came to pass....

CHAPTER 7

"Vanity of vanities; all is vanity!"

– Ecclesiastes 1:2

HAVING WEATHERED the social and economic upheavals following the Great War, by 1928 Christian Fritz was slowing down and even contemplating retirement – selling off his farmstead, most of his land, and building a new house at the edge of the village where he and his wife might live out their remaining years.

Christian and Luise Fritz of Heutensbach in 1927

*Bridal couple Emma
and Hermann Ettle
(1925)*

*Emma's wedding (1925). Christian and Luise are to the left of the bridal couple. Alfred stands
directly behind his father. Theo (left) and Rudolf are in the back row. Seated in the grass (left to
right) are Karl, Elise, Erika, then Gretel and Johanna. Hedwig and her husband did not attend,
and Frieda and Berta were already in America.*

Rudolf, his eldest son, had married the previous year at the ripe age of thirty-two. Uninterested in farming, Rudolf had started up a trucking and hauling business. Christian's other sons, Theodor, Alfred and Karl, had all 'deserted' him one by one; all three were now in Nebraska. Four daughters had also gone to America – Frieda, Berta, Hedwig and Elise. Of his older daughters, only Emma had stayed behind, marrying Hermann Ettle, a local farm lad from the adjacent village of Cottenweiler.

His source of labor thus severely depleted, Christian was now left with only three children at home – three young girls at that! Insight to his predicament can be garnered from village archives which show that in 1927, when both the schoolmaster and the pastor tried to introduce an eighth school year in addition to the then seven years of compulsory schooling, Christian Fritz was one of three 'influential' villagers to vigorously protest, emphasizing economic necessity – claiming that "children were needed at home, as their parents were dependent on their labor!"

Such was the situation when, in early 1929, Christian and Luise Fritz transferred ownership of their farm to a Mr. Gottfried Nagel. Together with their three young daughters, Johanna, Erika and Gretel, the couple then moved in with Rudolf and his wife while their new house was under construction next door. (Christian had built Rudolf's house as an investment property at the start of the Inflation. It was now considered Rudolf's inheritance, Christian having "sold" it to his eldest son at a reduced price.)

Christian could now look forward to a quiet retirement. In 1928, the economic outlook for Germany's fledgling democracy (the Weimar Republic) appeared promising; there was full employment. Germany had recently even been granted permission to join the League of Nations...

But alas, the Great Depression would soon hit Germany also, and with catastrophic force.

The Wall Street Crash in October 1929 affected all of Europe, but it hit Germany the hardest, because German businesses had come to depend on loans from banks in the U.S. for their survival. Thus, when the Great Depression crippled American banks, the economic engine driving German employment stalled. American banks began withdrawing their credit from Germany, calling in their loans. But Germany was in no state to pay back the money it had borrowed; it was just recovering from its last depression. Forced to give back what it had borrowed, Germany had no money to invest in its own economy. As a result, many businesses went bankrupt; there was no money left for them to borrow and put back into their businesses. The German economy began to collapse.

Stores and factories closed; mass unemployment followed. The government then had to borrow money from the banks to pay for all the unemployment benefits. Soon the banks ran out of money and had to close. As in the Hyperinflation of 1923, the German people again lost all their savings.

Rudolf's house, built by Christian in 1921, and located at the edge of the village, in the direction of Rudersberg (2007 photo)

The new house next door, built in 1931, where Christian and Luise would live out the remainder of their lives (2007 photo)

Once again there was hunger and despair. Many citizens blamed their weak democratic government for the situation and lost confidence in democracy. The mass unemployment, poverty and misery gave Hitler just the opportunity he needed. Hitler had blamed the democratically elected Weimar Government for the Hyperinflation of 1923. Now he blamed the Weimar Government for this second Depression. Soon he would convince the people of Germany that what they needed was not democracy, but rather a strong leader like himself who would make Germany great again!

The same thing happening with farmers in the U.S. as a result of the Great Depression was now taking place in Germany as well. With farm prices dropping, many farmers could no longer meet their debt obligations. Unable to obtain credit, many small farmers were losing their farms.

By 1932, Gottfried Nagel was also having trouble meeting his payments. Consequently, Christian was forced to repossess his farm in early 1933, shortly before his death. (Christian died of cancer on June 24, 1933. He was sixty-four.)

The year before, he and Luise had drawn up a will, naming each other as sole beneficiary. Luise, now sixty-three years old, no longer in the best of health (she was suffering from shingles), unable to afford outside help, and with only two daughters still at home (Erika had married Wilhelm Werf of Oberweissach in a quiet ceremony just weeks before her father's death), could no longer manage the farm. So she decided to turn over the farm to her youngest daughter, nineteen-year-old Margarete (Gretel). Although Johanna (twenty-two) was three years older than Gretel, she was not the least bit interested. Engaged to an auto mechanic, Johanna wanted nothing more to do with the hard farming life!

At the time, Gretel was being seriously courted by Karl Krauter, the son of a well-off farmer in Allmersbach who could bring sufficient resources into the marriage to clear the Fritz farm of debt and make it profitable again. Thus, Luise was certain that in making Gretel her sole heir, she was doing the right thing. The cash infusion her new son-in-law would bring into the marriage would not only be sufficient to cover any debts, but would also provide for her in her old age.

Historically, German laws of inheritance – in particular with respect to the family farm – were determined largely by tradition, with each geographical area following its own local customs. The large agricultural estates of northern and eastern Germany were customarily passed on to either the eldest or the youngest son, intact and undivided, whereas in Württemberg, farmland had historically been divided and subdivided until, over time, practically nothing remained except a patchwork of small plots – a strip of land here, another narrow parcel there.

German inheritance law must also be considered in three periods: pre-Hitler, under Hitler, and after World War II. Prior to the Third Reich, tradition (in southern Germany) dictated that all the sons had equal right to the farm; it was decades of this practice that had led to the parceling of the land. But in Hitler's Third Reich, this practice was halted by the enactment of the *Reichserbhofgesetz* (State Hereditary Farm Law) dated September 29, 1933.

The *Reichserbhofgesetz* was intended to improve the immediate condition of farmers as well as to preserve the farming community. Under the Law, the family farm was to be protected and preserved at all costs. Farms of a certain size (such as Christian's farm) were declared an *Erbhof*, or hereditary estate, and could not be split up or sold by quarreling heirs, nor could they be mortgaged or foreclosed for debts, but had to be passed down, intact, to a single heir.

Needless to say, this very much pleased Luise. In fact, farmers were some of Hitler's strongest supporters – at least in the beginning, as he promised them good prices for their products. Indeed, when Hitler came to power in 1933, he singled out farming as the nation's most honorable occupation. Farmers, he claimed, were of superior stock because of their pure Aryan blood. They were the backbone of the "Aryan" race, the guardians of the holy "soil."

(The glorification of the peasantry as well as the Nazi 'blood and soil' (*Blut-und-Boden)* ideology was a key component of Nazism or National Socialism. "Farmer peasants" were the heart and soul of the nation, and since the true strength of the German people was derived from its peasantry, it was important to save the peasantry and its Germanic heritage.

Of course, behind all this blood-and-soil ideology and racial posturing, something very important was at stake: Hitler needed to exert central control over agricultural production in order to prepare the country for war. During World War I, a British blockade had prevented food imports from coming in, resulting in widespread hunger followed by unrest in the cities. Hitler knew from history that Germany had to be able to rely on its own farmland to produce the food it needed, that Germany must never again be dependent on food imports from abroad. For this reason, The State Hereditary Farm Law underscored the health of Germany's farms as critical to the health and well-being of the German nation!

Luise assumed that she could bequeath the farm to whomever she pleased. She soon learned, however, that according to the *Reichserbhofgesetz* (which entered into effect three months after her husband's death), in order for her to appoint her youngest daughter as sole heir, she would have to specially petition the district Hereditary Court in Backnang, since the new law stipulated the line of inheritance as follows:

1. The sons of the testator; [Ideally, the eldest or the youngest son was favored, depending on local custom, since there was variation in this regard. In the absence of local custom, the youngest son was to be favored.]
2. The father of the testator;

Reichsgesetzblatt

Teil I

685

| 1933 | Ausgegeben zu Berlin, den 30. September 1933 | Nr. 108 |

Inhalt: Reichserbhofgesetz. Vom 29. September 1933... S. 685

Reichserbhofgesetz. Vom 29. September 1933.

Die Reichsregierung will unter Sicherung alter deutscher Erbsitte das Bauerntum als Blutquelle des deutschen Volkes erhalten.

Die Bauernhöfe sollen vor Überschuldung und Zersplitterung im Erbgang geschützt werden, damit sie dauernd als Erbe der Sippe in der Hand freier Bauern verbleiben.

Es soll auf eine gesunde Verteilung der landwirtschaftlichen Besitzgrößen hingewirkt werden, da eine große Anzahl lebensfähiger kleiner und mittlerer Bauernhöfe, möglichst gleichmäßig über das ganze Land verteilt, die beste Gewähr für die Gesunderhaltung von Volk und Staat bildet.

Die Reichsregierung hat daher das folgende Gesetz beschlossen. Die Grundgedanken des Gesetzes sind:

Land- und forstwirtschaftlicher Besitz in der Größe von mindestens einer Ackernahrung und von höchstens 125 Hektar ist Erbhof, wenn er einer bauernfähigen Person gehört.

Der Eigentümer des Erbhofs heißt Bauer.

Bauer kann nur sein, wer deutscher Staatsbürger, deutschen oder stammesgleichen Blutes und ehrbar ist.

Der Erbhof geht ungeteilt auf den Anerben über.

Die Rechte der Miterben beschränken sich auf das übrige Vermögen des Bauern. Nicht als Anerben berufene Abkömmlinge erhalten eine den Kräften des Hofes entsprechende Berufsausbildung und Ausstattung; geraten sie unverschuldet in Not, so wird ihnen die Heimatzuflucht gewährt.

Das Anerbenrecht kann durch Verfügung von Todes wegen nicht ausgeschlossen oder beschränkt werden.

Der Erbhof ist grundsätzlich unveräußerlich und unbelastbar.

Das Gesetz wird hiermit verkündet:

1. Abschnitt

Der Erbhof

§ 1

Begriff

(1) Land- oder forstwirtschaftlich genutztes Grundeigentum ist Erbhof, wenn es

1. hinsichtlich seiner Größe den Erfordernissen der §§ 2, 3 entspricht und

2. sich im Alleineigentum einer bauernfähigen Person befindet.

(2) Höfe, die ständig durch Verpachtung genutzt werden, sind nicht Erbhöfe.

(3) Die Erbhöfe werden von Amts wegen in die Erbhöferolle eingetragen. Diese Eintragung hat rechtserklärende, keine rechtsbegründende Bedeutung.

§ 2

Mindestgröße

(1) Der Erbhof muß mindestens die Größe einer Ackernahrung haben.

(2) Als Ackernahrung ist diejenige Menge Landes anzusehen, welche notwendig ist, um eine Familie unabhängig vom Markt und der allgemeinen Wirtschaftslage zu ernähren und zu bekleiden sowie den Wirtschaftsablauf des Erbhofs zu erhalten.

§ 3

Höchstgrenze

(1) Der Erbhof darf nicht größer sein als einhundertfünfundzwanzig Hektar.

(2) Er muß von einer Hofstelle aus ohne Vorwerke bewirtschaftet werden können.

§ 4

Entstehung von Erbhöfen durch Teilung

Die Bildung mehrerer Erbhöfe durch Teilung größeren Grundbesitzes ist zulässig, wenn

1. jeder Hof für sich den Erfordernissen der §§ 1 bis 3 entspricht und

2. der Gesamtbetrag der Schulden des Eigentümers einschließlich der auf den zu teilenden Grundbesitz ruhenden dinglichen Lasten dreißig vom Hundert des vor der Teilung zuletzt festgesetzten steuerlichen Einheitswerts nicht übersteigt.

§ 5

Entstehung eines Erbhofs durch besondere Zulassung

(1) Der Reichsminister für Ernährung und Landwirtschaft kann nach Anhörung des Kreisbauernführers und des Landesbauernführers von den Erfordernissen des § 3 Ausnahmen zulassen.

Law Gazette No. 108 of September 30, 1933 regarding the State Hereditary Farm Law (Reichserbhofgesetz) of 1933 (page 1). "The government seeks to preserve the farming community as the blood-source of the German people in accordance with cultural tradition. Family farms must be protected against undue indebtedness and fragmentation due to inheritance so as to remain a family's heritage – an enduring legacy of a family and its descendants." In addition: "A farmer must be a German citizen, of German or similar Nordic blood, and of honorable character." [The Reichserbhofgesetz remained in effect until 1947 (after WW II), when it was replaced by the former law in effect prior to 1933.]

3. The brothers of the testator;

4. The daughters of the testator. [Of greatest importance was that the farm should remain intact. In some instances, the farming male had married in; and although the daughter was the actual receiver, the property went under the name of the male head.]

Thus, it was up to the Hereditary Court to approve Luise's petition to make her youngest daughter the sole recipient, since in so doing, she was by-passing those individuals preceding her daughter in the line of inheritance – primarily, her sons!

Luise's petition was dated November 23, 1934. Upon receipt thereof, the Court set out to notify all the Fritz children of their mother's proposal. This notification process was delayed, however, since Luise was unable to provide addresses for all her children. (Several had left home years ago and she had not heard from them since!) Finally, on April 18, 1935 the Court was able to write to each of the Fritz children, directing them to state their position and/or comment on their mother's petition. The Court's directive, together with a copy of Luise's petition, was mailed to all twelve children:

Rudolf, age 39	Proprietor of a trucking business in Heutensbach
Frieda, age 37	Wife of Paul Kleinknecht, farmer in Cozad, Nebraska
Theodor, age 36	Farmer in Cozad, Nebraska
Berta, age 34	Wife of Emil Heller, farmer in Cozad, Nebraska
Emma, age 33	Wife of Hermann Ettle, farmer in Cottenweiler.
Hedwig, age 32	Wife of Gottlob Schwarz, tailor in Brooklyn, NY
Alfred, age 30	Farmer in Eustis, Nebraska
Karl, age 27	Chauffeur, or farmer (!!) in Brooklyn, New York
Elise, age 24	Wife of Henry Wagner, Brooklyn, New York
Johanna, age 22	At home in Heutensbach.
Erika, age 20	Wife of Wilhelm Werf, mason in Oberweissach
Margarete, age 19	At home in Heutensbach

The State Hereditary Farm Law also contained a provision whereby prior to transfer of farm ownership to a sole heir, any other siblings must have been provided for. Thus, in her petition, Luise not only had to justify her decision to bequeath the farm to her youngest daughter, but she also had to account for her other children's claims to compensation as well.

Luise explained to the Court that her eldest son, Rudolf, had relinquished all claims, having already received his inheritance. (His parents had sold him his house at a greatly reduced price.) In Luise's opinion, all the remaining children had also received sufficient compensation. The daughters had either received a dowry and/ or passage money to America, and all of them were now married. The sons, too, had received either passage money to America or had been outfitted with a new wardrobe prior to leaving for America, with the exception of Karl (whom she had not heard from in years). She would, however, honor any claims Karl might have in this regard.

The justification for Luise's decision to bequeath the family farm to her youngest daughter was obvious: the farm was in serious need of a good manager as well as a fresh influx of cash. Her youngest daughter's pending marriage with Karl Krauter would more than fulfill both requisites.

The Court advised the Fritz children of their rights under the law. All children were entitled to a fair start in life; either some type of training to enable them to support themselves once they left home or some other resources to help them get started in life – for girls, this meant a dowry. The Fritz children were asked to state whether they agreed with their mother's petition, whether they had, in fact, received compensation, and, if so, in what amount, and whether they were satisfied with the amount or would be asking for additional compensation at such time as title to the farm was transferred to their youngest sister. The deadline for responding was June 15, 1935. Failure to respond would be deemed as consent.

Karl's letter reached him in New York, where he was boarding with his married sister Hedwig, in Brooklyn. Karl had been unable to make a go of it in rural Nebraska. With the Depression and the dust storms, no one had any work for a hired man, or any money to pay him with. His sisters had encouraged him to come to New York in the hopes of finding work there. Since Karl had not received one penny from his parents when he left home, in his written response to the Court he sought assurance that he would be compensated by his mother, and in what amount. In his response Karl also stated that although he agreed in principle that the family farm should be passed down intact, he questioned why he himself should not be the one to inherit, since, as the youngest son, he was positioned well before his sister in the line of inheritance. He was, after all, both a farmer and a German citizen, and if he were designated heir to his father's farm, he would return to Germany. [In fact, Karl had no intention of returning, but was cleverly paving the way for Alfred's eventual return...]

On September 9, 1935 the Backnang Hereditary Court handed down its decision, based on the following line of reasoning:

> The Court could <u>not</u> approve Luise's petition since the first person in line to inherit was the youngest son, Karl, then Alfred, followed by Theodor. The Court might have approved of the mother's choice (to place her daughter before her sons), if convincing argument had been made. Such, however, was not the

case. In his response to the Court, the youngest son, Karl, clearly stated that if he were made heir, he would return to Germany. **Alfred in his response had also questioned why he could not be the heir to his father's farm and was petitioning the Court for his rightful inheritance. Alfred was also willing to return to Germany if he were made heir.**

The Court saw no reason to deny the sons their request. The fact that they had not written frequently after leaving home was no reason to deny them their lawful inheritance. Many people who had gone to America had written a few times at the onset and then had never been heard from again. It is true that in recent years the sons had not concerned themselves with the welfare of their parents or the family farm, but that in itself was not justification to discount them – at least not legal justification. Moreover, in her response, daughter Emma in Germany had written that their father's last wish was that Margarete should not marry Karl Krauter, and that one of his sons should inherit the farm. Furthermore, although the widow maintained that the children in America had been adequately compensated, several had claimed otherwise. Indeed, it was not sufficient that the mother merely expressed her intention to compensate; rather, the farm had to be protected from any future claims a sibling might bring against it.

For all of the above reasons, Luise's petition was denied!

The Hereditary Court's ruling reached Nebraska in mid-September. Alfred made up his mind right then and there to return to Germany!

Everyone thought he had lost his mind. After all, during Elise's visit that summer, the Fritz siblings had discussed their mother's petition at some length, but then the topic had been put to rest. But Alfred could not let it rest; the idea of inheriting his father's farm totally preoccupied him. All throughout that hot, dry summer he thought of little else. For him, the American dream had become a nightmare; the land of opportunity was now a place of desperation. He was so tired of the heat, the dust, and the unrelenting wind – *der verdammte Wind!* – the hot, dry wind that never let up and threatened to drive him mad. He was exhausted from the futility of trying to farm the parched earth. Alfred was homesick. How he longed for the lush fields and meadows of his *Heimat* – for the green, green grass of home!

That fall, there was no harvest, and Alfred saw himself confirmed in his decision to return to Germany, to give up his life in Nebraska and to part with all that he owned – his horses, the livestock (cows and heifers, hogs and chickens), his farm implements and machinery, his tools, all their furniture and household goods, his Model T – everything!

The idea of inheriting the family farm had become a blinding obsession, and although everyone cautioned him against the idea, Alfred was a determined man who had already made up his mind. Theo tried in vain to dissuade his brother; repeatedly admonishing him that Agnes was not a sturdy woman and not cut out for the hard life of a farmwoman in southern Germany, where women were expected to labor long hours in the fields. Agnes would never last, he warned. But despite everyone's misgivings, Alfred stubbornly plowed ahead with his plan. When it came time to applying for a passport, he completely ignored the cautionary advice of his concerned

Left: Family passport issued by the German Consulate-General at Chicago on January 17, 1936

Below: Inside cover of passport showing personal data and photos. Included are 2-year-old Rudolf and 9-month-old Nancy.

relatives to simultaneously apply for a re-entry visa to the States – just in case things in Germany didn't work out!

In December he began selling off all their worldly possessions – farm implements, horses and livestock, plus household goods. It was the worst time imaginable to try to sell anything – in the midst of the Depression and the Dust Bowl! Everything sold at a loss, as most folks were too poor to buy anything. There were so many tenant farmers just like them who were simply giving up, loading whatever possessions they could onto their cars and heading west to California, in the hopes of finding work there.

Agnes was miserable. Clasping baby Nancy tightly in her arms, and with little Rudy clinging to her apron, she stood by, watching as all the bits and pieces of her life were carried off by others: everything she had worked so hard for, all her possessions, the things she had saved up for and purchased one by one from her meager earnings – her kitchen items, her cooking pots and baking pans, the wooden kitchen cupboard with her nice set of dishes, the modern bed and dresser set she was so proud of. Worst of all was having to part with those precious items most dear to her – her embroidered tablecloths and hand-crocheted doilies, the cedar chest containing the linen sheets and pillowcases, hand sewn from yardage and which she had tediously hem-stitched and hand embroidered in the evenings by kerosene light during the many long years she had worked as a servant and a hired girl: the dowry that she had spent long years accumulating and which she had brought into the marriage.

Alfred (31) and Agnes (29) in January 1936

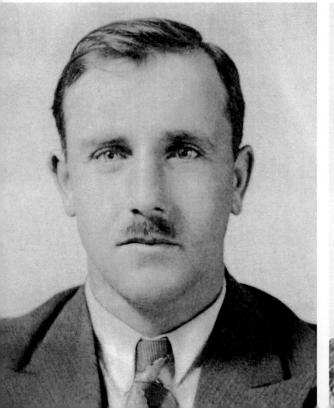

Distraught, her eyes overflowing with tears, unable to bear it any longer, she at last broke down sobbing, confiding to her sister-in-law, Dora, that she didn't know how she could go on. How she hated the idea of going back to Germany!

What was so utterly amazing about Alfred's decision is that essentially, he had nothing more to go on other than a copy of a lower court's ruling denying his mother's petition. Based on that alone, he made the momentous decision to uproot himself and his family and return to Germany.

Alfred had arrived in Nebraska in the spring of 1927. Now, eight years later, and with a reluctant wife very much opposed to the idea of giving up her adopted country, he was willing to abandon everything he had achieved in America, to put everything on the line for the opportunity to inherit the family farm in Heutensbach!

On Sunday, the twentieth of January, Agnes asked Pastor Schaum to drop by in the afternoon to baptize baby Nancy. A few days later, she and Alfred were gone.

From Cozad they traveled by train to Chicago, then on to New York and to Hedwig's flat in Brooklyn, where Agnes could at least wash the baby's diapers before boarding the ship on which they had booked passage.

Karl showed Alfred the most recent [undated] letter he had received from Rudolf:

"Dear brother Karl,

Thank you so much for your letter. Helene and I are both well, and I hope the same for you.

You asked about the situation at home with regard to acquiring the farm. Well, you should bring with you at least $1,000 in cash. That should be sufficient.

[In 1936 that would have been the equivalent of $17,000 today!]

You ask which fields and meadows still belong to the farm. Well, all the land is still intact with the exception of the *Burgacker,* which was sold.

I am keeping your driver's license status valid in case you return.

The harvest was good this year, with an especially abundant amount of fruit. Mother sold 3,000 marks worth and spent it all on the three of them at home, on clothes and such things. It appears that mother is now agreeable if one of you would come back to take over the farm. It looks like Gretel's relationship with Krauter is over; she's now being courted by someone else. That is why somebody should come soon, before the fieldwork starts in the spring.

It looks like you are not married yet. Well, Gottlob Fritz's Anna is still single, and if you do decide to return, you should marry a rich woman. Do what you think is best; I don't want to be blamed for anything.

Please give my regards to Hedwig and Gottlob and the children. Why do we not hear from them? Also give my regards to Elise. I think when she writes to mother she sends her regards to me as well, **but mother never tells me anything**.

I wish you all a Merry Christmas and a Happy New Year, and I hope to hear from you soon regarding your plans."

After re-reading Rudolf's letter, Alfred and Karl strategized that it would be a good idea for Karl to sign some kind of legal document in which he declares under oath that although he (Karl) is first in line of succession to inherit, he relinquishes his right in favor of his brother, Alfred, who is on his way back to Germany and will be arriving shortly.

In everyone's life there are times when we question whether we actually have control over our own lives or just how powerful chance can be in shaping our lives. Are we really in control of what happens to us in life, or are we mere victims of circumstance, of fate? Do we really have free choice, or are we driven on a path marked by destiny? Who can tell? Perhaps we are mere pawns in this strange game called 'LIFE', the outcome of which is already predestined, no matter what shrewd moves we might make.

Do the decisions we make in the course of our lives actually originate from somewhere deep within ourselves, or are they essentially just a reaction to outside influences and events? Would Alfred have decided to return to Germany if there had not been a prolonged drought? Would he still have been that keen on inheriting the family farm if the economic situation in Nebraska had been more promising in the mid-30s?

Alfred was disappointed in America; he was disillusioned with farming in Nebraska, where all his dreams had turned to dust. For him, America was no longer "the promised land." And yet, there were his brothers, Karl and Theo, certainly no better off than he. Theo, too, was but a tenant farmer struggling to hold on, and Karl had even been obliged to leave Nebraska to try to find work in the city. Yet neither Theo nor Karl had any desire whatsoever to return to Germany.

Alfred's decision, it seems, was the result of a combination of many factors, both from within and without. But why was he consumed with such longing to return to Germany? What was he homesick for? Certainly not for his family members or the bleakness of the life he had left behind! Can it be that in the end, he simply longed for the green fields and meadows of his youth, and for the abundant rainfall that always ensured a plentiful harvest?

On the last day of January 1936, Alfred Fritz took his small son in his arms, and together with his wife and baby daughter, stepped onto the gangplank of an ocean liner bound for Germany, certain that he was on his way back home to claim his rightful inheritance. Rudolf's letter had left him more confident than ever that he had made the right decision.

But destiny, the "Game of Life," was about to play him a very cruel trick…

*   *   *

A F F I D A V I T

Vor mir, dem oeffentlichen Notar des Staates New Kreis und Stadt New York, erschien heute Karl Fritz wohnhaft 61-29 Cooper Ave., Brooklyn, New York und sagte Folgendes aus:

Ich, der endesunterzeichnete Karl Fritz, erklaere hiermit unter Eid, dass ich am 29. August 1907, zu Hautensbach, Backnang Land, geboren bin. Im Juni 1933 verstarb mein Vater Christian Fritz, und nach dem jetzt gueltigen deutschen Erbhof-Gesetz bin ich nunmehr der ärste in der Erblinie. Da mein Bruder, Alfred Fritz, in Kurze nach Deutschland zurueckfaehrt, und die zur Uebernahme des Hofes faelligen Zinsschulden bezahlen wird, trete ich an ihn hiermit mein erstes Erbfolgerecht ab,--bis zu solcher Zeit, dass mein Bruder sich eventuell entschliessen wuerde, nach den Vereinigten Staaten von Nordamerika zurueckzukehran. In diesem Falle soll das Erbfolgerecht wieder an mich zurueckfallen.

Ich gebe diese Erklaerung ab, damit mein Bruder sein Recht der Erbfolge nachweisen kann.

New York City, den 27. Januar 1936.

STAAT NEW YORK

KREIS NEW YORK

STADT NEW YORK:SS

Vor mir, dem oeffentlichen Notar des Staates New York, Kreis und Stadt New York erschien heute Karl Fritz, aus 61-29 Cooper Ave., Brooklyn, N.Y., wurde gesetzesgemaess vereidigt und vollzog seine Unterschrift eigenhaendig, was hiermit beglaubigt wird.

New York, den 27. Januar 1936.

Karl's Affidavit dated January 27, 1936

ALFRED HAD LONG AGO ceased corresponding with family members in Germany, and since at the time there was no trans-Atlantic telephone communication, he had no way of knowing that at the very same time he had been busy parting with all his worldly goods in Nebraska, his mother, back in Germany, had been vigorously appealing the lower court's ruling!

As fate would have it, and irony of ironies, Alfred and Agnes boarded the ocean liner bound for Germany not realizing and totally unsuspecting that, just days prior to their departure, the lower court's ruling had been reversed!

Undaunted by the lower court's decision, and not about to be cheated of her rights by some newfangled inheritance law, Luise had immediately sought out the leader of the local farmers organization, the *Ortsbauernführer,* pleading her case.

The *Ortsbauernführer* was a powerful man during the Hitler era, responsible for implementing Nazi agricultural policy at the local level. Being a member of the local community, he was sensitive to the mood of the locals and was very much aware of the fact that Hitler was keen on keeping the farmers content and on his side. The *Ortsbauernführer* was personally acquainted with Luise, who, as the widow of Christian Fritz, still enjoyed considerable standing and influence in the village. It was thus in his own best interest that he align himself with her.

In its Judgment dated January 25, 1936, the *Oberlandesgericht* (Stuttgart Regional Appeals Court) explained its decision to overturn the lower court's decision "because a complaint had at once been entered against it." The Appeals Court further decreed "that since in fact no set local inheritance custom exists in the Backnang area, the mother is entitled to pass her property on to whichever child she chooses. The mother is also correct when she states that the sons now living in America had not shown any interest in their parents or the farm during all the years since they left home, so why now the sudden interest? Furthermore, the sons in America could not supply convincing evidence of their farming capability, whereas the farm in Heutensbach was in desperate need of a competent individual, and the fiancé of the daughter to whom the mother wishes to transfer ownership is just such a competent person."

The time-limit for filing an appeal was set to expire at the end of February.

Of course, Alfred and Agnes were blissfully unaware of this fateful turn of events; they had already disembarked by the time the Appeals Court's ruling reached Karl (by mail) in New York. It was too late; Karl had no way of contacting his brother, to give him a warning heads up!

In Cuxhaven, Agnes was delighted and relieved to be met by her sister, Meta. Meta had remained single; she was employed as head housekeeper for the Adamis, an affluent merchant family in the port city of Stade, near Hamburg. Adelheid, her younger sister, whom Agnes barely knew, was employed as *Kinderfräulein* in Hamburg, and her employer had granted her a few hours off. Thus, the three sisters

Erbhofgericht beim
Oberlandesgericht Stuttgart.

— Geschäftsstelle —

An Herrn

Karl <u>Fritz</u>, Chauffeur
<u>oder</u> Landwirt

in <u>B r o o k l y n</u> (New York)
61 - 29 Cooper Ave.

Stuttgart-O, den <u>25. Januar 1936.</u>
Urbanstraße 18.

Geschäftsnummer: We. F/ Nr. <u>451/35.</u>
(bei allen Eingaben anzuführen.)

Betreff: Erbhofsache der Bauerswitwe
Luise **F r i t z** in Heutensbach
Kreis Backnang.

Beil.: **0.**

Weisungsgemäss wird Jhnen mitgeteilt, dass vom
Kreisbauernführer der Kreisbauernschaft Murr gegen den
Beschluss des Anerbengerichts Backnang vom 9.9.35 sofortige
Beschwerde eingelegt wurde. Zur Begründung der Beschwerde
wird vorgetragen, die Mutter habe, da im Kreis Backnang
seither keine Anerbensitte bestanden habe, das Recht,
den Hofnachfolger unter ihren Kindern frei zu bestimmen.
Den Söhnen in Amerika, die sich heute so lebhaft für den
Hof interessieren, halte die Mutter mit Recht entgegen,
dass sie sich seither um das Ergehen der Eltern und des
Hofes nicht gekümmert hätten; die in Amerika lebenden
Söhne könnten auch ihre Bauernfähigkeit nicht einwandfrei
nachweisen. Der Hof verlange dringend einen tüchtigen
Wirtschafter; ein solcher sei in der Person des Bräutigams
der Hofübernehmerin vorhanden.

Es wird Jhnen Gelegenheit gegeben, sich zur
Beschwerde bis spätestens Ende Februar 1936 zu äussern.

25. 9. 35. 1000.

Appeals Court Ruling dated January 25, 1936 (Page 1)

were able to rendezvous and celebrate a reunion of sorts in the third-class lounge of the Harburg-Wilhelmsburg railway station. They had not seen each other in over twelve years!

They sat around a wooden table in the drafty lounge, waiting for their connecting train, with Meta and Adelheid adoringly admiring Agnes' children. Over hot cups of tea, the three sisters were soon happily conversing in rapid-fire *Plattdütsch*. Alfred, of course, could not understand a word, and Agnes, sensing her husband's growing discomfort, tried to draw him into the conversation. But, as so often before, he failed to connect. After listening for some time in silence, he suddenly erupted, berating Agnes' astonished sisters that, whereas they were still stuck in the old ways of thinking and doing, he had gone to America and gotten ahead in life. What's more, he would soon own his own farm, and, as if to emphasize that he was a man of consequence, he took the calling card Adelheid handed him and wrote on the back, with proud flourishes, his future mailing address, handing it back with the casual comment: "Everybody knows me there."

Such impudence and arrogance did not sit well with the younger sister. Indeed, Adelheid's impression of her sister's husband was that he acted and behaved like a peasant – coarse and rude, lacking in manners, even resting his feet atop the table, cowboy-style!

Continuing on by train, Meta guided them to the home of Ernst Bartels in Zeven. Onkel Ernst, their mother's eldest brother, was the patriarch of the family. In Zeven they could rest and regroup before continuing on to their final destination, a day's journey south via the German Reich Railway.

What were their thoughts during the final stretch of their long journey? Alfred, agitated and on edge, was nervously anticipating the overwhelming sight of his boyhood village, totally caught up in the dream of owning his own place, his father's farm where he was familiar with every inch of the soil. At last he would be able to work his own fields! And he would surely prosper, for had he not learned a great deal about farming during the many years he had spent laboring in Nebraska – first as a hired man and then as a tenant farmer, coaxing crops from the dry soil, praying for rain, the same rain that had always been so plentiful in his home country? Soon he would be able to apply the agricultural methods he had learned in Nebraska. His "modern" farming techniques would revolutionize the old way of doing things in Heutensbach. Why, he would even introduce the planting of corn instead of fodder root crops! In his mind he was already planning the necessary additions to the farm buildings….

Agnes sat opposite him, busy with the children, trying to keep them still. Rudy had just turned two; Nancy was nine months old. All the while, she kept wondering how it could be that she, Agnes, was sitting here opposite this obstinate, driven man who had been so adamant about returning to Germany. Sitting in the third-class compartment of a train speeding southwards towards Stuttgart was certainly not where she wanted to be! She loved America! America was her country, and she had never wanted to leave. How she hated and had fought the idea! But Alfred was stubbornly set on a future for them in Germany.

With both children now asleep, she allowed her thoughts to wander, imagining herself back on the other side of the Atlantic, back in Nebraska. She thought of her friends there, of Blanche Kiesel, to whom she had poured out her heart during those last rushed days in Eustis.

But then she suddenly recalled the story of Ruth in the Old Testament, Ruth's promise of fidelity to her mother-in-law, Naomi, to go with her back to her home country and to take care of her. She was a bit like Ruth, she thought, going to live among people she did not know.

"*Wo du hingehst, gehe ich auch hin!*"

Agnes knew the Bible verse so well, silently continuing in English: "For whither thou goest, I will go; and where thou lodgest, I will lodge. Thy people shall be my people…"

Agnes would go with Alfred, would return with him to his home and to his people, even if he was taking her to a place where she could barely understand the dialect, much less speak it, a place where she knew no one, and where she would be at the mercy of her husband's estranged family.

She recalled what she had once overheard Theo telling her husband, that life was hard for farmwomen in that part of Germany. Well, she was used to hard work, and besides, if everything went well, it would be nice to have a place of one's own at last, and who knows, maybe Alfred would find contentment, would finally be happy. If Alfred could only be happy and content, it would all be worth it! And yet, it was with growing trepidation that she approached the end of their journey. What would await her there?

With what eagerness they finally pulled into the tiny Backnang station, and with what high anticipation Alfred arrived in his home village!

But the prodigal son was greeted only with hatred and derision.

Never one known for his tact, Alfred, in his highly charged emotional state, headed straight for his childhood home and ordered everyone out, as he was now the rightful owner. Unaware of the recent ruling of the Appeal's Court, Alfred was acting as though he had every right to claim what was lawfully his.

Alfred was confronted with the deep resentment of his mother, who wanted nothing to do with him and treated him with indignation and contempt. And his rash behavior created such animosity in the village that he had to tread very carefully during the weeks that followed, as the villagers all sided with his mother against him, and there were men in the village who were itching to beat him up, not least of whom was Karl Stirm, Gretel's fiancé.

Poor Agnes! Not only did she have the ravings of a desperate, half-crazed husband to deal with, but she was also made to feel totally unwelcome. Her mother-in-law flatly refused to speak to her – the outsider, the "foreigner" who dared show up and try to take the farm away from her daughter.

Intimidated by her irate mother-in-law, who treated her with open disdain and who made life miserable for her, Agnes suffered in silence. Powerless in the face of her awkward and embarrassing position, she watched with growing alarm as her frantic husband chased from one legal authority to another, from one court of law to another, from Backnang to Stuttgart and back again, trying to make sense of what had happened.

So there they were: Alfred's hopes and dreams shattered! And such deceptive dreams they had been, inducing him to believe that he could go home again! He and Agnes had traveled thousands of miles, all for naught. What were they to do now? Where could they go?

Alfred's mother finally relented (if only for gossip's sake) and allowed them to stay temporarily in the old farmhouse alongside the other family living there. How demeaning that must have been! They were assigned one of the cold, unheated bedrooms, and Ages was grudgingly allowed to share the use of the kitchen stove...

Then there was the matter of their survival. Since arriving in Hamburg, Alfred had begun drawing from their savings (a letter of credit in the amount of 6,650 *Reichsmarks*, or $1,500). But given the mounting court costs and legal fees, he was spending much more than he had anticipated. Finally, when it became clear that he would inherit nothing, and with their life savings rapidly being depleted, Alfred had to find work. Rudolf advised him to purchase a hauling truck. There was money to be made in short-distance hauling.

They moved away from Heutensbach, to a place halfway between the town of Backnang and the village of Erbstetten. Alfred had found a small deserted house for rent at the edge of an abandoned quarry which they furnished scantily with a cookstove and just enough furniture to get by – a kitchen cabinet, a table and chairs, and a bed.

Unlike the United States, which was still in the midst of the Great Depression, Germany's economy was booming. When Hitler came to power in 1933, there were over six million unemployed, but he promised to end the depression and make Germany prosperous again. By 1938, less than four years later, there was almost no unemployment – an impressive achievement. The other world leader of the '30s who tried to revamp a whole society was our own American President, Franklin Delano Roosevelt, but he did it less effectively under the constraints of democracy. Also, while millions of conservative Americans were critical of President Roosevelt's New Deal for the "common man," labeling it socialism, Hitler found much wider acceptance.

The Depression of the early 1930s was Germany's second such disaster within a decade. (The 1919 Treaty of Versailles had not only left Germany embittered and humiliated, but the resulting inflation and unemployment in 1923 had wiped out not just the working class, but Germany's middle class as well.) Thus, the Germans were not only grateful, but also impressed with Hitler. Hitler was restoring German pride and putting people back to work. Even if you were totally apolitical or did not agree with his political ideology, still you had to be impressed with his success in restoring full employment, economic order and social stability. Hitler was a popular dictator at first. In fact, many Germans found the idea of a one-man leadership very appealing. They longed to return to the good old days, *die gute alte Zeit*, when things would be as they were before the War, under the monarchy of the Kaiser, or so they hoped…

With his truck, Alfred found work hauling gravel for road construction. Hitler's most famous public works program was in full swing – the construction of the Autobahn, the major highway system that would soon connect every major German city. This massive road construction project served two purposes at once: it helped solve the problem of unemployment by creating work; and it provided the means to enable Hitler in the future to move troops and war machinery quickly across the country, in all directions.

Alfred worked on just such an Autobahn construction site – Highway 14, the by-pass road around Backnang.

Agnes spent long days alone with the children, as the house they were renting was isolated, far from the nearest village. Rudolf, feeling partly guilty for their misfortune, did as much as he could to help them get settled, but there was only one person to whom Agnes, in her outcast situation, could turn – her sister-in-law, Emma Ettle. It was Emma who befriended her and came to her aid. Emma would often send her ten-year-old daughter, Gretel, to visit Agnes in Erbstetten and to babysit Rudy and Nancy.

Neither of them was content. The only reason Alfred had returned to Germany was to inherit the family farm. As soon as it became apparent that this was not going to happen, they both wanted nothing more than to return to the United States. Although Alfred had found work, he considered it only a temporary solution. His real interest lay in farming; his dream was to own his own farm. In Germany, that was all but impossible, but in America he still might have a chance to start over again.

Agnes had never wanted to go to Germany in the first place. Was Alfred to drive a truck the rest of his life? Were they never to have a place of their own? Not only that, but Herr Hitler was rearming the country, and everything, even daily life, seemed so militaristic. In town, there was constant marching and flag waving. The Nazi banner was now the official flag, and Agnes learned soon enough that she was expected to give the Nazi salute whenever one of those swastika banners was carried past. She marveled how people with whom she came into contact, even the shopkeepers in town, no longer greeted her with the familiar *"Guten Tag"* or *"Grüß Gott"* but with *"Heil Hitler!"*

The situation was indeed troubling. Hitler had reintroduced military conscription, which meant that there was a good chance that Alfred could be drafted into the *Wehrmacht*! In March, German forces had invaded the Rhineland, and there was talk of even more aggression. Then there was Hitler's plan to make Germany self-sufficient in agriculture, with the result that dairy products were to be rationed, since *der Führer*, unwilling to spend precious currency, refused to continue to import from Denmark and Holland.

Agnes and Alfred, used to being self-sufficient, now had to purchase the major share of their food at the local market, which is how Agnes found out that butter was to be rationed. The idea of rationing food, in peacetime, made her suspicious. Politically naïve, Agnes sarcastically remarked to anyone willing to listen that in America, at least, there was plenty of butter!

Alfred, for his part, had his own problems readjusting to life in Germany – the restrictiveness, the bureaucratic pettiness. *"Armes Deutschland, kleine Füchse!"* was his favorite disparaging remark.

Their discontent grew. Daily life in Germany seemed so confining after having experienced the vastness of America, the freedom of opportunity, the sense of personal liberty and the lack of restrictions. In America, you could come and go as you pleased without being constantly asked to show your papers, plus you could speak your mind without fear of being reported.

They were desperate to return to the States, but how? They didn't have a visa! Alfred's siblings in Nebraska had pleaded with him to secure a re-entry visa at a cost of just a few extra dollars (!) so that he and Agnes could re-enter the United States in case things didn't work out as planned. [As an alien, Alfred would have been required to swear under oath that he was leaving the United States only *temporarily* and to state the length of his intended absence, and the reason for his departure].

But Alfred had stubbornly refused to listen to reason, blinded as he was by homesickness and the absolute certainty that he would never want to return. Now his

Otto Esenwein,
Gustav Grimmer,
Alfred and Rudy
in Heutensbach
(September 1936)

shortsightedness came back to haunt him. Indeed, as German citizens with a German passport, their situation appeared hopeless; they had hardly any chance of obtaining an immigrant visa to the United States. Agnes recalled her own brother's experience, how in 1929 the new regulations limiting immigration had prevented Jonny from securing an immigrant visa. Since that time, the situation had only gotten worse. With the Depression raging, President Roosevelt and the U.S. State Department had essentially shut down immigration, allowing an annual quota of only 27,000 German and Austrian immigrants, and the quota, they learned, had already been met until the year 1940!

Enter Otto Esenwein onto the scene! In September 1936, he and Päule and their two sons, Erich and Otto Jr., visited Heutensbach. (Most likely it was Rudolf who then enlightened their old childhood neighbor about his true origin when he told Otto what Christian had confessed to Rudolf on his deathbed: that Otto was actually his son!)

Otto Esenwein had done very well for himself in America. He had left Germany as an impoverished farm laborer in 1927 with his wife and then five-year-old son Erich. Sponsored by his wife's brother, Gottlieb Haegele, who owned a German bakery in Philadelphia, Otto had initially worked as a milkman, delivering fresh, glass-bottled milk to people's doorsteps in the early morning hours. Now, nine years later, he owned and operated his own successful milk delivery business in Philadelphia.

Otto had done everything right – had applied immediately for citizenship papers – so he and his family were now American citizens holding American passports. Otto, it was rumored, was acquainted with people in high places. As an active member of a number of German-American associations, and having professed contacts to German consular officers in Philadelphia, he could conceivably exert some influence. Thus Alfred, painfully aware of the hopelessness of his situation, approached Otto Esenwein, his half-brother, and begged him for his help. Otto promised only that he would do his best, since it was up to the discretion of each individual American consulate whether an exception would be made in granting a particular person a visa or not. He would, however, through his affiliations and personal contacts, try to put in a good word.

Thus it was solely through Otto's intervention and efforts, and, in turn, through the intercession of the German Consulate in Philadelphia, that Alfred eventually secured an immigrant visa from the American Consulate. My parents would remain grateful to Otto Esenwein *("Onkel Otto")* for the rest of their lives.

The process took a year. Not until September 1937 was Alfred finally issued an immigrant visa. Sister Hedwig, in Brooklyn, had agreed to sponsor him. In order to finance the return voyage, Alfred sold his truck. Then, after saying their farewells to Emma and Rudolf, they boarded a train heading north, towards Hamburg.

On October 8, 1937, Alfred took hold of the small hand of his three-year-old son as they made their way up the gangplank of the *S/S Europa*. Known for its speed, the *Europa* was set to arrive in New York Harbor in record time, on October 14. On the passenger manifest, Alfred had listed his occupation as "farmer."

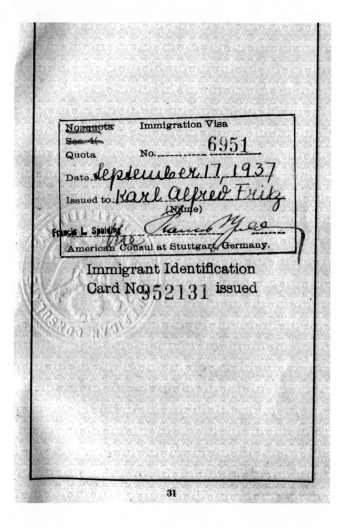

Immigrant visa issued to Karl Alfred Fritz by the American Consulate General at Stuttgart on September 17, 1937

Agnes, nearly seven months pregnant, had to remain behind! Thus plans were hurriedly made for Agnes and two-year-old Nancy to stay with Meta in Stade until after her baby was born. Meta was happy to share her room in the Adami household with Agnes and little Nancy, glad for her sister's company, to have someone to talk to at the end of her long workday.

Even as an old woman, Meta recalled with fondness their time together in Stade, recalling little Nancy's cute *Schwäbisch* speech, how *das kleine Deern* would awake in the middle of the night and call out to her:

"Dande Meta, Wasser trinkle und kleine Küchle esse!"

Meta recollected how for such a young child, Nancy was remarkably confident in herself and who she was. Laughingly, she recalled how one time Nancy came running to her complaining, indignant that the neighbor's child, Wilma, refused to play with her:

"Dande Meta, d'Wilma will nedd mit mir spiela, und i bin doch die Nanzi Fritz!"

Frau Adami had agreed to let Agnes stay, but not out of the goodness of her heart. Agnes would have to pay room and board. Meta, aware of Agnes' dire financial situation, quietly paid out of her own wages, later asking Adelheid and Jonny to chip in. Their sister, Meta explained, was under enough stress already, and should be allowed to await the birth of her child without additional anxiety. Adelheid was incensed. How could Alfred leave his wife behind with no money!

One wintry afternoon, Meta returned home from her errands to find her sister gone.

"Wo ist Agnes?" she asked in alarm.

"Well, where do you suppose your sister could be?" replied Frau Adami, teasingly. "Agnes was taken to the hospital!"

Agnes' time to deliver had come, and on December 17, 1937 she gave birth to her third child – a boy. She gave him the double first name Ernst-Erich: "Ernst" in honor of Onkel Ernst Bartels of Zeven, and "Erich" because she had always liked the name, plus it reminded her of Otto Esenwein's pleasant, handsome young son, whose name was Erich.

Thus, Ernst-Erich was born into Hitler's Third Reich; but he would not remain there for long. On February 8, 1938, Agnes was issued her visa. Two days later, she and the children set out from Bremerhaven aboard the German passenger liner *SS Deutschland*. They would arrive in New York eight days later, on February 18, 1938. Agnes was thirty-one, Nancy almost three, and the baby just two months old.

Agnes was thrilled that Jonny, a machinist with the Borgward-Werke in Bremen, was able to come to Bremerhaven to see her off. Jonny, Meta and Adelheid all came on board the ship and helped her get settled. But all too soon the announcement was made that it was time for non-passengers to disembark. As the ship's anchor went up and the giant ocean liner slowly moved away from the dock, the brass band on the pier played farewell songs. Agnes stood at the railing with little Nancy, waving goodbye. The band

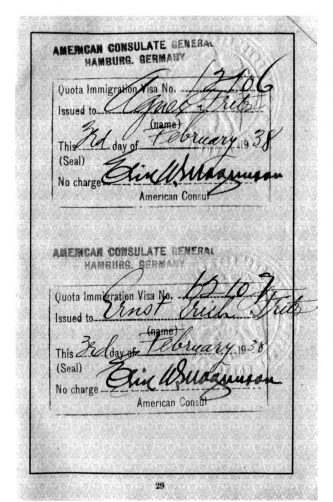

Top: *Agnes, visibly stressed and exhausted (January, 1938)*

Left: *Immigrant visas issued to Agnes Fritz and Ernst-Erich Fritz by the U.S. Consul General at Hamburg on February 8, 1938*

played *"Auf Wiedersehn, auf Wiedersehn…"* But neither Agnes nor her siblings thought it probable that they should ever see each other again.

Agnes was lucky to have secured passage; the *Deutschland* was almost fully booked. Her sisters had accompanied her by train to the departure pier in Bremerhaven. There they had the opportunity to observe the first- and second-class passengers, who boarded first, her sister Adelheid noting with some resentment the elegant women dressed in furs, many of them German Jews, quietly desperate to get out of Germany, to escape while they still could. Under Nazism, things had grown steadily worse for Jewish people. Accused by Hitler of being responsible for all of Germany's problems, Jews no longer felt safe in Nazi Germany.

It is thought that half of the five hundred thousand Jews living in Germany in 1933 fled prior to 1939. The Jews who remained in Nazi Germany were either unwilling to leave or unable to obtain visas. Some could not get sponsors in host countries or were simply too poor to be able to afford the trip. Many foreign countries, such as the United States, made it even harder to get out due to strict immigration policies designed to prevent large amounts of refugees from entering, particularly in the wake of the Depression.

One month after Agnes' departure, Hitler annexed Austria, and a year and a half later, in August 1939, in anticipation of Germany's invasion of Poland, all German merchant ships were ordered back to German ports immediately. Agnes was lucky to have left Germany when she did, before all trans-Atlantic ocean travel came to a halt.

The return voyage was not a pleasant one – the ship encountered severe winter storms and very rough seas. Baby Erich was the only one who did not get seasick. Agnes had tied his "bassinet," a wicker clothes basket, to a rope suspended between two bunk posts. Rocking gently side to side, he "floated" above the storm-tossed passengers below.

Booked under the cheapest fare, packed sixteen to a dormitory deep in the bowels of the old ocean liner, the air in the stuffy, confined quarters was so rancid that it made Agnes' stomach churn and only helped to start the cycle of being sick all over again. Due to the rough seas, she only managed a few times to take little Nancy above deck for some fresh air, climbing the many flights of stairs. From there, she could catch a glimpse of the wealthy passengers in the upper sections of the ship. She wondered if the day would ever come when she would be able to travel above-deck, in comfort, instead of in third-class...

Agnes had no idea what awaited her in New York. But there was one thing she did know for certain: She was so glad to be returning to America! In her mind, she was returning home; America was home. She thought of herself as American, not German! On the ship's passenger manifest, she even listed her nationality as American and gave her last permanent address as Eustis, Nebraska! Agnes would be so glad to see Lady Liberty! Instead of the swastika flag, she could not wait to see the Stars and Stripes flying overhead again!

Alfred had written and provided an address to list as her final destination: Box 121, Laurel Springs, New Jersey. Agnes had no clue where that was. How she wished that she could simply return to Eustis! But Eustis was thousands of miles away, and she knew that Alfred would never go back to Nebraska. Besides, they had nothing there to return to.

Their financial situation was dire; they were nearly destitute. Agnes knew that hard times awaited her. She and Alfred would have to begin anew, with three small children and not much more than the clothes on their backs. They had managed to bring along their bedding, but not much more. Alfred had financed their return passage by selling his truck, and the little cash remaining she had cleverly hidden, sewn inside the lining of Alfred's jacket and inside the ticking of their *Federdecken* (feather comforters). It was law that only 10 *Deutschmarks* (approx. 4 U.S. dollars) could be carried out of Nazi Germany. Otherwise, you could be accused of trying to smuggle currency.

Agnes could only guess at Alfred's current state of mind. His pride and self-confidence had taken such a beating, and she knew how worried he was for their welfare. He had been so deeply humiliated, and he was now so disillusioned and bitter.

We can only imagine their sad plight, their predicament! People with lesser physical and mental stamina might have broken. In Alfred's case, it was his strong, determined Germanic character – his *Dickköpfigkeit!* – which helped him to endure, while Agnes, with her unending patience, took comfort in her faith, praying for the necessary strength.

Her destiny was, after all, inexorably linked to that of her husband, and this was no time to give in to despair. She needed to be strong, not weak. From now on, she would have to be extra tough, not only for her husband's sake, but also for the sake of her three little children, whom she loved so dearly.

Was it then that she remembered? Sitting on her bunk on the lower deck of an ocean liner bound for America, balancing herself against the rocking of the ship, quietly nursing her newborn and calmly pondering her fate, Agnes suddenly recalled the old comic strip with its philosophical saying. It would become her mantra, and she would quote it again and again for the rest of her life: "WHAT A LIFE, IF YOU DON'T WEAKEN!"

For there were to follow long years of bitter poverty and deprivation, and she did not dare weaken.

CHAPTER 8

"A man without land is nobody."

– Mordecai Richler, the Apprenticeship of Duddy Kravitz

ALFRED RETURNED to America on October 14, 1937. Thirty-three years old and near broke, he would now have to start all over again from scratch. Hedwig and Elise were waiting on the pier. (Immigrants no longer routinely went through Ellis Island. After 1924, the only people who were detained at Ellis Island were those who had problems with their paperwork.)

Alfred's Immigrant I.D. card had already been stamped "Admitted" when the immigration examiner abruptly pulled him and Rudy aside and, upon further questioning, wrote "Claimed" above Rudy's U.S. citizenship and refused them permission to disembark!

Labeled as "Aliens Held for Special Inquiry," they were on the following day, "Delivered to Ellis Island" by ferry where they were held over the weekend until a "Witness" made it possible for them to be "Discharged" early Monday morning. Alfred's Immigrant I.D. card was re-stamped "Admitted" on October 18.

Why were they detained at Ellis Island for three days? And who was the witness who cleared things up?

A closer inspection of the family passport provides a clue. It states that Rudy is a U.S. citizen, born in Nebraska, but mistakenly lists his year of birth as 1931, when actually he was born in 1933. The ship's manifest correctly states that Rudy is three years old, but according to the passport, he would have been five years old! Obviously, the immigration examiner didn't catch the discrepancy until the last moment. He might have thought that Alfred was smuggling in a child, and that Rudy was not even his son, much less a U.S. citizen. A flustered Alfred would not have had any documentation to prove otherwise. Perhaps someone from the German Consulate was the witness who authenticated Rudy's U.S. citizenship?

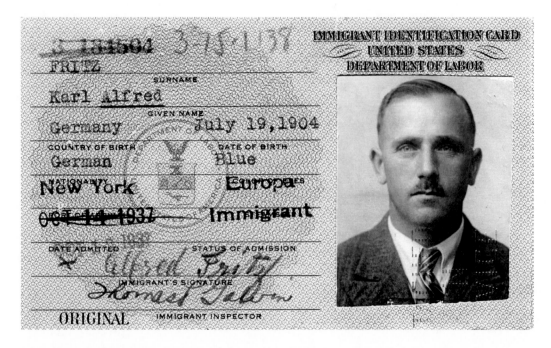

When Alfred and Rudy were finally released, his sisters were waiting. Elise took Rudy home with her, gladly volunteering to look after the little fellow until Agnes could come from Germany. In

The coveted "green card", granting Alfred permanent resident status

fact, in the months to follow, she and Henry would grow very fond of the little *Schwäbisch*-speaking boy and would gladly have kept him longer, although Elise did have her hands full with him, especially in the beginning.

Mimicking what he had seen back in Germany, little Rudy liked to click his heels together and give the Hitler salute! Not only that, but Elise would often catch him standing on the front steps of their two-flat, holding his small body erect, standing at attention, his right arm raised in the "Heil Hitler" greeting. All this in bright daylight, in full view of their neighbors and passers-by on the street, in Queens, bordering Brooklyn! Elise would run to snatch him up and bring him inside in a hurry!

Alfred went home with Hedwig to her and Gottlob's flat in Glendale, in Queens, where Karl had also stayed for awhile. With jobs very hard to come by, Karl had been very fortunate to find work as a handyman for an apartment complex in Brooklyn, where he continued to work until shortly after the Japanese attack on Pearl Harbor in December 1941, when he was one of the first men to be drafted, even though he was a German citizen and thirty-four years old!

Alfred was a determined man and anxious to get started. Onboard the *SS Bremen* he had listed his occupation as "farmer," and farming is what he wished to pursue.

Otto Esenwein again came to his aid. Otto had already told Alfred that compared to out west, the countryside and farming style in the eastern part of the country was similar to that of their homeland in Württemberg. Fields were smaller in size, and, unlike in Nebraska, rainfall was adequate and reliable.

Otto knew of a small 'farm' – forty acres, in rural New Jersey. The property was actually a former peach orchard now covered in a thick growth of shrubs, brush and small trees. The owner of the property was in the process of fixing up the house. At present, there was only one room that was fit to live in; the "house" was actually a one-room shack, but in return for clearing the land, the owner was willing to let him live in the house, rent-free.

Alfred grabbed at the opportunity and went straight to work. The owner supplied him with the necessary hand tools, and throughout the fall and winter, he was all alone by himself on the property, hard at work clearing the land.

Agnes arrived in mid-February. Elise and Henry met her at the pier. Exhausted from seasickness, Agnes sobbed for joy to see her little Rudy again. The following Sunday, Elise and Henry drove her and the children out to the country to join her husband. Alfred broke down when he held baby Erich in his arms for the first time. Agnes fought back tears of her own when she saw the condition of the house where she would be living...

There was now a spirit of hopefulness... New York relatives and friends from Philadelphia gathered at the farm (July 10, 1938). Back row (left to right): Winnie Schmiemann, Erich Esenwein, Otto Esenwein, Otto Schmiemann, Joe McGuinness and Hinrich Otto Schmiemann. Front row: Alfred and Agnes, Gottlieb and Päule Haegele, daughter Ruth, Päule Esenwein, Elise Wagner and Anna Catharina Schmiemann (Agnes' aunt). (Photo taken by Anna McGuiness)

Elise had given Alfred money to buy a horse to help with the work. Now she bought him a cow so that the children could have milk. Every other Sunday, the city relatives took turns driving out to the country – Karl, Hedwig and Gottlob, and Elise and Henry. Time and again they drove the long distance, bringing with them foodstuffs and such items as a poor immigrant family might need: used housewares of all kinds, chipped, mismatched dishes, kitchen utensils, cast-off furnishings, old clothes, and hand-me-downs for the children. In short, anything and everything the New Yorkers, their friends and acquaintances could manage without, although most folks had very little to spare during those depression years.

Late that spring, having already cleared quite a bit of land, Alfred took his last remaining cash (the money hidden inside their *Federdecken*) and purchased seed for planting. Agnes laid out a vegetable garden.

There was now a spirit of hopefulness about the farm – a feeling of guarded optimism. In June, Hedwig's young daughter, Almida, came to baby-sit for several weeks. Almida recalled that the house was just a shack, with no indoor plumbing – quite an adjustment for a fifteen-year old city kid! She also recalled how Onkel Alfred

would brew his own beer. It was warm, tasted terrible, and would sometimes explode!

Alfred continued to work all that summer, clearing more land and tending to his crops, all the while anticipating the fruits of his labor. But before he could actually harvest anything, they were suddenly and abruptly given notice to vacate! Now that the place had been made livable, the owner wanted to live on the property himself!

At risk of losing everything he had invested in time and energy, seeing all his hard work going for naught, Alfred saw himself forced to take the owner to court. But all he managed to recover was his seed

Alfred and Agnes Fritz with baby Ernst-Erich (July 10, 1938)

Rudy, Nancy and Ernst-Erich Fritz (July 10, 1938)

money. (Without a written lease, Alfred was considered a month-to-month renter and thus had no legal recourse against the landlord.)

It was a bitter setback that drove them both to the brink of despair. Now they had nothing left – no money and nowhere to go. How would they survive?

Unlike in Germany, the United States in 1938 was still stuck in the Great Depression. With unemployment hovering around 19 percent, how could Alfred hope to find work? Alfred was desperate. How could he support his family?

Many years later, I recall coming upon my father in a pensive mood, his eyes welling with tears, as he stood in the doorway to our dining room, surveying the pleasant scene before him – the table nicely set for Thanksgiving dinner, adorned with fresh flowers, a fine linen tablecloth, and my mother's good china. He just stood there, slowly shaking his head. Then, in a voice choked with emotion, he turned to me and said: "*Wir hatten damals nichts; damals hatten wir nichts!*" ("Back then, we had nothing, nothing at all!")

Immigrants were not to become a burden to society, which is why an immigrant was required to have a sponsor! Thus the New York relatives rushed to the rescue of the family in what was to become an all out effort to save them from starvation.

Onkel Henry, who had a printing machine repair business in downtown Manhattan, had his ears to the ground. His business partner had a friend who knew of a place for rent just east of Trenton, near the borough of Hightstown, centrally located between New York and Philadelphia. The property was quite small, only sixteen acres. On it stood a small bungalow, a chicken coop and a shed – not large enough to farm, but it was another start.

Once again, Elise withdrew from her own meager savings to loan them money. Nobody was rich in those late Depression years, but everyone tried to help. Word spread of the family's sad plight. Soon friends from Philadelphia – Gottlieb and Päule Haegele, Karl and Helene Pfaehler – were driving the forty-odd miles from Philadelphia on Sundays, bringing with them stale breads as well as leftover, unsold baked goods from their bakery shops. To this day, Rudy can recall the delicious German bakery treats; the children thought they had died and gone to heaven!

Alfred's mental state did not improve with the stress of this added setback. The years of continuous drought in Nebraska, the humiliation of what had occurred in Germany, the deprivations he and his wife had to endure, combined with the uncertainty of their very survival, now threatened to replace his strong instinct to endure with emotional collapse. Seemingly unable to cope with this last in a long series of reverses, he would often explode in rage, would literally go berserk, for it seemed no matter how hard he worked, no matter how hard he drove himself, no matter how frugally they lived, he could do nothing right, could not achieve anything, could not "get ahead" like others, could not even support his family.

Inside, he was seething; he was a man full of indignation at the injustice he had once again experienced, on top of the countless degradations and humiliations he had been made to endure, it seemed to him, all his life.

Alfred had never been able to verbalize his frustrations. Not only had he been raised to keep everything inside, but long, lonely years as a shepherd had left him unable to communicate. Now, with his back against the wall, and unable to put his emotions into words, he would keep his feelings of frustration, helplessness and fear penned up inside until they reached a point where his mind would seemingly explode.

One never knew when some minor incident would trigger an onset, and he would be beside himself with rage. It was at home that he usually "let go," and those closest to him would bear the brunt of his aggression – more often than not some unfortunate farm animal that happened to be close at hand. Once, Elise found him inside the shed beating the horse unmercifully with a board.

Screaming at the top of her voice, she pleaded with him to stop.

"How can you beat a poor animal that has done you no harm?" At which Alfred, his eyes fiercely glaring and in "manic" mode, snapped back. "Sometimes I get so mad I could walk up the side of a house!"

No, Alfred was not always a likable guy. Gruff and short-tempered, he could be mean and coarse in his everyday dealings. But perhaps he could not help being how he was. Over his (inherited) temperament he had little control, and what other kind of personality could he have developed after the harsh discipline and emotional neglect he had endured? In hindsight, and over more than a half-century later, it is obvious that his adult character reflected his early childhood experiences, and that he emerged from the deprivations and abuse of his formative years emotionally crippled. His father, Christian, was brutally strict. His children were produced for one reason only: to work and to be useful. Made to work from the time he was five years old, Alfred's "permanent" chore about the farm, starting at the age of nine, was to herd sheep. His father would even fetch him out of school. Deprived of love and affection (if he returned home because he was scared or lonely, his father would beat him), it would be an understatement to say that Alfred missed out on the "golden years" of childhood.

According to Garrison Keillor, "culture is what you know is so by age twelve." Similarly, our childhood experiences shape us forever and set the tone for the rest of our lives. In turn-of-the-century Württemberg, once a child completed compulsory grade school, and then following confirmation at age fourteen (the traditional "coming of age"), he was considered an adult. Alfred at age fourteen thus became his father's full-time shepherd, sent as far away as the *Schwäbische Alb*, hundreds of miles from home, with only the company of his dog. He was kept in this capacity for many years – alone with sheep and dog, with little or no socialization.

Thus his anger, his frustration, was fostered at an early age. It grew out of childhood abuse in the form of emotional neglect and social deprivation, and most of all, the powerlessness to change his situation. Instead of being nurtured by his parents, he was exploited and at the same time treated with callousness, indifference and cruelty. Although clever in school, especially with numbers (he could do complicated mathematical calculations in his head), he was deprived of further educational prospects or even the opportunity to learn a useful trade. Alone for years with sheep and dog, he had neither books at his disposal nor the opportunity to learn, to nourish his inquisitiveness. As far as anyone was concerned, he was nothing more than a lowly, unpaid farm hand.

Alfred's resentment and frustration accumulated into adulthood, resulting in his "unique" personality and behavior. Between periods of "normalcy," his moods would fluctuate. He could be sullen and irritable, or hot-tempered, exploding violently without warning. *"Keep Your Temper, Nobody Else Wants It"* read the wording on the small wooden plaque Agnes hung on the kitchen wall.

Or the episodic pendulum would shift, and he would become withdrawn and depressed, with spells of crying, feeling sorry for himself, and suicidal thoughts. Seemingly powerless against these mood fluctuations, neither he nor later his sorely tested family ever knew in advance which would prevail, or how long it would last. Any kind of acute stress, however, would almost certainly trigger a flare-up.

Today, his condition would likely be diagnosed as some type of personality disorder. He would be treated with mood stabilizing drugs and would receive psychological counseling. [It is thought that between a third and a half of adults diagnosed with bipolar disorder report traumatic/abusive experiences in childhood. Alfred may also have been genetically predisposed; an alcoholic uncle in Germany had hung himself...]

In the 1940s, however, people generally didn't bother with therapists or psychologists; there was no public awareness of mental diseases such as mood disorders, bipolarism or manic depression, and modern day medications were unknown. Besides, people would not even have dreamed of consulting a doctor to discuss how to cope with mental distress. It was not deemed medically necessary. The very idea of opening up to anyone would have been dismissed as personal weakness, as silliness. After all, everyone knew the trials of Job in the Old Testament! People were expected to cope as best they could on their own. Plus there was the social stigma associated with any type of mental disorder, as psychological impairments were thought to be genetically predetermined or inherited defects.

Amazingly, very few people, even close relatives, were ever aware of the extent of Alfred's mental disarray, his unpredictable moods that would shift from extreme anger and irritability to sadness and despair. Agnes, a very private person, did her best to keep her husband's choleric outbursts of rage hidden, always concerned about what other people would think. Dreading her husband's explosive, unpredictable temper, she tried her best not to upset him and to keep anyone else from upsetting him as well. She became a peacemaker *par excellence,* constantly trying to "keep the lid on." Often she simply kept things from her husband – anything that might potentially upset him. She became so adept at "'keeping the peace" that it eventually became second nature. And to a large degree she succeeded. Alfred's brother, Karl, the sibling to whom he was closest, went to his grave without ever really knowing...

In later years, when we children were no longer young, we would occasionally find good reason to pass judgment: "Mama, why did you ever marry him; how can you stand to put up with him?" we would ask. "Why don't you get a divorce?"

But Agnes, horrified at such talk, and intent on instilling respect for their father in her offspring, would each time counter with the same reply: "How can you talk about your father like that? You should be ashamed! Don't you see how hard he works for you?"

And it was certainly true. Alfred did work extremely hard; nobody would ever question how hard he worked to provide for his family and to get ahead. Besides, Agnes believed in the sanctity of marriage. Had she not vowed, "until death do us part?" One did not simply throw away a marriage; you tried harder. Brought up in the tradition of women's subordination to men, she considered it primarily the woman's duty to make a marriage work.

Alfred was desperate for work. Once again, Otto Esenwein came to his aid. Even with so many men jobless, Otto's brother-in-law, Hermann Pfaehler, a butcher in the retail meat industry, through personal and business connections, was able to get Alfred a job at Derby Meat, a processing plant that produced sausage, scrapple and other processed meat products. During the week, Alfred roomed with Karl and Helene Pfaehler in Philadelphia on the second floor of their bakery shop at Marshall and Luzerne, within easy walking distance from the plant. Friday afternoons he took the train home to spend the weekend with Agnes and the children, returning to the city late Sunday afternoon in order to begin his shift early Monday morning. Alfred was very fortunate to get this job, although from then on he refused to eat hotdogs, after seeing first-hand what animal by-products and other "mysterious" ingredients went into their making. Himself an excellent butcher, Alfred was all too aware of the difference between a fine quality, small butcher, handmade *Bratwurst* and the mass-produced, all-American hotdog!

Thus Agnes and Alfred began anew, from scratch, slowly building a new existence in America. During the following years they saved every penny towards buying the implements, tools and livestock they would need as tenant farmers – gradually acquiring several milk cows and a pair of mules, a hog for butchering and a small flock of hens. With Alfred gone during the week, Agnes was alone and on her own, with three children to look after, plus the farm animals. Rudy recalls how she could even handle the big mules!

Agnes would later admonish her daughters that, as a woman, you must learn how to do everything, since you never know when you might have need of a certain skill. "Once you learn something, you never forget it!" she would insist. "It always comes back to you." Whether it was learning how to milk a cow, ride a bicycle, drive a car, or use a typewriter, she always found application for her advice. It certainly applied to her in her own life – a farmer's wife had to know how to do everything. Her family's very survival depended on it!

They were living in Hightstown when they learned of Germany's invasion of Poland in September 1939. The following August, they had to go to the local post office to register as aliens with the U.S. government.

> The Alien Registration Act, passed by Congress on June 29, 1940, made it illegal for anyone in the United States to advocate, abet, or teach the desirability of overthrowing the government. The law also required all alien residents in the United States over 14 years of age to register with the U.S. government and to file a comprehensive statement of their personal and occupational status and a record of their political beliefs.

Like most German-Americans in the 1930's, Alfred and Agnes were by and large apolitical. Caught up in the fierce, daily struggle to make a living, they had only a cursory interest in what was happening in the outside world, including Hitler's Germany.

With Otto Esenwein, however, it was a different story. Otto was an active member in the German-American Bund, an organization sympathetic to Germany and National Socialism. He had even persuaded Alfred to allow rallies of the Bund at his farm – mainly social gatherings, with German-American families from the city gathered together for a day's outing in the country where they picnicked, sang German folk songs *(Heimatlieder)*, drank beer, and listened to pro-German and 'right-wing Americanism' speeches.

The German-American Bund achieved limited popularity in the 1930s (at one point staging a rally with over 20,000 people). However, it did succeed in gaining lots of media attention, and thus made many enemies, some of them powerful special interests who successfully sought to create the image of a sinister, frightful menace in the Bund, a "lunatic fringe" "infected" with the "Nazi virus." The "Bund," however, was never a danger or in any way unpatriotic or subversive. Members of the German-American Bund simply rejoiced in their ethnic and cultural roots, admired Hitler's economic successes, and dreaded what they foresaw as another war with Germany. In fact, the Bund's enthusiasm for the recovery of German pride and self-confidence after 1933 was a natural enough emotion in an ethnic and cultural minority, especially one that had suffered great humiliation and persecution during the anti-German hysteria of the First World War.

The Bund appeared to be more powerful than it was. It actually represented an extremely small number of individuals; however, what it lacked in numbers it made up for with parades, rallies, and rhetoric. In fact, the Bund attracted so few members, but aroused so much antagonism in the United States, that the Third Reich severed its ties with this stupid and noisy organization, which it recognized to be more of a liability than an asset. Thus, there never was a close relationship between the German-American Bund and the Nazi government in Germany. The only ties with Germany were those of sympathy for Germany's emancipation from the oppression of the Versailles Treaty. The Bund was definitely not "un-American" and, although provocative in nature, never posed a danger to the United States. Its leader, Fritz Kuhn, however, failed to convince the House Un-American Activities Committee of that. After his imprisonment in December of 1939 (on trumped up charges of embezzlement of Bund funds) and with the onset of World War II, the Bund rapidly faded.

At any rate, with 32 million! German-Americans living in the United States, Bund membership at its height in 1938 never exceeded 10,000, of which only 4,000 were German-born or German-American. The majority of German-Americans never accepted the Bund or its attempts to win them over to Nazism.

Indeed, by 1938 the overwhelming majority of Germans in the United States considered Nazism an embarrassment and disgrace.

[Excerpted from Peter H. Peel, "The Great Brown Scare: The Amerika Deutscher Bund in the Thirties and the Hounding of Fritz Julius Kuhn," *The Journal for Historical Review.* Winter 1986]

Agnes thought the Bund members ridiculous – their endless speeches, all that marching and saluting. Alfred, on the other hand, was more open to the Bund's far-right ideology, and besides, he was glad that he could do Otto Esenwein a favor, plus he was grateful for the extra income to be made by holding the rallies at the farm. Somewhat naïve, it never even occurred to him that by hosting these gatherings he might come under suspicion by the FBI, not until Elise brought it to his attention …

They didn't stay long in Hightstown. Sixteen acres was simply too small. The following spring they moved to Pennsylvania where they rented a farm just outside Bucksville, near Ottsville, about fifty miles north of Philadelphia, in Bucks County.

[According to the 1940 U.S. Census, Alfred's annual income was $600, from which he paid $13 in monthly rent (as compared to Otto Esenwein, who paid $45 in monthly rent for his house on North 5th Street in Philadelphia and whose yearly income from his milk delivery business is listed as $1,800.]

Otto and Päule Esenwein with milk delivery truck

In the spring of 1941 they moved again, this time to a tenant farm outside Hatfield, near Souderton, just twenty-five miles north of Philadelphia. The New York relatives continued to visit, but less frequently, especially once gas rationing began. The following year they relocated to a "second" farm just up the road. Years later, when they learned that the "first" farmhouse had caught fire and burned to the ground, Agnes' only comment was: "Good, that place was full of bedbugs anyhow!"

It was while they were at the "first" farm in Hatfield that all three children came down with the dreaded childhood disease – scarlet fever. The Department of Health posted a large red warning sign on their front door placing the entire family under quarantine; for six weeks they were not allowed to sell their milk! "Scarlet fever" certainly sounds like a life-threatening illness, and in those days it was. It was considered a serious, highly communicable disease among young children that, if left untreated, could lead to rheumatic fever and even death. Alfred could recall his little five-year-old brother dying of scarlet fever. Although antibiotics were being developed for medical use in the 1940s during the War, penicillin would not become available to the general public until the early 1950s. Today, we can only imagine how scary life must have been without antibiotics, where every cold, every inflammation or even an infected sore could turn into something serious...

The children developed a sore throat, accompanied by high fever and vomiting. A rash appeared on their chests and spread, their tongues swelled up and turned strawberry red (hence the name, "Scarlet" Fever). Without modern medicine, the disease had simply to run its course. The children clamored for elderberry juice, made from the wild, black elderberries that Agnes had picked and canned the previous summer. She was totally exhausted, what with the sleepless nights, keeping watch over three very sick children. But slowly, patiently, over a period of six weeks, little by little she nursed them back to health. How many times did she go up and down the stairs; how many bedpans did she empty; how many countless pails of freezing water did she heat on the stove; how many vomit-soaked sheets did she rinse out, then wash out by hand; lifting the heavy, dripping linens into the pot of boiling water atop the cookstove in order to sterilize the infected bed linens, all in a valiant effort to make her children well again!

At last, they all pulled through and recovered. Tucked under their warm *Federdecken*, the children recited their nighttime prayers in German:

> Ich bin klein,
> mein Herz mach rein.
> Es soll niemand drin wohnen
> als Jesu allein.

Müde bin ich, geh zur Ruh
schließe meine Äuglein zu,
Vater, lass die Augen dein
über meinem Bette sein.

And the classic children's prayer Agnes had taught them in English:

Now I lay me down to sleep,
I pray the Lord my soul to keep;
If I should die before I wake,
I pray the Lord my soul to take.

On December 11, 1941 the United States declared war on Germany. The mood in the country was definitely anti-German. As German nationals living in the United States, Alfred and Agnes were now classified and viewed as "enemy aliens" and subject to certain restrictions. But even naturalized American citizens of German descent came under suspicion, especially those who had shown any sympathy for the government in Germany. Otto Esenwein fell into this category.

Otto was active in several German-American organizations and had been a member of the now defunct German-American Bund. The FBI had followed him out to the farm several times; his phone had been wiretapped. Based on anonymous accusations by informers, the FBI had composed a file on him, questioning his loyalty. When FBI agents came knocking at their front door one day, Päule Esenwein quickly grabbed her husband's copy of "*Mein Kampf*" off the bookshelf, ripping it apart and flushing its pages down the toilet. Later, a plumber had to be called in to unclog it!

It is easy to understand why Otto Esenwein was attracted to National Socialism. He had visited Germany in 1936 and had seen first-hand how Hitler's party had saved Germany from economic collapse. Being himself of peasant stock, Otto would have bought into the Nazi "blood-and-soil" ideology – that the German peasant class embodied the finest qualities of the German race. From there it was just one step further to embrace the Nazi ideas of Aryanism and of Nordic supremacy – that Germans were naturally superior.

Thus, from the mid to late 1930s, Otto truly had believed that Hitler was a good thing for Germany. He may also have believed that Hitler could possibly save the United States from economic ruin, and might even establish a German nation in this country some day. By the time the United States entered World War II, however, Otto, like most Germans in America, no longer supported the Nazi regime.

In 1942, Otto was unjustly placed on the FBI's list of German sympathizers "engaged in subversive activities." At this point, had he not been a naturalized

American citizen, he would have immediately been interned in a camp for "dangerous enemy aliens" for the duration of the war.

> Most Americans have heard about how the entire Japanese population living on the West Coast was uprooted and incarcerated in relocation camps during World War II. But what most Americans appear to be totally ignorant about – largely because our media and history textbooks, intentionally or otherwise, overlook, ignore or just simply kill with silence – is the fact that **at least eleven thousand German-Americans were also interned in U.S. concentration camps between 1943 and 1947.**

In February 1942, President Roosevelt, reacting to wartime hysteria, issued Executive Order 9066 which declared that the U.S. armed forces could designate military zones from which certain people were to be expelled. EO 9066 thus cleared the way for the mass deportation of Japanese-Americans to internment camps. All Japanese Americans (including those born in the U.S.) living on the West Coast were to be relocated.

With German-Americans making up the largest ethnic minority in the United States (there were more than sixty million Americans of German heritage living in the United States!), the government could not possibly carry out a mass internment on a scale comparable to that of the Japanese relocation and internment. Instead, German nationals were to be 'selectively' interned on an individual basis, while "potentially dangerous" U.S. citizens of German ancestry were to be excluded from residing in so-called military zones and forced to relocate elsewhere. By making an example of a few, selective internment and exclusion were meant to frighten and intimidate the entire German-American community.

Otto Esenwein was one of those individuals singled out for selective exclusion. Forced to relocate away from Philadelphia, a high-security zone, Otto sold his milk delivery business and purchased a small farm outside Birdsboro, eight miles southeast of Reading, in Berks County.

Otto's move away from Philadelphia, however, was soon deemed insufficient. His file had been forwarded to a military review board, and relying on unconfirmed FBI reports, the Army now directed that he vacate the entire Eastern Defense Command Zone. Otto had to relocate away from the eastern seaboard to at least five hundred miles inland!

He ended up in Toledo, Ohio, but thanks to the efforts of his lawyer, who could prove that his client was no threat at all, Otto was able to return home in less than a year. During his forced relocation, a neighbor agreed to look after Otto's small farm so that Otto's wife and twelve-year-old son could join him in Ohio as "voluntary relocatees."

What is truly absurd about this story is that all the while Otto and Päule and their younger son, Otto Jr., were being forcefully relocated five hundred miles inland, their older son, Erich, was an active member of the U.S. Army fighting for America's freedom! Tragically, on September 29, 1944, twenty-two-year-old Private Erich Esenwein was killed in action on a battlefield in France where he was serving as a front line army medic, caring for and evacuating the wounded.

Erich Esenwein lies buried in the American Cemetery at Epinal, France, recipient of both the Silver Star and Purple Heart. For his bereaved mother, however, there was no consolation in these medals; for years, she cried herself to sleep every night. Päule Esenwein never got over the loss of her eldest son, the handsome boy she so loved and adored.

With America now officially at war, Alfred and Agnes were cautious and tried to avoid calling attention to themselves. Agnes was nervous because of her German accent whenever she went to town. It became almost a crime or humiliating to speak German anymore. At home, less and less German was spoken. Soon, the only time the children heard German spoken was when relatives came to visit. By now, Rudy and Nancy were both in school, putting up with ethnic slurs, being called "Krauts" and "Nazis". In the evening, after the supper dishes were put away, Agnes sat with them at the kitchen table, helping with reading and spelling, taking advantage of the opportunity to improve her English.

Even though Alfred and Agnes would always retain their German accent, they made every effort to blend in, and soon their assimilation into American culture would be complete. As was the case with most all German-Americans, they willingly and effortlessly "melted" into the great American pot.

During World War II, all contact with relatives in Germany was lost. Initially, letters were censored; then all correspondence ceased. The last

*Päule Esenwein in happier days
(son Erich at right)*

Right: Agnes' siblings, Jonny, Meta and Adelheid, in mourning after the death of their Onkel Ernst Bartels in 1938

Below: Initially, letters were censored, then all correspondence ceased. (Meta's letter dated August 1940, opened by the German Wehrmacht)

Agnes had heard, Meta was still housekeeper for the Adami family in Stade, just outside Hamburg. Her younger sister, Adelheid, had completed two years of nurses training and was working in an army field hospital. Adelheid had taken advantage of Hitler's 1938 "Law for Reorganization of Nursing," which stated that only a grade school (*Volksschule*) education was required for getting into nursing school.

Agnes was uncertain of her brother Jonny's whereabouts, but assumed he was still in Bremen.

In July of 1943, after reading about the terrible firebombing of Hamburg, Agnes feared for Meta's safety. Psychologically, the war between her homeland and her adopted country was very difficult to bear.

Agnes knew what war was like. War brought misery and hunger. As a child, she had experienced hunger first-hand – during the *Hungerwinter* of 1917-18 and the year before, when the townspeople had collected wagonloads of turnips for the people in Hamburg and Bremen and when the turnip, which normally was fed to pigs, became their food of last resort. Even though her family had a garden plot and milk from their goats, Agnes could recall always feeling hungry…

After the Second World War ended, and before the Marshall Plan came to Europe's rescue, the German population again was threatened with starvation. Agnes put together CARE packages to send to her sister, Meta, in which she included such items as canned meat, lard, dried milk, flour, sugar, coffee and soap.

In later years, whenever Agnes witnessed the excesses and wastefulness of American society, she would offer these words of caution:

"In America people don't know what war is. They don't know what it's like to go hungry; what it's like to experience war on their own soil."

After the attacks of September 11, 2001, I sensed her words of warning beginning to ring true.

Alfred and Agnes had moved five times in the last seven years – from one tenant farm to another, each move with the idea of bettering their situation. Now, finally, things were beginning to look up. During the Depression there was hardly any money to be made from farming. But now the war was quickly bringing an end to the Depression; farm products were again in demand – prices for agricultural products sky-high. With so many men enlisting or being drafted, unemployment disappeared almost overnight. Alfred had long since left his job at Derby Meat in Philadelphia. Now, he often assisted Mr. Clymer, the local butcher in Hatfield. But mainly he hired out for cash, as there was now a real shortage of experienced farm workers.

With gas now rationed, more farm labor had to be done by hand. It also became difficult for farmers to obtain spare parts; they had to learn to make do and be creative. Rubber was scarce, so iron-wheeled tractors were in common use.

It was early on a mild spring afternoon in 1943 when Agnes happened to glance out the kitchen window and noticed Alfred's old 1931 DeSoto standing still in the

Iron-wheeled tractors were in common use.

shallow ditch at the end of their lane. Thinking it strange that her husband was home so early, and, after a while, curious why he didn't get out of the car, she decided to walk out the lane to investigate. She found Alfred slumped over the steering wheel and unconscious, bleeding profusely. Her screams for help brought the neighbor from across the road running…

That morning, Alfred had been plowing on a distant farm when by some freak move the cuff of his wide-legged overhauls caught in a cleat of the rear tractor wheel, jerking his leg forward, yanking him down to the ground. Unable to free his caught leg in time, it was quickly dragged beneath the wheel, the cleats of the heavy iron wheel puncturing and fracturing his lower leg as the weight of the tractor passed over it.

It all happened so quickly! In shock, his leg badly mangled and bleeding, Alfred somehow managed by a superhuman effort to both crawl and drag himself to the far corner of the field where he had left the DeSoto, to hoist himself up, to get the car started, and to drive home – clutch, brake, and gas pedals – before losing consciousness.

Agnes was beside herself. Once again the fragility of their lives was all too obvious. Alfred remained hospitalized for fourteen days; there were hospital bills to pay, and since they lived a hand-to-mouth existence, they were now at the mercy of the landlord, as Agnes, on her own, could not possibly pay the monthly rent. Luckily, the owner of the farm liked Agnes, commiserated with her and gave them a break. Although it eventually healed, it was several months before Alfred would have full use of his leg again. Once again, the greater burden of the farm work fell upon Agnes.

They were in Hatfield long enough to acquire a sense of belonging. Although there was plenty of anti-German sentiment, they were not made to feel unwelcome; many of their neighbors were themselves hyphenated-Americans (Polish-Americans, Rumanian-Americans, etc.) Just down the road lived the Leathermans, a young Mennonite family. Their eldest son, Daniel, was the same age as Erich (now anglicized to "Eric"); the two little boys were playmates. Mr. Leatherman made his living as a bookkeeper and was a pacifist. He and Alfred enjoyed playing a game of checkers, both men being about equally matched in skill.

That winter, the children attended their first funeral. There had been a sledding accident. In spite of the light traffic and slower traffic speeds, Bobby Weiss, the neighbor's son, not much older than Erich, was hit by a car and killed when his sled slid onto the road at the bottom of a hill.

"Safe in the Arms of Jesus," the congregation at the little boy's funeral sang. From that time on, Agnes forbid her children to go sledding on the road. Nor could she ever shake her fear of losing one of them to drowning. (Among her keepsakes was a photograph of a young child lying in a coffin – Alfred's three-year-old nephew, Walter Kleinknecht, who just a few years earlier had drowned in an irrigation canal in Nebraska...)

Nancy (8), Rudy (10) and Erich (6) dressed up for Christmas (1943). No matter how poor they were, Agnes always saw to it that her children had Christmas. There was always a tree on Christmas morning, and each child received some kind of a present.

Alfred and Agnes (Christmas 1943)

By the summer of 1944, they had been tenant farmers going on seven years – seven long years since Agnes had brought Erich as an infant in a laundry basket to America. Now she was about to give birth again. In June, Hedwig and family drove out from New York bringing along used baby items. Almida's husband, Frank Trapp, recalled driving them all out in his old Model A Ford with the little rumble seat. In those days it was at least a five-hour trip from New York. You had to drive through all the small towns that are by-passed today, plus the wartime speed limit (to save on gas) was only 35 mph. In fact, due to the strict gas rationing, theirs had been an almost impossible trip. To top it off, their car broke down with a timing gear that was "kaputt," although one of Alfred's neighbors not only repaired it (a monumental task), but even refused payment.

Agnes, eight months pregnant, aided by Eric and Nancy, caught two chickens for dinner. Agnes had perfected her method of slaughtering a chicken: holding tightly to its legs with one hand, grabbing its head with the other, and then twisting the neck, pulling the legs and ripping off the head in one fell swoop. The headless chicken would then "run" around the farmyard, spurting blood, until its body finished dying. Watching her kill a chicken always made a big impression on the city folks; they never ceased being amazed at how one could simply "harvest" a chicken for dinner.

On July 9, 1944, one month after her thirty-eighth birthday, Agnes gave birth to a baby girl in the hospital at Sellersville. They named the baby Frieda Anna – Frieda after Alfred's sister (who had died in childbirth six years earlier), and Anna after Agnes' own middle name.

This time she was very ill after giving birth. Diagnosed with "milk fever," she was not only feverish, her breasts sore and inflamed, but also so run down, so mentally and physically exhausted and drained, that she completely lost the will to go on. She just didn't care anymore if she lived or died.

Sick, unable to nurse her newborn, Agnes herself was gradually nursed back to physical and spiritual health by her kindly Mennonite neighbor, Mrs. Ruth Leatherman. Agnes would remain friends with Ruth Leatherman. She would, over the years, continue to exchange Christmas cards with the kind Christian woman who had helped her through a very dark time indeed. [Daniel Leatherman was later ordained minister and pastor of Lansdale Mennonite Church. Both he and Ruth are remembered by the congregation as being humbly and sacrificially helpful to people in need.]

Karl and Katren Jancsics were also friends who lived close by. The Jancsics, German-Rumanians, had emigrated from Rumania as newly-weds in 1923 (the same year that Agnes emigrated from Germany). The Jancsics were extremely hard-working people. Karl Jancsics was also a shrewd businessman who by thrift and diligence had succeeded in becoming the proprietor of a paint supply store in Philadelphia. The

Depression, however, had put him out of business, forcing him to change his line of work; he now preferred to buy old farms, fix them up and sell them at a profit.

It was late that summer when Mr. Jancsics, always on the lookout for a good investment, mentioned a farm he had read about for sale – eighty-six acres, in Berks County. Together, he and Alfred drove out to have a look at the property. Alfred very much liked what he saw, but how could he ever hope to buy it?

Given their status as "enemy aliens", plus realizing full well that without collateral, no bank would ever loan them money, Alfred and Agnes decided to drive into Hatfield to discuss their vexing situation with their butcher friends, Howard and Emily Clymer. Mr. Clymer knew the Fritzes were honorable, hard-working immigrants, and that Alfred was good at farming,

"Not to worry," Mr. Clymer assured them. "Where there's a will, there's a way." Never once doubting my father's ability to repay him, Mr. Clymer offered to purchase the farm and initially hold title on their behalf until some future date when the war would be over and restrictions on their movement and property ownership rights as "enemy aliens" would be lifted. In other words, Mr. Clymer's trust was such that he agreed to loan the Fritzes the full purchase price of the farm: $5,500 (a huge sum in today's money).

Alfred sold all the steers he had been raising as a down-payment; the outstanding balance of the debt he would pay in monthly installments. The two men sealed their deal with a handshake.

Alfred and Agnes had long since realized the futility of tenant farming. Since their early years in Nebraska, their goal had always been to own their own farm. Agnes had hung on the wall an old framed painting that someone had discarded. It was a painting of a bucolic scene – a small, rustic farmstead, in the foreground a grassy meadow and several grazing cows. She would often gaze wistfully at the peaceful pastoral scene, longing for the day when she and Alfred might finally have a place of their own. Indeed, whenever she sang the words to "Home, Sweet Home," she meant them with all her heart: "Be it ever so humble, there's no place like home!" Agnes didn't care how humble, she just simply wanted a place of her own that she could finally call "Home."

With her health slowly improving, Agnes' desire to live also returned. **"What a life, if you don't weaken!"** Now, just three months after having given birth, she was packing up their few belongings once again, only this time was different. Their years as tenant farmers were finally over. This time they were moving to a place that they could at last call their own!

AUNT FRIEDA'S STORY
A reflection

F RIEDA LUISE, eldest daughter of Christian and Luise Fritz, of Heutensbach, was born at the close of the nineteenth century, on March 6, 1897. Of solid Swabian peasant stock, she was nevertheless graceful in her bearing, slender and petite. Unlike her many siblings (there were fifteen children, of whom twelve survived childhood!), Frieda had brown eyes, whereas the Fritzes were known for their strikingly blue eyes.

Frieda was already in her mid-twenties and still without a suitor. So many of the young men from her village and the surrounding rural communities, men who might otherwise have courted her, had either been killed or crippled in the carnage of 1914-18. Indeed, the Great War had taken the lives of an entire generation of German men.

Frieda was trained as a cook and was employed in the household of a well-to-do family in town.

She was the first of the Fritz children to emigrate. Like thousands of other young people, Frieda left Germany during the height of the German Inflation, in August 1923, at the age of twenty-six. Encouraged by her next-door neighbor and friend, 22-year-old Pauline Pfaehler, who had emigrated two months earlier, Frieda boarded the steamship *Westphalia* at the port of Hamburg and arrived at Ellis Island thirteen days later, on August 15, 1923. From there she continued on by train to Hatfield, Pennsylvania, to the home of her sponsor, Mrs. Carrie Pfaender, Pauline Pfaehler's aunt. For several months, Frieda worked as a nanny in Philadelphia, but then joined her recently arrived younger sister

Frieda as a young girl in Germany

Berta in New York, where the two sisters readily found employment. German maids, as well as German cooks and *Kinderfräulein*, were very much in demand. It was said that they made the best housemaids and were especially valued for their cleanliness, efficiency, and strong work ethic.

Frieda and Berta spent the next several years gainfully employed as live-in nannies in the homes of affluent, upper class New Yorkers.

In 1926, Frieda decided to leave New York at the prompting of her brother, Theo, who, acting as matchmaker, had encouraged her to join him in rural Southwest Nebraska. For a short while she was employed in a Nebraskan household; she

Frieda and Berta as Kinderfräulein in New York (1925)

was an excellent cook and seamstress. Theo introduced her to an acquaintance, a young bachelor who farmed in the hills north of Cozad. Paul Kleinknecht, a fellow-countryman (from Necklinsberg), was looking for a wife. Frieda had just turned thirty when she and Paul were married.

Berta soon followed suit. The very next summer she married Emil Heller, also a bachelor and fellow-countryman (Emil hailed from Mittelbrüden). Thus the two sisters settled into married life, but on isolated farms quite some distance apart – Frieda in the hill country fifteen miles north of Cozad, Berta on the Platte River Valley, nine miles south of town.

*Frieda and Paul
Kleinknecht
(March 1927)*

Theo soon came to regret his decision, admitting that recommending his sister to Paul Kleinknecht was a mistake he would later regret many times over. Paul was a blustering fellow, loud-mouthed and coarse, and although Frieda was a small, exquisite person, Theo had the distinct impression that her husband made her work like a man, and that it was Frieda who did most of the work around the farm, the chores – he once even caught her digging holes for fence posts! – while her husband spent a great deal of time in town. According to Theo, it was because of all the hard work that Frieda suffered so many miscarriages.

The first baby she brought to full-term was a little girl, Ruth Martha, born in August 1931. Frieda's joy was boundless, and little Ruthie was a happy and perfect child.

In those days, farm families did their own butchering. As rural farms were not yet connected to the electricity grid, there was no refrigeration, and for this reason butchering usually took place in the late fall or early spring. With temperatures in mid-March still wintry, Paul Kleinknecht decided to butcher a pig. Butchering was a lot of work, and, as was customary, a neighbor had been invited to assist.

Frieda shows off her baby in the spring of 1932. In front: Emil & <u>Berta</u> Heller, Dora & <u>Theo</u> Fritz, Agnes and <u>Alfred</u> Fritz. In back: Bachelors Ernst Heller (with niece Dorothy Heller) and <u>Karl</u> Fritz

It was a full day's job plus, working together to scald and clean the animal, to remove its head and hooves, to hoist it up off the ground, to cut it open and remove the innards, to saw it apart, to

Ruth was a happy child.
Here with the family dog…

cut up the meat into the appropriate pieces, to preserve the meat, to clean and prepare the intestines for use as casings for the sausage, and finally to prepare and season the sausage meat.

The carcass would be hung outside, hoisted up off the ground, cut open lengthwise from top to bottom, and then the actual butchering process would begin – slicing the pig up into various cuts of pork, with some cuts reserved for the smokehouse to be salted down and cured into bacon or ham. The liver and heart would be set aside for making sausage, and the abundant fat, trimmed from various parts of the pig, would be placed in a large kettle and 'rendered down' into lard.

To preserve the meat that would not be cured, Frieda would be busy all day keeping the wood stove in the kitchen hot, removing the bone from the cuts of pork the men handed to her, frying down the pork in a large skillet and then preserving the meat in its own grease (the rendered lard) in a large ten-gallon crock.

Some of the fresh trimmed meat would later be put through the meat grinder. Once ground, it would be seasoned with various spices and then used to stuff the casings, the prepared intestines, which had been flushed, turned inside out, scraped and washed with salt and hot water.

In short, they had a full day's work ahead of them. The animal would first be killed (shot in the head with a 22 rifle), and then bled (its throat slit, catching the blood in a small crock and stirring it until it cooled so it would not clot.) The blood would later be used to make *Blutwurst*. Then the pig had to be scalded by means of lifting it into a shallow trough, pouring boiling water over it, and then rotating it in the trough of hot water until all sides had been scalded. Scalding was necessary so that the pig's coarse hair and bristles could more easily be scraped from the hide, thus avoiding bristles on your morning bacon!

While her husband went to fetch the pig, Frieda was busy in the kitchen gathering together all the knives, scrapers, and various other butchering utensils and containers they would need, all the while stoking the fire, getting the water in the large boiler atop the cookstove to boil. Soon the pig would be ready to be hoisted into the trough, and she needed to have the boiling hot water ready.

With Frieda thus preoccupied, the little girl, playing alongside her busy mother, was easily neglected for a moment. Frieda failed to keep an eye on the child for just one brief moment…

On butchering day, March 16, 1933, little Ruth, now one-and-a-half years old, was playing alongside her mother in the kitchen. The family dog outside was barking; by now the neighbor had arrived. The pig squealed loudly in protest, followed by a rifle shot, and then Frieda's husband Paul came into the kitchen to help his pregnant wife lift the heavy boiler from the stove onto the floor. The two of them were about to carry it outside to the waiting trough when the dog in its excitement bounded through the open door, bumped against the toddler, knocking her off balance, causing the little girl to stumble and fall headlong into the boiling hot water.

Ruth was fatally scalded…

It was too much for a mother to bear!

Five months later, in August, Frieda gave birth to an infant son who was stillborn.

Frieda's third child, Walter Sam, was born during the hot, drought-stricken August of 1936. Walter, also, was a beautiful, happy baby. The doctor warned the couple, however, against having any more children, as Frieda had nearly died during the delivery.

Frieda's husband took no notice, or perhaps neither one of them paid much attention. When Frieda found herself pregnant again, she had a premonition that she would die. For this reason she made her sister-in-law Dora, Theo's wife, solemnly promise that she would look after the baby should anything happen to her.

Frieda died in childbirth on the morning of April 9, 1938. The delivery itself had gone well, and afterward the family doctor stayed on for breakfast with the father. But when the doctor returned to the bedroom to check on the mother, he found her dead. While the men were in the kitchen having breakfast, Frieda had hemorrhaged to death.

*Berta and Emil Heller with daughter
Dorothy and little Walter*

True to her promise, three days later, at Frieda's funeral, Dora took the boy infant, Fritz, home with her and proceeded to nurture and to raise him as one of her own.

The distraught father entrusted two-year-old Walter to Frieda's sister Berta. Since Berta and Emil Heller had only one child of their own, the little boy was a welcome addition in their home.

Berta and Emil were busy raising the little boy when another tragedy struck. Walter was just a little over three years old at the time. During the evening chores, the inquisitive little fellow had wandered off unnoticed, apparently to inspect some wild ducks that had attracted his attention earlier in the day.

Walter fell into the irrigation "ditch" (Thirty-Mile-Canal) that flowed close by their farm. Its banks were wet and slippery from a recent rain, and the three-year-old would have struggled in vain against the swift-flowing current. Once the icy water had the struggling child in its grip, it swept him along, sucking him into the large cement culvert through which the canal water then flowed underground for some distance and from which there was no escape. His small, lifeless body was later found a mile or so downstream.

Walter's drowning occurred just nineteen months after Frieda's death. To preserve his memory, Berta took a picture of her nephew and sent a print to each of his aunts and uncles. My mother always kept that small, black-and-white photograph of little Walter lying peacefully in his small white casket.

Walter Kleinknecht lying in his casket (November 1939).

In 2009, octogenarian George Johnson shows the spot where Walter Kleinknecht fell into the irrigation canal and drowned.

Thus, Frieda's only surviving child now was her infant son Fritz, to whom she died giving birth.

From the day she first carried the newborn home from her sister-in-law's funeral, Dora had raised little Fritz as one of her own. Both she and Theo grew very fond of him. Then one spring day, when little Fritz had just turned two, Paul Kleinknecht suddenly showed up at their farm, unannounced, to reclaim his son. Two years after burying his wife, and five months after burying Walter, the bereaved father had now come to take his little boy home. It seems Paul Kleinknecht had traveled back to Germany in the meantime and fetched himself a new wife. Fritz was to have a new mother…

Young Fritz, raised and nurtured first by his Aunt Dora, then by his caring stepmother Lina, grew up to be a fine boy, good-natured and even-tempered, always willing to lend a helping hand. Over the years, the aunts and uncles who watched him grow into manhood often remarked how much he resembled his grandfather, Christian Fritz.

Frieda lies buried in a country cemetery one mile east of Cozad.

Her siblings were deeply moved by their sister's untimely death. Frieda was only forty-one years old when she died – the first of the Fritz children to depart this earth.

Her story is surely a tragic one.

Little Fritz Kleinknecht in December 1940 (Age 2 years, 8 months)

CHAPTER 9

"Was lange währt, wird endlich gut."

- German folk saying

THE FARM, eighty-six acres, was located in the northwestern corner of Berks County, in Tulpehocken Township. Situated near the foot of the Blue Mountains, a mile and a half south of the village of Bethel, ours was the first farm on the left after turning south onto Wintersville Road.

Not until decades later would we learn of the farm's historical significance, that it was the homestead of the Christian Frantz family, an immigrant family who arrived at the port of Philadelphia in 1732 seeking refuge from religious intolerance and a chance at prosperity in the woodlands of William Penn. They were among the original German immigrants (the "Pennsylvania Deutsch") to settle in the interior of Pennsylvania. When Christian's son (Christian II) arrived in Tulpehocken Township around 1745 to claim title to his tract of land, the Blue Mountain Ridge was the Indian frontier. Behind those mountains was Indian country.

Remnants of an old "springhouse" were still evident in the meadow below the farmhouse. The roof was gone, but the thick fieldstone walls were still standing, and in one corner of its dirt-packed floor, fresh cold water still flowed from the spring over which it had been erected. The springhouse, which had provided the settlers with a cool, frost-free space in which to store their harvested vegetable and fruits, was all that remained of the Frantz homestead.

The original log/stone dwelling, a rough-hewn, one-room cabin erected quickly for frontier shelter, had long since been dismantled, the stones and lumber used elsewhere. At one end of the structure was a shallow (sleeping) loft, the only access to which was through a trap door, by means of a slender ladder. For safety at night, in the event of an Indian attack, the loft ladder could be drawn up and the trap door securely fastened down.

Indian attacks were a frequent occurrence, particularly at the time of the French and Indian War (1756-1763), and it was the poor, peace-loving German settlers on the frontier who suffered the most, living under constant fear for their lives. Although a line of forts were established along the Blue Mountains where the terrorized settlers might go for refuge (one of which was Fort Henry, located north of Bethel at the foot of Round Top, some five miles distant), Indian raids usually came without warning. They were sudden and swift, and an isolated farmstead was easy prey to Indian attacks.

It was somewhat reassuring to learn that no Indian massacre ever took place on "our" farm. Christian's brother, however, was not so lucky. The John Frantz homestead was located even further away from Fort Henry, closer to Mt. Aetna. On a June morning in 1758, while John was working in a distant field, a band of Indians attacked the family's cabin. John and his neighbors heard shots and came running, but by the time they arrived at the scene, the Indians had tomahawked John's wife and stolen his three young sons, disappearing with them into the forest. Only the two eldest boys were ever returned, many years later, in a prisoner exchange. John Frantz never gave up the search for his youngest son.

Up until the start of the 20th century, when (in 1906) the land passed out of the possession of the Frantz family for good, the property had been the home of succeeding generations of the Christian Frantz family. They had been born there, had died there, and had been carted away for burial at the Frantz family cemetery across the road.

At the time of the closing of the sale (November 9, 1944), both the farmhouse and the barn were well over a hundred years old, their design and construction having been overseen by Matthias Frantz (Christian II's grandson) sometime prior to his death in 1829. By then, the wilderness encountered by the early German settlers had long since been converted into arable fields of grain and hay. In fact, from 1790 to 1840, the state of Pennsylvania was known as the "breadbasket of America"; German farmers in Berks County were getting rich from the sale of wheat. It was during this time of great prosperity that many elegant farmhouses and large, substantial barns were constructed.

Matthias Frantz, a potter by trade and both a potter and farmer by occupation, cleverly sited the farmstead to take advantage of springs (there were at least three) and solar heat. Rather than oriented toward the roadside, the buildings, located at the end of a long lane, all faced south.

The farmhouse, with its fieldstone foundation, was constructed of red brick from Matthias' own pottery works, from clay extracted from the lower back meadow. It had remained largely unaltered for more than a century.

It was still a splendid house, impressive even in its neglected state. Built sometime between 1810 and 1825, its early nineteenth century German builders had copied the then popular Georgian ("English plan") architectural style: two and one-half stories, gable-roofed, with two end chimneys, a perfectly balanced, symmetrical façade (central entrance, with two windows on each side, five above) and a four-room, center-hall floor plan.

A raised wooden porch, high off the ground, ran the full front length of the house, with five wide steps leading up to the center front half-glass entry door. On entering you came into a wide, center hallway that ran the depth of the house, bisecting the main floor into two pairs of rooms. At the far end, an exposed staircase, with a landing mid-way, rose to the bedrooms above, again two large rooms on each side of a similarly wide second-floor hallway. From there, an open stairway with wooden balustrades led to the attic above.

Downstairs, to the left of the staircase, the hallway narrowed into a short corridor with a half-glass door that opened to the back porch, while a small, narrow door to the right of the corridor, underneath the staircase, opened onto steep wooden steps leading down to the cellar.

With its earthen floor, the full-length cellar was always cool and damp. In a closed-off cold room area directly below the kitchen, a spring had been channeled into the dark, dank space (Germans liked to build their houses on top of springs), a handy way to keep milk, butter and other food items cool. It was the closest thing to refrigeration.

The back porch, a half-porch low to the ground, had an attached woodshed where the fuel supply for the kitchen stove was stored. The crumbling woodshed was later torn down, the half-porch enclosed in glass and converted into a light-filled "greenhouse" for Agnes' many houseplants.

There was no fireplace, and growing up, I often wondered why our farmhouse, since it was so old, did not have one. It seems the Germans were not impressed with open fireplaces; they wasted too much heat. Thus, the German builders did not copy all the "English plan" architectural elements. Unlike the interior of an "English plan" house, the Germans preferred their rooms heated by stoves rather than fireplaces. To them, a room without a stove was not a *"Stube"* and a house without a cozy, stove-heated room was unthinkable. ("No stove, no *Stube*, no *Stube*, no home!")

Everything in the farmhouse was "original" – the floors were of wide oak boarding, the kitchen and center hallway were wainscoted, and the slatted wooden shutters could be closed to keep out the winter cold or the summer heat. There were no closets. People hung their few clothes in the open, on pegs, when not folded into chests. A row of wall-mounted coat hooks lined each side of the center hallway.

Like many homes in rural America in the 1940s, the farmhouse had not yet been brought into the modern age; there was no indoor running water, no plumbing, no electricity, and no central heat.

Just beyond the back porch was the well. Covered by wooden planks, on top of which stood an old-fashioned hand pump, the well was the only source of water for the house. The wood-burning Majestic cookstove in the kitchen, its flue pipe connected to the chimney, was the only source of heat, and a smoky kerosene lamp was the only source of light after dark. There was no bathroom; the outhouse, with its ever-present Sears-Roebuck catalog (used as toilet paper) was conveniently located in the backyard, just a few steps away…

The barn was huge – a two-story, rectangular structure several times the size of the farmhouse. The lower story was built of fieldstone, the upper story of wood. My brother Rudy, who once had the job of painting it, can recall the exact dimensions: 85 feet long and 50 feet wide!

The early Pennsylvania Germans combined the type of barn forms that they had known in Germany and Switzerland and adapted them to suit their needs. The resulting design eventually became identified as the Pennsylvania German bank barn, of which "our" barn was a perfect example. Built in the early 19th century, it had two essential features: It was banked, which means that the foundation was built into the sloping bank of a hill, allowing wagons to be driven into the upper floor of the barn; and the front side of the barn had a projecting forebay (8 to 10 feet), a sheltered space beyond the stable doors. Since the barn faced south, taking advantage of solar heat, the forebay provided shade in the summer, when the sun was at a high angle, and heat and sunlight during the winter, when the sun was more slanted.

The upper floor of the barn contained two large haymows for storing hay and straw, two central threshing-floors, and a large granary for storing the threshed wheat and oats. In the winter, the upper barn was a wonderful place to play, either hide-and-seek or crawling up the ladders to the mows, jumping from the high wooden beams into the soft hay or straw below, or simply sliding down

Butchering day (beneath the forebay of a PA Dutch Bank Barn)

the loose piles, being careful not to fall through the hay holes, those perilous openings through which hay or straw was tossed from the upper level to the barn floor below and which sometimes were left uncovered!

On the lower level, the stalls with wood partitions for the cows and horses were organized crosswise and separated by walkways or passages. Doors from the barnyard opened into each stable section and into the feed passages between them. The main floor of "our" barn was large enough to be divided into eight such separate compartments, each with its own access door. Plans would soon be made to convert it into a modern dairy barn.

Alfred was forty; Agnes was thirty-eight – both quite old (for their time) to be starting out all over again...

Without a doubt, the move to the farm was a giant step forward. It had taken all this time – ten years – for them to catch up to where they had left off in Nebraska as a result of Alfred's ill-fated decision to return to Germany. Ten long years of trying to rebuild their lives! But now they had finally "made it"; they were about to realize their dream. It had taken a long time, but *was lange währt, wird endlich gut!*"

"Made it" is somewhat of an overstatement. For, not only were they penniless, but in many ways the move was a step backwards in time, since the farm was without electricity, which meant a return to the farming lifestyle they had known back in Frontier County, Nebraska.

In early November, Alfred began the tedious process of transporting his harvested crops, one load at a time, from one farm to the other. His friend, Karl Jancsics, owned a small farm truck and kindly volunteered his help. But when Jancsics arrived at the farm with the first load of hay, the outgoing tenant, Miles Brown, threatened him and tried to chase him off!

It seems there was a good deal of antagonism on the part of the Browns toward the new owners, the Fritzes. In August, the farm on which the Browns had been tenants for decades had been sold to one Charles Weiser, who turned out to be nothing more than a shrewd land speculator. After bidding up the purchase price to an exorbitant $3,500, Weiser then turned around and (after listing the property in newspapers as far afield as Philadelphia), sold the farm less than three months later for the then unheard of price of $5,500! Quite a profit in only a few months' time! Miles Brown, the farm's hapless tenant who had wanted to purchase the farm for himself, saw himself significantly outbid by a slick opportunist who realized that with the Great Depression over, farm prices would soar. This then would explain Miles Brown's ill-will and attempts at intimidation towards the new owners.

But Brownie ("the Dumbfounded Dutchman") was no match to Jancsics ("the Resolute Romanian"), and the first hay transport was eventually unloaded and safely stored. Ill feelings between the Browns and the Fritzes, however, continued and were never resolved. Miles Brown and his son, Rufus, later farmed the adjoining property to the east, but though neighbors, the two families avoided all contact and never spoke.

Even with the help of Mr. Jancsics' truck, it would take many a long trip back and forth to transport the contents of one farm to another – first the grain, corn and hay, then the farm implements and tools, and lastly the farm animals – five milk cows, a calf, three pigs, and several crates of chickens.

As for household items, other than their two (handed down) beds, their bedding, and a few assorted pieces of kitchen furniture, there was very little in the way of household goods to transport. They were not burdened by much "stuff"; most of the rooms in the farmhouse would remain bare and unfurnished for nearly a decade.

On moving day, the children, Rudy (11), Nancy (9) and Eric (7) were so excited they could barely contain themselves as their father slowly steered the old Desoto down the long, rutted lane and into the farmyard. Jumping from the back seat, they dashed off to explore their new home. Racing up the pathway to the house ahead of their mother, who was carrying baby Frieda, they couldn't bear to wait. Finding the outside cellar door already flung open, they hastily descended the stone steps into the murky darkness. But soon they came running back out of the dark, scary cellar, making a dash for the back porch, following their mother through the back porch door and the rear hallway and then immediately scampering up first one, then the second flight of stairs until they reached the giant attic from where they peered out all the windows and discovered the creek! They had never had a creek before! Down both flights of stairs they raced, out the front door, into the bright sunlight and down across the meadow to explore the shallow winding creek. Then back up again to inspect the barn, the haylofts, the granary, and finally the out-buildings: the chicken-house, the pig pen, the corncrib and the milk house. Wow!

To Agnes' great dismay, instead of finding a nice, clean house, she was "welcomed" with dirt and filth, including one downstairs room filled floor to ceiling with coal dust, wood ash and trash! This she never forgave the former tenants, the Browns.

When the tired children went to bed that first night in their very own home, they methodically recited their prayers:

> Ich bin klein,
> mein Herz mach rein....

And their exhausted mother prayed too. Silently, fervently, Agnes prayed for the strength she would need to transform this filthy, neglected old farmhouse into a clean, comfortable home. But most of all she prayed that the farm might prosper, that she and Alfred would be able to pay off their debt to the Clymers, the $5,000 they had loaned them to buy the farm, and that they would never, ever, have to move again.

CHAPTER 10

"We spend our years as a tale that is told."

Psalms 90: 9

ALTHOUGH PLEASED to be settled in her own home at last, Agnes, still weakened from her recent illness, exhausted from the care of a newborn, plus the move, which had zapped the remainder of her strength, was increasingly lonely. How she missed having someone to talk to! A friend was the only outlet she might have, and such a friend she did not have in her husband.

The original German settlers, the "Pennsylvania Deutsch," had preceded our family by over two hundred years, yet their descendants had managed to hold onto their unique Pennsylvania Deitsch dialect. Living mostly without electricity, on isolated farms far from any large urban center, their exposure to the outside world was minimal, so that as late as the 1940s, they were still clannish and wary of newcomers.

The newly arrived Fritzes were suspect, not only because they were newcomers to the area, but also and especially because they were Germans! In November 1944, with American soldiers dying on the beaches of Normandy and the final outcome of the war still uncertain, there was plenty of anti-German feeling.

Thus their neighbors were not exactly eager to welcome them; it would take a long time before they would be accepted. My mother later told me that during that first year on the farm, nobody spoke to her. She might have made contact sooner had she been able to attend church, a place where she had always found both solace and kinship. But they were so poor in those days, so very poor! Agnes was unable to attend church services since, in her own words, "I didn't have shoes to wear." We are not talking fashion here, but rather the sad fact that my mother's shoes were beyond repair and she could not afford a new pair. In 1944, a pair of leather shoes cost five dollars, but five dollars then were the equivalent of one hundred dollars today. Better to put that money toward paying off their debt to the Clymers...

Envelope of a letter from Tante Emma of Cottenweiler dated November 1946. Since Württemberg was under the control of the American forces, Emma's letter was opened by U.S. military censors.

Thus, Agnes, who thrived on her friendships and had always found it easy to make friends, now endured poverty-induced isolation while simultaneously suffering the humiliation of being ostracized because she was German. Depressed and lonely, she later confided to me how, during that first year on the farm (my first year of life!) she often wanted to die. It must have been us children that kept her going.

Alfred, by necessity, did have outside contact, especially since a lot of farm work in those days was reciprocal, and a farmer could hardly get by without the good-will of his neighbors. There was Dawson Harnish, their neighbor to the south, who had the milk hauling route. Each morning, after the morning milking, he would pick up Alfred's milk cans for delivery to the receiving station. Then there was their neighbor to the west, whose bull Alfred used to service his cows. He and Rudy would walk the cow down Wintersville Road and over to the neighbor's ready bull. And of course, Alfred would interact with other men whenever he drove into town on some necessary errand. But being the tight-lipped, socially inept person that he was, such encounters never lead to anything, much less an invitation to "come and meet the misses."

In May 1945, Germany surrendered and World War II finally came to an end, at least in Europe. It would take another year, however, before civilian foreign mail service to and from Germany was resumed and Agnes was able to re-establish communication with their relatives in Germany, to learn if they had survived the Allied bombings ...

During their first summer on the farm, and with the war finally over, Dawson Harnish saw to it that the Alfred Fritz farm was included in the neighborhood threshing circle. When it came Agnes' turn to cook for the threshing crew, she heeded the advice of the Nebraska farmwomen and put all her skill and energy into serving her delicious fried chicken with all the trimmings. At least the men would go home and tell their wives that they had eaten well at the Fritzes!

As the years went by, and beginning with Dawson and Mary Harnish, folks discovered just how amicable and sociable Mrs. Fritz was, the ice was eventually broken and they became acquainted with their other neighbors on the adjacent farms – the Trautmanns, the Muths, the Katzmanns, and later the Burkholders.

For the first eight or nine years, the kitchen (later also the room adjoining) was the only downstairs room occupied. Daily life was centered around the cookstove in the kitchen. Fueled by corncobs, chopped wood and coal, it was used for cooking and baking and was the sole source of heat. In the hour or so between evening chores and bedtime, family members gathered around the kerosene lamp in the warm kitchen to challenge each other at a game of checkers or *Mühle* (mill), the German board game of which Alfred was particularly fond. Upstairs, the bedrooms were unheated and in winter freezing cold. Before the children got undressed and into bed, Agnes would heat heavy flatirons, wrap them in old sheeting (rags), and then slip them underneath the feather comforters to use as a buffer between their feet and the icy sheets.

Although "empty," the two downstairs rooms on the opposite side of the center hallway were put to good use. During the winter, the north-facing room was where the home-made sausages from butchering were kept: links of *Blutwurst* and *Leberwurst* hung on suspended poles, along with stored *Schinken* (salt-cured ham), *Speck* (bacon), and *Schmalz* (lard). In the springtime, I recall coming home from school thrilled to find the sunny, south-facing room filled with dozens of golden, freshly-hatched chicks, delivered that same day from the hatchery. Inside their sawdust-filled enclosure, the downy, softly peeping chicks would be kept warm inside for several weeks until they were old enough to be transferred to the henhouse.

My mother always liked Pennsylvania – she especially loved the view of the mountains. And I can imagine my father feeling very much at home in a landscape not unlike that of his *"Heimat,"* the rolling countryside still rural and unspoiled – what we would now call 'charmingly bucolic.' Wintersville Road was still a dirt road. In fact, all rural roads back then were more like tree-shaded country lanes, and the fencerows, the boundaries between adjoining fields, were lined with trees and overgrown with bushes and undergrowth, which sheltered wild game (pheasants, rabbits and squirrels) in abundance. With a shotgun and a steady hand, one need never go hungry for lack of meat. My brother Rudy recalls shooting and eating lots of squirrel and rabbit.

In the 1940s, farming was still a way of life, not an industry. Farms were run by hard working families engaged in agriculture, not corporations engaged in agribusiness. The simple agricultural life still prevailed. Farms were not yet specialized, and on their clayey soil, farmers in Tulpehocken Township grew wheat, rye, oats, corn and hay to feed their livestock – eight or ten milk cows, plus several pigs and a flock of chickens. The farmer's wife planted a garden full of vegetables to feed her family – potatoes, cabbage, beets, peas, green beans, lettuce, cucumbers, onions, carrots, sweet corn and tomatoes – and also grew fruit trees (cherries and plums). Plus, there were all kinds of berry bushes and wild berries used for preserves: strawberries, raspberries, blackberries, currants, gooseberries and elderberries. Almost every farm had a few apple and pear trees. All this provided a steady supply of chicken, pork, eggs, milk, butter and surplus vegetables and fruits for canning.

So many people lived on farms! The 1927 farm census of Tulpehocken Township counted 169 farms! Since we know that not much changed 'down on the farm' in the 1930s (due to the Great Depression), the farm census of 1927 could just as well be considered representative of the early 1940s. It showed that the average-size farm was 83 acres, that most farmers owned a small tractor and an automobile or other vehicle of some sort in which they transported their milk cans to the local creamery. Many still owned horses. (We know that Dawson Harnish still kept horses, as my brother Rudy recalls how in winter, Mr. Harnish avoided the snowdrifts on his milk route by cutting across the fields in a horse-drawn sled.)

The area remained predominately rural, and farming was still THE occupation, until the 1950s, when everything began to change. The 1950s brought prosperity and "progress" – rural electrification, telephone, indoor plumbing, and modern appliances such as refrigerators, electric ranges, hot water heaters, washing machines, central heating, etc. Under President Eisenhower, Interstate 78 was built, bringing with it new industries, commercial development (especially along the Interstate and along Old Route 22) and the seemingly unstoppable encroachment of the outside world. Then, during the 1960s, single family prefabricated ranch style houses began lining the roadways, trailer parks popped up, and, starting in the 70s and 80s, housing developments appeared, gobbling up the pristine farmland, so that by the end of the 20th century, the quiet rural roads of the 1940s had been replaced by highways, the once bucolic landscape disfigured not only by suburban sprawl, but also by unsightly and seemingly haphazard industrial and commercial development, including the latest 21st century eyesore and blot on the landscape: warehouse distribution centers. (Even worse, there is seemingly still nothing being done to counteract this loss of prime farmland to unsightly suburban sprawl.)

Distances seemed greater in those days; you didn't just hop in the car and go somewhere. Trips to town were made infrequently, perhaps to pick up or have mended some tool or hardware item, or to purchase a few grocery staples, on the way home stopping by Mt. Aetna to pick up some cuts of butchered meat from our rented frozen meat locker. The only other place our family drove was to church on Sunday, and occasionally, a Sunday afternoon drive which would often end with a spontaneous visit.

Alfred loved to drive through the countryside to look at the crops, especially the corn. Agnes never learned to drive herself; women of her generation often did not. But she enjoyed the Sunday afternoon drives when she and Alfred went to see how everyone else's crops were growing.

Prior to the Interstate, the trip to New York City took four to five hours! Relatives who lived at some distance wouldn't see each other sometimes for years, especially not if you were a farmer, because cows had to be milked twice a day, in the morning and in the evening. For this reason, it was easier for friends and relatives from New York and Philadelphia to drive out to the farm to visit.

In August 1945, Alfred's younger brother Karl, fresh out of the army, drove out from New York to introduce his lovely young bride, Helene. Although Onkel Karl had been stationed in New Guinea during most of World War II, our relatives in southern Germany, knowing that Karl was with the U.S. Army, had searched for him in the faces of the conquering American soldiers as they came marching through their defeated German villages, hoping that they might find Karl among them!

We have Karl's wife, Helene, an amateur photographer, to thank for these photographs from August 1945:

The Bank Barn Alfred and Agnes (at right) with Eric, Nancy, Onkel Karl and Rudy

The Farmhouse Alfred and Agnes with Nancy, Eric, Rudy and Onkel Karl

Onkel Karl performing his morning toilet at the outside pump

Agnes with one-year-old Frieda

234

Sunday afternoon at the Esenweins From left: Otto Jr., Onkel Otto Esenwein, Onkel Karl and wife Helene, Alfred, Rudy, Nancy, Eric and Agnes Fritz (with baby Frieda) and Päule Esenwein

Karl and Alfred Fritz with Eric and Rudy

On November 8, 1945 Alfred became a naturalized citizen, and on April 2, 1946 Howard and Emily Clymer transferred the farm's deed of title over to Alfred and Agnes Fritz.

Encouraged by his visit, Karl decided to try his luck at farming also. By year's end (1945), he had purchased a dairy farm in nearby Bethel Township, along Old Route 22, the two-lane highway that was then the main thoroughfare from New York to Ohio.

Tante Helene was a career secretary. Having lived in New York ever since coming to America with her parents at the age of twelve, she knew nothing about farming, about milking cows or tending chickens. But Agnes was glad to give advice and to help when help was needed. Tante Helene recalled the first time that she had to cook for a crew of ten threshers and Agnes came to assist. Fried chicken was for dinner, and Helene watched in awe and amazement as Agnes smoothly dispatched several unlucky hens – stepping on their necks, pulling on their legs, and then letting them run!

Young Nancy was charged with looking after baby Frieda, which allowed Agnes to get on with her work. But sometimes, when Agnes could spare her, she would send Nancy over to help her sister-in-law. Rudy, too, would occasionally disappear on the pretext of having to "help" his uncle. Onkel Karl was good-natured and likable; Rudy and Eric enjoyed his company.

Alfred's Certificate of Naturalization

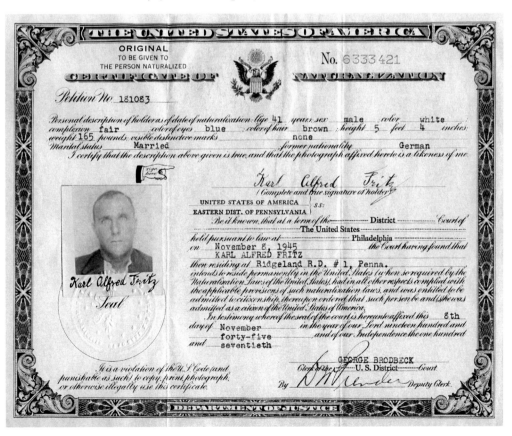

Onkel Karl, Rudy and Eric out mowing hay with the Farmall B

It took two years for rural electrification to reach our farm, during which time kerosene lamps provided the lighting, and all the water for cooking and washing had to be pumped at the outside well, then carried into the kitchen and heated on the stove. Agnes had to run her household without any of the modern conveniences we now take for granted, doing everything laboriously by hand. She cooked over a hot stove, scrubbed the dirty sheets and clothes by hand on a washboard, hung them to dry, and ironed using heavy flatirons heated on the stove.

Like most women of her day, she tried to follow a weekly schedule. Monday and Tuesday were for washing and ironing, while Wednesday was for patching and mending. There were always work pants to patch and clothes to mend or alter. Thursday was sort of an open day. Perhaps she and Alfred needed to drive to town to take care of some business or run some errands. Since most of their food was home-grown, they did not need to buy many groceries. Nor did Alfred and Agnes go "shopping." Our clothes were hand-me-downs from relatives and friends. In the fall, we drove to Swope's General Merchandise Store in Frystown where we were fitted for new shoes for school after a summer of going barefoot.

Agnes looked forward to the twice-weekly visit of Albert's bakery truck and the affable, chatty driver who was always a discreet source of neighborhood news. Although she usually stuck to the purchase of a set number of loaves of bread, if we (children) were around, we would inch up behind her skirt, and, standing on the bottom steps of the open truck, from where we could eye the shelves filled with cakes and pastries, we would then pester her until she bought us each a 5¢ Hershey bar from the candy display.

Friday was for cleaning house, and Saturday was baking day. Saturday morning, Agnes kept strictly to her kitchen, filling the house with the fragrant, yeasty smell of homemade dough – big batches of it – from which would then emerge a *Hefekranz,* a sweet yeast braided bread, along with several sheets of *Butterkuchen* sprinkled with cinnamon and sugar. On Saturday she always served pancakes for noon dinner, as there was no time to prepare a regular meal. On Sunday morning, instead of the usual eggs, bacon and toast for breakfast we were treated with slices of braided sweet yeast bread with butter and jam.

Saturday night was bath night. Family members took their weekly bath in a washtub placed in front of the kitchen stove, one after another, in the same bathwater, Agnes being the last person to bathe, after which she used the dirty bathwater to scrub the kitchen floor.

Except for preparing Sunday dinner after church, Sunday was Agnes' day of "rest." Nor would she allow her husband to do any work on that day, other than the daily milking – not even during the busiest months of the summer – convinced that if a farmer worked on the Lord's Day, surely no good would come of it.

Sometimes on a Sunday we would have company, but company or not, on that special day of the week, at four o'clock in the afternoon, Agnes would take out a clean, ironed tablecloth, set the kitchen table with cake plates, cups and saucers, and then, as a special Sunday treat, whip up the cream she had earlier skimmed off the top of a milk can (we children taking turns with the manual beater until the cream stiffened) and serve it atop the fresh cake she had baked the day before. Sunday afternoon *Kaffee und Kuchen* was a German tradition that my mother made sure to keep.

Of course, the above weekly schedule was in addition to all her day-in, day-out duties of meal preparation (breakfast, dinner and supper, cooked from scratch), gardening, canning food for the winter, plus tending her growing flock of chickens, grading eggs, plus sharing in the farm work when necessary. Thank goodness she had young Nancy to help, although Nancy disliked housework, especially ironing! Nancy preferred being outdoors: gardening, fieldwork, milking cows, and caring for the livestock.

Alfred constantly fretted over the lack of electricity; he wanted to modernize so that he could step up milk production and "get ahead." In New Jersey and in Bucks County, where they had lived before, close to the major urban areas of Philadelphia and Trenton, access to electricity had not been a problem. During the Great Depression, President Roosevelt had addressed the issue of lack of electricity in rural areas. Hoping to help boost agricultural production by modernizing farming, Roosevelt had created the Rural Electrification Administration to bring electricity to rural areas. That was back in 1936. However, government crews were slow to string electric lines to isolated rural areas. Onkel Karl's farm, along Route 22, was wired for electricity long before Alfred could (finally!) persuade his neighbors to join him in connecting to the grid. It would take two full years before electrical lines were finally strung to our farm and an electrician added wiring to the house and barn. (It would take another several years for telephone lines to follow, so even though Agnes and her sister-in-law lived only a few miles apart, they communicated by letter.)

Once the farm had been wired for electricity, a plumber came to install water lines and an electric pump to serve both the house and barn. Although it would take several more years before they could afford to modernize the kitchen, Agnes now had the luxury of running water! No more backbreaking hauling! Her first major electric appliance was a refrigerator, which she called an icebox. The icebox proudly stood in the corner of the kitchen, opposite the cookstove. This major purchase was then followed by a wringer-style washing machine (no more laboring over a washboard!) and an electric water heater, both located in the cellar.

In September 1946 Agnes invited the pastor of Salem Reformed Church, Reverend Charles Rissinger, to Sunday dinner to baptize their now two-year-old daughter, Frieda. It was customary to be baptized as an infant, and they had never waited this long to have a child baptized – proof that until then, poverty had kept them from attending church. Two years after moving to the farm, they chose to become members of the Reformed Church in Bethel because, in Agnes' words, "it was the closest."

That Christmas, Agnes invited Karl and Helene for Christmas dinner, thereby establishing a tradition that would continue throughout the years – alternating Christmas dinner between our house and theirs.

With milk prices steadily rising, Alfred saw his future in dairy farming. Alfred milked his handful of cows by hand. He then carried the milk in buckets to the milk house where the milk was kept chilled in 100-pound milk cans lowered into a cement trough filled with cold running water, fed by a spring. After the morning milking, Dawson Harnish came by with his truck (in snowy winters, with horses hitched to a sled), loaded up the milk cans from the morning and from the previous evening's milking and transported them to the Hershey receiving station outside of Mt. Aetna.

Christmas Day, 1946. Alfred and Agnes with Nancy (11), Frieda (2), Eric (9) and Rudy (13)

Christmas, 1946 with Onkel Karl and Tante Helene

But the dairy industry was rapidly modernizing; bulk milk tanks and insulated bulk tanker trucks would soon make the old-fashioned milk cans a thing of the past. Alfred wanted to sell his milk in bulk also, but to do so, he would first have to increase his milk volume, i.e. the number of milking cows, and he would have to modernize the lower level of the barn, converting it for dairy purposes.

Thus, in the winter of 1947, Alfred began the massive project of converting the old-fashioned bank barn into a modern dairy barn. The entire inside of the lower level – all the crosswise dividing walls – would have to be torn out, and everything reoriented lengthwise rather than crosswise. The dirt floors would have to be cemented, with indentations for manure gutters and feed troughs. Metal stanchions would replace the stalls – two rows on either side of a central isle, which would extend the length of the barn, with large sliding doors cut into each end, wide enough for a tractor and wagon to pass through.

In order to achieve the proper depth needed in order to stanchion two rows of cows, Alfred would have to extend the front barn wall outward to enclose the forebay. In order to achieve this, he had to first dismantle the stone wall and then reconstruct the stones flush with the upper barn.

In reconstructing the front barn wall, he ran out of stones, so he used the fieldstones from the old springhouse, which matched the barn's own fieldstone foundation. Expertly he lined up the stones, so that when the remodeling was complete, you could hardly even tell that the barn had been altered.

The Dutch doors in the front were replaced with a row of windows that provided light and ventilation and

Dairy Barn Interior

also allowed the barn swallows access. (My father was fond of these birds that returned every spring to their nests on the sides of the wooden beams overhead.)

The entire project was completed in less than a year. Alfred had not only worked out all the design and remodeling calculations on his own, but he had also completed the work by himself, with the help of his two capable young sons. No small feat, but rather a testament to his intelligence, skill and ingenuity.

Once completed, the interior of the barn was whitewashed; electrical wiring was installed, and the stanchions were fitted with a pipeline connected to automatic drinking cups between the stanchions to assure that each cow could drink her fill whenever she was thirsty. The daily chore of watering the cows by bucket or leading them outside to drink at the water trough was thus eliminated.

Alfred later had a vertical silo of wood and concrete erected, with access through the barn's "cellar," underneath the banked driveway. The silo was for putting up corn silage, which made good winter feed for the cows.

During the winter, Alfred kept his cows inside, warm and free from drafts, until the coming of spring and when the grass had grown tall enough for grazing. The annual spring event of letting the cows out to grass for the first time was an exciting occasion not to be missed. Turning them loose from their stanchions, releasing them to the outdoors, and watching even the most sedate milk cows prancing about and acting like young heifers again was such fun! Even the older cows would act "half crazy" before eventually settling down and becoming their usual placid selves.

Alfred put all his farming know-how to work to make his farm one of the best. He was a careful, conservative farmer who farmed the old-fashioned way, using time-honored traditions – spreading lime and manure and practicing crop rotation. And although he later farmed with large, modern farm machinery, he still insisted on employing old practices of thrift. My brothers, often exasperated by his seemingly excessive frugality, would scoff and call it a "waste of time" when he went around raking up hay by hand, clumps of hay the baler had missed, or when he would use his scythe to neatly trim around the buildings and the edges of the fields. They were not able to appreciate his Swabian ethos of tidy frugality, nor did they realize that he was simply following the ingrained behavior patterns that had been passed down from father to son over generations. It was the frugal and industrious way his Swabian forefathers had farmed for centuries, where each plot of earth was precious, where nothing was ever wasted, and every little nook where grass grew was carefully cut with a sickle and then carted home.

Alfred might have thought on a grand scale, but his methods were often the old-fashioned ones ingrained in him as a boy by his father, and his father's father – the methods of the *Schwäbishe Bauer* who could not bear to waste anything.

My father was a man of few words. He seldom spoke, not when you were helping with some task or other – his instructions were minimal; you were supposed to anticipate what was required – and not if you were alone together, in the car for example. He never told you what he was thinking. You hardly dared ask him a question, and even then you could not be certain that he would answer.

And yet, he must have communicated something to us. My brother Rudy, in later years, readily admitted his admiration for his father: "He taught me the difference between right and wrong, the value of hard work, and the satisfaction derived from it."

On May 28, 1947, a few days short of her 41st birthday, Agnes gave birth to a baby girl. She was given the name Ruth Elise – Ruth after Agnes' dear friend, Ruth Leatherman, and Elise after Alfred's younger sister, to whom they owed so much. This, her last child, Agnes half-jokingly implied, would one day look after her in her old age…

Alfred was in the midst of his barn modernizing project at the time. One evening after milking, Onkel Karl stopped by to check out the work in progress. Tante Helene, who had come along, remarked that she was going into the house to visit with Agnes. Alfred, characteristically, did not bother to mention that Agnes was not at home, that she had just given birth to a baby girl and was in the hospital in Lebanon. Only after Tante Helene stepped inside the house did the children greet her with the news.

This is just one more typical example of my father's reticence, his inability or failure to communicate. Of course, it might have been taken as a practical joke. Perhaps he simply wanted his sister-in-law to be surprised once she entered the house? But that, unfortunately, would be reading too much into his disjointed thought process. Alfred was not a joker! In short, you had to READ HIS MIND; he didn't deem it necessary to open his mouth and inform his brother and sister-in-law that Agnes had given birth. After all, years earlier, in Nebraska, he had not bothered to tell his brother that he was getting married either! Perhaps it never even dawned on him that his failure to communicate might be taken as a slight, might really hurt someone's feelings.

In the end, Alfred was best left alone and told only what was necessary so as not to upset him. He was most content when he was silently going about his work, and when everyone else around him was busy and hard at work also.

With the barn modernized, Alfred next turned his attention to building an addition to the old milk house, making it large enough to house a bulk milk tank. He had barely finished, however, when disaster struck the farm!

Bang's disease can enter a herd of cows when a farmer purchases an infected cow at a sale, which is what happened in Alfred's case. *Brucellosis Abortis* is highly contagious and can also be transmitted to people if the milk is not boiled. The disease affects the uterus of the cow; infected cows abort their calves prematurely, around seven months, and the calves are born dead. This in turn upsets the natural cycle of the cows, and they don't produce any milk for awhile. The farmer has to sell the infected cow, but since the cow is diseased, it must be destroyed and can only be sold as slaughter meat for dog food. The only way to try to prevent the disease is to vaccinate the healthy calves against it and to only buy cows that have been blood tested and have a clean bill of health. According to Dr. Haverstick, our veterinarian, "test and slaughter" was the motto of the day. Alfred would lose many of his best milk cows before he could finally rid his herd of the disease.

The situation was dire. Once again, Alfred found himself confronted with a major set-back just as he could see a light at the end of the tunnel, an end to their wretched poverty. Why? What did life have against him? No matter how hard he tried, everything always seemed to go against him!

The consequences of Alfred having to sell his valuable milk cows for grade "0" butcher meat were catastrophic, and my earliest childhood memories are somehow associated with Bang's disease – the frequent mention of the disease. I was too young to grasp its damaging financial impact, or its devastating affect on my father's fragile mental state.

My sister Nancy recalls the day when our anguished mother, not knowing what to expect next and losing heart, at last got up the courage and made up her mind to leave. Gathering the children around her, Agnes resolutely began to walk out the lane, only to hesitate once they had reached the road. There she stood, looking down at them, her resolve unbearably dissolving in the realization that her attempt to get away was hopeless.

"It's no use," she sighed, with such an utter and complete resignation even the children could grasp. "There's no place we can go!"

And with that, Agnes reluctantly turned and retraced her steps back towards the house, for there was nowhere for her and the children to go, and no one to whom she could turn. Even now, I am moved to tears at my sister's story.

But Agnes was quick to put the past behind her, conveniently forgetting or not wanting to recall.

"*Vergiss es!*" she would usually answer back, whenever we prodded her to tell us something of her past. "Forget it!" It was as if the past had been so bad it was better not to speak about it.

Alfred had a bad and unpredictable temper, it was true, but as a wife, Agnes felt it was her duty to stick it out because she had made those vows. You didn't just throw marriage away. Not only did you try harder, but it was the wife who made a marriage work. In fact, Agnes would have been deeply ashamed to tell anyone about her situation. And besides, in those days, even if she had dared to approach a pastor, in all likelihood he would have reminded her of her vows and instructed her to go back to her husband and to make the best of it.

She was, of course, not alone. For centuries, wives had always been ashamed and remained silent, their secrets well guarded. And as children, we too learned to keep quiet about our father's occasional violent outbursts. We also learned instinctively not to upset him if we could help it, and we disciplined ourselves, since we knew if we upset him, not only we, but also our mother, would have to suffer the consequences.

A decade and a half later, Agnes' sister, visiting from Germany, would comment on how 'tough,' how unsentimental Agnes had become.

"Was ist Eure Mutter aber hart geworden!"

Yes, Agnes had become hardened. Life had made her that way. I recall an event from my childhood when my little sister, Ruthie became hysterical after her kitten was run over by a tractor and Mama, exasperated that Ruthie would not stop screaming, dismissingly remarked: "I hope you make such a fuss over me someday when I am dead!"

Agnes made certain that we children were baptized and confirmed, attended Sunday school and church, were taught the Golden Rule, and knew the difference between right and wrong. As a mother, she looked after and cared for us, braided our hair, made certain that we were neat and clean for school, and nursed us through chicken pox and the measles. When we were ill, she read aloud to us and rubbed our backs until we fell asleep. She made certain we knew our lessons, and she herself earned to spell by listening to us spell the words on our vocabulary list. But she was not demonstrably warm and tender as once she had been as a girl and later as a nanny. Her "Germanness" came through. She never hugged or kissed us; nor did she ever express her love for us in words.

But most certainly, she was not a cold or distant person either. She was sort of … she was there. In our minds, we always knew that we were loved; of that there was never a doubt! But always busy with one task or another, she had no time for us. If we tested her patience, she would tell us to go outside and play, or (once we were older), to go help in the barn. She was our ever present, no-nonsense, forever busy, hard-working mother. We took her for granted and loved her without even knowing it, and she loved us without ever demonstrably expressing her love.

School Pictures – Academic year 1946/47
Rudolf (13), Nancy (11) and Eric (9)

In time, the decimated dairy herd was replenished, and life on the farm returned to "normal." But every so often, Alfred would snap; his brain would "burst" it seemed, whenever the perceived pressure was too much for him to deal with.

Such might be the case, for example, during the summer if there was insufficient rain. Farming is always a gamble, a risky business. No matter how carefully he plans, a farmer is constantly at the mercy of the weather for the success or failure of his crops. Often during a hot, dry Pennsylvania summer, the leaves of the corn would shrivel up for lack of moisture. At such times, Papa would grow increasingly frantic. The hot, dry, westerly winds would bring back all the painful memories of the 1930s. My father could never eradicate the memory of the anguish he had endured during those desperate years of drought in Nebraska.

Eric once found him in the haymow with a knotted rope tied around his neck, sobbing. At other times, Papa would get out his double-barrel 12 gauge shotgun and threaten to put an end to himself. His threats to end his life, however, were just that; his attempts at suicide feeble; they were more a call for help. I don't believe my father ever had the courage or intent to actually "do it," although as children, ignorant and spiteful and fed up with his violent temper and erratic moods, we often wished he would hurry up and get it over with. During such flare-ups, Mama would be beside herself with concern, and we children would wonder why. Wouldn't she be better off without him?

But Agnes never said an unkind word about her husband; she never disparaged him in any way. On the contrary, she forever defended him, constantly tried to make us see the good in him. She insisted that we respect him, and she never ceased pointing out how hard he worked to provide for us. Whatever we had in life, we had our hard-working father to thank for it.

Agnes was the great peacemaker, always trying to appease her husband and to restore harmony in our home. It was she who held the family together and kept the peace. After her death, I received a condolence card from Päule Haegele. "Your mother was a saint." she wrote.

Eventually, Papa would calm down and things would again return to "normal." Thus, there are lots of nice memories of him also. Seeing him descend the stairs on a Sunday morning, dressed in his Sunday suit, even we children couldn't fail to notice what a handsome man our father was. Sometimes he would take the older kids to see a movie – "Roy Rogers" or "The Lone Ranger." My brother still recalls the day Papa treated him to an ice cream cone as a reward for memorizing the words to *Backe, backe Kuchen,"* an old children's rhyme.

Given the differences in our ages, we siblings all have divergent childhood memories of him. Mine are mostly pleasant. In particular, memories of watching over the cows with him behind the barn on a lazy Sunday afternoon, sitting beside him on the grass while he played a tune by placing a flat blade of grass between his tongue and his teeth. Or observing how he wove the pliable stems of a certain weed together to form a miniature 'chair' – skills he had undoubtedly learned while a shepherd in Germany. When he was in a pensive, contented mood, he would sing or whistle the tune of a *Heimatlied,* one of the beautiful German folksongs from his youth. Often, he would sit and listen appreciatively, nostalgic tears welling up in his eyes, while I played these same melodies for him on the piano.

Alfred's mood swings became less frequent as the farm prospered. Was it because there was less frustration in his life, less feelings of helplessness, less insecurity, less fear? Considering the type of childhood he had endured, the privations of his youth, the hard life he had been dealt, and with not the slightest understanding of the mental disorder with which he was seemingly plagued, it is not at all difficult, in retrospect, to understand "where he was coming from" and to appreciate, finally, the man who worked so hard for us and who taught us the qualities that would serve us so well in life: respect, self-discipline and hard work.

Summer thunderstorms were usually a blessing, as they would bring with them the needed rain. But they could be scary as well. If a storm occurred at night, Mama would awaken us and make us go downstairs until the thunder would abate. Her fear of lightning stemmed from her youth; her childhood home had been a thatched roof cottage, and you can bet they all got out of bed during a thunderstorm in case lightning should strike!

We sat in silence in the living room (away from the metal kitchen pipes; away from the windows!) and Papa would eventually venture outdoors to make certain that the barn had not caught fire and that the cows were unharmed. The cows would always huddle together underneath a tree for shelter from the rain, which was, of course, the most dangerous place for them to be.

One time, our farmhouse almost did catch fire, but it was many years later, and in winter – on a cold, blustery night as Ruthie and I sat with our parents, watching the Lawrence Welk Show on television. (We only got TV in 1956, when I was twelve.) During the program, Papa kept getting up at frequent intervals and stepping out into the backyard. True to form, however, he did not say why. Curious as to why he kept going outside, I decided to tail him. Once outside, I followed his gaze upwards towards the roof, where, to my horror, a bright shower of orange sparks was shooting from the chimney. How long had this been going on already – for hours? Why had Papa not said anything? Back inside, a large, vertical crack opened in the kitchen chimney. Fearing the worst, I ran to the phone, dialed "0" and, shaking so violently that I was barely able to speak, stammered into the receiver that our farmhouse was on fire! Thankfully, the Bethel All-Volunteer Fire Company, siren blasting, soon arrived, despite the blowing snow, and smothered the fire.

The next morning at breakfast, Agnes could be heard chiding her uncommunicative husband: "Be sure you give those men at the firehouse some money!"

In the winter of 1948, Alfred would test his skills and ingenuity with another major project – constructing an indoor garage. Our old car, a 1931 four-door Desoto acquired second-hand from Otto Esenwein and used for everything from hauling calves to market to driving the family to church, was giving out. Alfred had been saving up in order to buy a new one. (He always paid in cash!) It occurred to him that it would be convenient to have an indoor garage for his new car. Agnes was more than a little bit nervous about digging out the cellar, afraid the foundation might collapse. But Alfred set to work, first removing half of the porch that ran the full length of the front of the house, and then digging out a driveway that would lead to an opening in the cellar's stone foundation. He then cemented the cellar floor, installed a sliding garage door and, using the fieldstones removed from the foundation, lined both sides of the driveway leading to the garage with a fortifying stone wall. Another major construction achievement!

How proud Alfred was when he drove home from the dealer in a brand new 1949 Ford Mercury (his first new car ever!) and parked it in the indoor garage that he had designed and built himself!

Lots of people admired his work and envied the fact that we now had an indoor garage. That year, in a Christmas letter to her sister-in-law, Berta Heller, in Nebraska, Agnes enclosed a photo, on the back of which she proudly wrote: "Alfred with his new car in front of our new garage."

Nowadays, it would be nice to own a 1931 Desoto, but in 1949 it was a boost to the ego and definitely a sign that you were coming up in the world if you owned a new Ford!

Rudy and Eric help to build the driveway to the garage (Spring 1948)

Berta and Emil Heller stop to visit on their way back from Germany.. (From left: Tante Helene with Margaret, Tante Berta, Onkel Karl, Tante Elise with baby Linda, Onkel Henry and cousin Joanie Wagner, then Rudy, Eric, Agnes with baby Ruth, Nancy (hidden), Alfred and Frieda (Spring 1948)

Karl, Berta, Elise and Alfred Fritz (Spring 1948)

Time passed. Alfred put all his farming know-how to work and the farm prospered. A strong German work ethic prevailed, and the older children, like farm children everywhere, were viewed as productive members of the household and were kept busy helping in the barn, in the field and about the house. In the summer of 1949, Rudy (15 1/2) and Nancy (14) were teenagers; Eric was 11 1/2. Ruthie (2) and Frieda (5) were still little.

Alfred with his new 1949 Ford Mercury

Making fence

Out making hay

Nancy, Frieda and Ruthie and Rudy and Eric (Summer 1949)

Alfred and Agnes with Ruthie and Frieda (1950)

By 1950, there were fifteen cows to be milked. Nancy was responsible for milking certain cows that would allow only her to come near them! Rudy milked five or six cows, and Papa the remainder. (Eric would later replace Nancy with the milking.) In the evening, they would hurry to finish with the milking chores in time to gather in the kitchen to listen to their favorite radio programs: *The Shadow* and *The Lone Ranger*. By nine o'clock, the house was dark and everyone was fast asleep.

Cows must be milked twice a day. After helping with the milking in the morning, and before boarding the school bus, the children would quickly change from their "barn clothes" into their school clothes. But if they still smelled of barn, of manure and hay and cows, nobody much noticed, since most of their classmates were farm kids as well.

When the family now gathered at mealtimes, all the places at the table were filled: Rudy, Nancy and Eric on one side, then Mama, Ruthie and I opposite. Papa, at the head of the table, would recite the centuries-old German table prayer:

"Komm Herr Jesu, sei du unser Gast
und segne, was du uns bescheret hast."

Then each child, in turn, beginning with the oldest, would respond with *"Abba, lieber Vater! Amen."* Hurriedly and mechanically we children mumbled this response, never even curious to know its meaning. ["Abba" is the Aramaic word for 'father.' Biblical references show that "Abba" is the way Jesus affectionately addressed his heavenly Father.]

Agnes, seated next to the stove, then passed the dishes of food, beginning with her husband, followed by Rudy, the oldest, and on down the line. There was little or no conversation at the table. Papa liked to eat in quiet, and we children knew to respect that!

There was always plenty of food: meat and potatoes, Spätzle or noodles, a cooked vegetable dish, and in summer a fresh green salad and tomatoes as well. What was brought to the table was eaten, and since we were hungry, we cleaned our plates. Besides, everything always tasted delicious. The idea of requesting something other than what Mama had prepared, or complaining that you didn't like a particular dish or cut of meat (other than *Speck*!) would never have occurred to us; we ate everything that came to the table. The only exception was Papa's adamant refusal to eat corn. Mama would prepare fresh sweet corn from the garden for the rest of us, but Papa would not touch it, claiming that corn was only for pigs!

Our own pasture-fed meat was on the menu daily. Years later, it occurred to me that fish never appeared at our table, not even canned tuna. Agnes had eaten pickled herring growing up, but I suppose she knew that her husband would object to fish, after the old saying; "*Was der Bauer nicht kennt, das frisst er nicht!*" ("A peasant only eats what he knows!")

When we had finished eating, Papa might mention whatever work was planned for the remainder of the day, or he might simply get up and the two boys would follow. When he spoke, we paid attention; no one dared interrupt. While he listened to the farm report on the radio, no one was allowed to talk. If he needed to place a telephone call, we all had to remain as quiet as a mouse. Being a man of few words, a typical telephone conversation, for example with the veterinarian, would go something like this:

"Hallo, Dr. Haverstick? Fritz calling. I got a sick cow. Ja, Ja, Ja, Ja ...."

Years later, Dr. Haverstick recalled with a smile my father's infatuation with his all-purpose medicine: LARD! Kept close at hand, Papa smeared lard on everything from dry, cracked skin and cuts and bruises to swollen udders, split hooves, or a cow's broken horn. Lard was his cure-all home remedy for man and beast alike. (Today we are discovering what my father always knew – that pastured pork lard is healthy and has many uses!)

Agnes saw her older children growing up. Rudy was a terrific worker, although he was rebellious and prone to mischief, involved in all kinds of (by today's standards harmless) pranks. And on top of everything, he managed to wreck Papa's brand new Ford! Often he would stay out all night, even though he had to get up early for the morning milking. Rudy was certain that nobody heard him when he sneaked in the kitchen window in the wee hours of the morning, but his mother heard him. Lying awake, Agnes worried that Rudy would not heed his father when Alfred went to awaken him at 5 o'clock. And Alfred, she knew, only spoke once; he never repeated himself.

Nancy had boundless energy and was full of life. After the evening milking, she would bribe Papa into driving her and a girlfriend to the roller-skating rink in Lebanon. The two girls didn't worry about finding a ride home; there were always lots of young soldiers stationed at the Gap who were more than eager to drive them! On Sundays, Nancy worked as a waitress at Haag's Hotel in Shartlesville, buying lipstick, dresses and fancy, high-heeled shoes with the money she earned in tips. Agnes had hoped that Nancy would choose nursing as a career after graduating from high school. She would have liked to see her own big dream fulfilled through her daughter. But Nancy, her head full of boys and having fun, had never been keen on studying, and a career in nursing was definitely not for her.

Agnes had neither the time nor the inclination to sit down and chat with her adolescent children. Not only was that not the "German" way, but also she was simply too busy from the time she got out of bed in the morning until she fell into bed at night, exhausted. She knew how to direct and instruct her children on how to behave, but lately, whenever she admonished them, they would argue and insist that things were different in America. Unlike her own strict upbringing, young people in America seemed to feel free to do as they pleased, something unheard of in her own youth. She had always tried to instill in her children a sense of propriety, but now, their smart-mouthed attitudes stunned her. Their ideas of self-expression and individualism, their claims that America was a democracy where people were free to do as they pleased, were totally foreign to her. When she scolded them for staying out late, when she warned them about getting into trouble, they would laughingly dismiss her concerns. And Agnes was aware that things were more lax in America. So as long as the children did their work, she did not want to risk saying or doing anything that might upset the peace

She had always harbored the secret hope that her eldest son would study for the ministry. But Rudy did not apply himself at school. In fact, he insisted on dropping out of the tenth grade, much to Agnes' dismay. Obviously, her eldest son was not cut out to be a "man of the cloth." But since Rudy would most likely follow in his father's footsteps, and since neither she nor Alfred had gone beyond the eighth grade, she reluctantly acquiesced.

Eric never caused any trouble. Already, he had taken his place helping with the milking. Eric was a quiet, sensible boy – earnest, like his German name, Ernst-Erich. He was very smart, and in spite of the fact that he never brought home any books or homework, he did well at school.

Then there were the two younger ones: Frieda had just started school, and Ruthie was three. Agnes didn't really have time for them, but Nancy was a big help, making certain that her little sisters were looked after.

Occasionally, Agnes would catch herself thinking back to her childhood in Sittensen – her dear mother and her father, now dead these many years; her brother, Jonny, who had wanted to join her in America; and her two sisters, Meta and Adelheid.

In January 1951, Hedwig's husband, Gottlob Schwarz, passed away suddenly. Gottlob was very well liked; all the Fritzes, even Theo and Berta from Nebraska, made a special effort to travel to New York for his funeral…

Fritz siblings Theodor, Karl, Alfred, Elise, Hedwig and Berta at the funeral of Gottlob Schwarz (January 1951)

Hedwig's husband, Gottlob Schwarz (1898-1951)

Rudy was finding it more and more difficult to get along with his father, whose strict, patriarchal approach just didn't sit well with an American teenager. Rudy didn't exactly wish to challenge his father's authority, but he didn't want to be treated like a slave either. Alfred, for his part, found himself confronted with an American teenager who talked back and argued – something unheard of in his own youth!

Fed up with his work-obsessed, uncommunicative and exacting father, Rudy decided to "leave home." At age seventeen, he hitchhiked all the way out West to his Onkel Ted in Nebraska. Once there, however, he discovered that working for his Onkel Ted was every bit as hard as working for his "old man." After several months he returned to Pennsylvania, resolving to enlist in the Navy once he turned eighteen.

Sure enough, in July 1952, Rudy enlisted in the U.S. Navy. Agnes didn't know whether to laugh or cry when he wrote her from boot camp: "Mama, get me out of here!" Six weeks later, at Rudy's basic training graduation ceremony, she and Alfred looked on with pride as their son lead his whole division in marching. When Rudy set out on his first trip at sea, Agnes secretly tucked a small New Testament into his sea bag…

Raising small flocks of chickens was very profitable in the 1950s, and Agnes, like many farmwomen of the day, saved most of the income she earned from selling eggs to buy things for the house, whereas the income from the sale of milk was always ploughed right back into the farm. Whenever she had a free moment, Agnes could be found down in the cellar, grading the many dozens of eggs she collected each day. At feeding time, no sooner would she step off the back porch than a flock of clucking hens would come surging towards her – hundreds of white Leghorns scampering across the barnyard to greet her!

In the fall of 1952, eight years after moving to the farm, Alfred and Agnes were finally able to turn their attention to their home. It was time to bring the old farmhouse into the modern age – installing an indoor bathroom, replacing the old wood-burning kitchen stove with a shiny new electric range, installing a furnace in the cellar to provide central heating, covering the old wooden plank floors with hardwood, fitting the windows with storm windows, etc. Needless to say, it was mainly Agnes' "egg" money that made all this possible, in particular fixing up and furnishing the two downstairs rooms that had stood empty all those years – converting the north room into a family room, the south room into a formal living room *(gute Stube!)*, complete with an upright piano. Of course, my parents had no sense of historical preservation, but they were keen on self-preservation. The farmhouse may have sacrificed its originality, but our family now had all the modern comforts.

From time to time, city relatives would announce their visit. Agnes always looked forward to having company. She would be out early in the morning, selecting a few plump candidates for the skillet, catching them, and then expertly ripping off each unsuspecting bird's neck. Then it was down to the cellar to scald them, pluck off their feathers and pull out their innards. At exactly noon, dinner would be on the table, and the appreciative city relatives would remark that Agnes' fried chicken was more delicious than any they had ever tasted. Of course, the fact that our chickens were not packed tightly into wire cages or crowded together in windowless buildings, but spent their days in the fresh air and sunshine, wandering around the barnyard, had a lot to do with their tastiness...

Agnes' New Yorker relatives, cousin Anna and sister-in-law Winnie, would stay for several days, bringing with them goodies from a German bakery and delicatessen – all kinds of German sausage, plus fresh yeast breads, cakes and pastries. Agnes, in turn, would serve up huge amounts of fried chicken for dinner, or simmered steak with mashed potatoes along with fresh vegetables and lettuce from the garden. Our city relatives all seemed to enjoy the country – appreciatively commenting on the quiet, the fresh air and the spectacular sunsets. We would make fun of their strange Brooklyn accents and wonder why everyone didn't live in the country, if that was the preferred place to be.

Agnes was a gracious hostess; she had the knack of making people feel welcome. Quick and efficient, she enjoyed feeding guests and making them comfortable. Her kindness was sincere; everyone liked her. "If you want a friend, you must be a friend," she would instruct us. And Agnes knew how to be a friend.

Alfred and Agnes with Cousin Anna McGuiness and Cousin Otto's wife Winnie Schmiemann, along with newlyweds Henry and Marilyn Schmiemann. In front, Ruthie and Frieda (August 1953)

With Rudy now in the Navy, Papa decided to switch to automatic milking (Surge milkers) machines. This would ease the chore of hand milking, so that he and Eric could essentially manage the milking by themselves. After a cow was milked by machine, the milk was poured from the machine into waiting buckets. Two people could alternate tending to the automatic milkers, wiping clean the udders and preparing the next cow, and carrying the heavy buckets of milk to the milk house and emptying them into the bulk milk tank.

Eric would spend his high school years plus two more years after high school working alongside his father on the farm. A precious time capsule is to be found in the form of a letter that Agnes wrote to Gretel Ettle, Alfred's niece in Germany, on March 10, 1953. Here in translation is a portion of her letter:

> "… Soon it will be Easter. Today it is snowing, but the winter has been mild. Rudy [in the Navy] is in Cuba and other points to the south. I believe his ship will arrive back in Norfolk in time for Easter. Rudy is tall, much taller than me or Onkel Alfred. Nancy will soon graduate from high school after twelve years of schooling. You ask what she plans to do after graduation. Well, it's difficult to say. At the moment, she has a steady boyfriend. He is here visiting this afternoon. I think they will get engaged this summer. I will soon send you her [high school] graduation picture. You won't recognize her anymore.
>
> There is always plenty of work, but farm work here is different than in Germany. We are currently milking twenty cows, but we milk them by machine. I also have a flock of over three hundred chickens.
>
> Eric helps Onkel Alfred with the milking. He is now fifteen years old and in the tenth grade. Next in line is Frieda, who will be turning nine, followed by Ruthie, who will be six years old in May. Pretty soon they'll all be grown …"

With her innate sense of style, Nancy might have gone to New York to study fashion and design, but this was the early 1950s, and Nancy's only goal in life after graduating from high school was to get married and be a homemaker. Engaged to be married, and earning good tips as a waitress, she was diligently saving up for her trousseau…

The highlight of 1954 was Nancy's wedding. Nancy had always wanted a home wedding, and with the modernization of the farmhouse now complete, Alfred and Agnes were able to grant their daughter her wish. How proud they were to welcome far-flung relatives and friends to their renovated farmhouse, now with all the modern amenities.

It was a perfect afternoon wedding. A pianist played the wedding march as the veiled bride, lovely in white, descended the stairs and was met by her father, who ushered her into the living room, where the groom and the assembled guests awaited her. In our matching white silk and lace dresses, our hearts thumping with excitement, Ruthie and I couldn't wait for the moment when the groom lifts the veil and kisses the bride!

Alfred and Agnes at the home wedding of their daughter, Nancy Meta, to Anthony Christos Wenger (April 10, 1954)

Throughout the spring, summer and fall, our herd of dairy cows ate mostly green grass; in winter, they were fed stored dry hay and corn silage. Making certain the cows had enough hay to last through the winter was of utmost importance and financially imperative. If a farmer had to purchase additional hay, it could be very expensive and his profits would all go down the drain, which is why, that February, Alfred had jumped at the opportunity to buy the Al Gallery farm, the farm adjoining ours to the west. The extra forty-eight acres would provide more tillable ground and extra pasture land so that he could have more dairy cows. Plus, Nancy and her future husband, a lineman with Bell Telephone Co., would have a ready-made place to live! Nancy and Tony, the quintessential '50s couple, originally rented, and then soon purchased the old farmhouse on the property, making it their permanent home. It was nice to have Nancy and Tony living so close by.

The large, airy chicken house that came with the property was a God-send, as the dairy to which Alfred shipped his milk (Freeman's Dairy in Allentown) had recently given notice that other livestock or fowl would no longer be allowed in or near the dairy barn. Thus, the chicken house across the road was the ideal solution for housing Agnes' free-range chickens, at least over the next several years, until, by the end of the 1950s, small-scale egg production was no longer viable. Agnes could no longer

Picnic at Otto Esenwein's farm (Summer 1954). (L to R) Onkel Theo, Onkel Karl, Gottlieb and Päule Haegele, Onkel Otto (with Frieda), Tante Dora Fritz, then Tante Päule Esenwein and Tante Helene Fritz (both standing). Children in front: Walter Specht and cousins Dorothy, Ruthie and Margaret Fritz

compete with commercial poultry farms that packed thousands of laying hens into cages. How well I recall the day when Mama prepared and served her first store-bought chicken. Needless to say, it failed the taste test!

Sad news came in March of the following year: Onkel Otto, Alfred's half-brother, the man who had made their return to America possible, died of a heart attack on March 15, 1955. He was only fifty-eight! Why, only the year before he and Päule had danced to the strains of the accordion at Nancy's wedding, and just last summer, relatives and friends had gathered at his farm for a picnic.

Otto Esenwein's passing was sad indeed, his untimely death a reminder of their own mortality. But 1955 would prove a very distressing year for another reason. That year, they would see their eldest son saddled with a paternity suit!

In his third summer in the Navy, Rudy hitchhiked home on a one-month leave – all the way from California. But no sooner had he arrived home than the township constable came looking for him. It seems that Rudy, like his paternal grandfather before him, was very popular with the ladies. The previous year, while on a weekend leave, he had hitchhiked home from Philadelphia. Now, one year later, the girl he had hung out with that weekend was claiming he was the father of her newborn daughter!

When no amount of denying on Rudy's part would make the young woman change her story, Alfred advised his son to just go ahead and marry her and get it over with. But Rudy refused, swearing that he never even slept with the bitch! But even more telling, the girl was not that keen on marrying Rudy either. Instead, the conniving female (who came from poor mountain folk), sensing a financial opportunity (the Fritzes owned a farm and were "well-off"), was demanding a one-time monetary settlement of five thousand dollars!

Alfred, at that point, and in front of the Justice of the Peace, decided to wash his hands of the whole affair, stating simply that since his son was over the age of eighteen, he could take care of himself. A stunned and chastened Rudy returned to his naval base in California under a court order to pay child support until "his" child turned sixteen.

In time, the whole sordid affair was forgotten. Agnes, however, could not put it out of her mind, afraid of what people would say or think. It was her one "weakness" – her desire for others to think well of our family.

Her longing for respectability was deeply rooted. Having been raised in a social milieu of strict class distinctions as well as strict norms of behavior, her actions were guided by the code of ethics by which she had been raised, especially as it pertained to marriage and sex: Having a child out of wedlock was a disgrace and brought shame to a family. You simply did not have sex outside of marriage. Agnes forever preached the same refrain: "If you get pregnant, you are on your own; don't even think of coming home!" And we knew she meant it.

The same code of moral ethics also applied to divorce. The saying, *"Wie man sich bettet, so liegt man"* she translated for our benefit: "The way you make your bed is the way you must lie in it." Agnes never would have divorced her husband. She might have fled from him on occasion, IF she had had a place to go, but Agnes took her wedding vow seriously. To her, marriage was forever, a covenant, entered into in the sight of God. It was not a romantic, feel-good, temporary condition, but rather a lifetime commitment, both unconditional ("for better or for worse, for richer or for poorer, in sickness and in health") as well as permanent ("as long as we both shall live, till death do us part"). And she lectured her daughters accordingly: "After you are married, don't expect to come running home to me!" As a result, both her sons-in-law adored her; she always defended them and took their side! Indeed, if it had ever come down to it, she would have sided with her sons-in-law, not her daughters, in any marital conflict.

In the end, Agnes' fears proved unwarranted. Nobody seemed aware of Rudy's patrimony case, and if they were aware, it didn't seem to matter. Our family was not shamed; Agnes could still attend church with her head held high. But her constant preaching paid off in the end. None of her children would have a child out of wedlock, and all but one would enter into marriages that would last a lifetime.

Wedding of Rudolf Alfred Fritz and Louellyn Duayne Driscoll in California (December 15, 1955)

Rudy had barely returned to California when he wrote home with the astonishing news that he was engaged and that he and his fiancée, a girl he had met near his naval base, were soon to be married. A stunned Agnes wrote back, offering congratulations and enclosing a hundred dollar bill (the same amount Nancy had received as her wedding gift).

The following July, after completing four years in the Navy, Rudy returned home to Pennsylvania with his nineteen-year-old (Mormon!) bride who not only knew nothing about farming, but was also clueless when it came to cooking and keeping house.

"Oh, why couldn't Rudy have married a nice farm girl from around here!" thought Agnes, in dismay. It took all of her patience to be accepting of this "alien" daughter-in-law, not to reject her as she herself had been rejected by Alfred's mother many years earlier....

With Rudy and his pregnant young wife temporarily living with us on the farm, Agnes saw a chance for her and Alfred to get away for a few weeks – their first vacation, ever! Taking widowed Päule Esenwein along, they drove out to Nebraska to visit Alfred's relatives (Berta and Emil Heller, Theo and Dora Fritz and Paul Kleinknecht) as well as friends and acquaintances from long ago...

Agnes was having such a good time and would have liked to stay away longer, but Alfred started getting restless and wanted to go back home. Thank goodness for that, because even though nothing "major" happened during their two-week absence, the farm was just not the same without them. The whole house was upside

Agnes and Alfred in Nebraska with Berta and Emil Heller and Päule Esenwein (October 1956)

down, and Agnes was so embarrassed when she couldn't find a single clean sheet to put on Päule's bed.

Soon everything was running smoothly once more, and our mother's voice again filled the house. Mama always sang as she went about her work. On Sundays, sitting alongside Papa in the front seat of our car on the way home from church, she would invariably sing her heart out.

In 1953, the Clymers had given us their old upright piano, as I had been eager to learn to play. After a while, I was able to accompany the singing at Sunday school. How Mama enjoyed listening to the beloved old hymns!

Christmas dinner at home on the farm, 1956. From left: Tony and Nancy (with Kathy and Renee), Agnes, Alfred, Ruthie, Frieda, Tante Helene, cousins Margaret and Dorle, Lou, Eric and Onkel Karl (Rudy is missing…)

Alfred and Agnes at home (Christmas, 1956)

Rudy and his wife Lou were now living in a rental apartment in Bethel. Employed full-time at the Bethlehem Steel foundry in Lebanon, Rudy also helped on the farm between shifts. Thus the stage was set: For a period of two years, from 1956 to 1958, Alfred enjoyed the luxury of having both his sons working for him. With the farm now flourishing, Alfred dusted off the custom sign he had ordered:

DAIRY FARM

ALFRED FRITZ & SONS

Our farm was now a veritable showplace. Taking advantage of a spring-fed stream in the upper meadow, Papa had a large pond dug, reinforcing the sides with rocks and cement. Attractively landscaped with young firs and flowering trees, the pond not only beautified our front yard, but became an endless source of summer fun. And in the fall and winter, you could glance out the kitchen window and be treated to an exquisite sunset, reflected in the pond.

Agnes continued to work her green thumb magic. She was proud of her large garden, a blend of vegetables and old-fashioned cottage garden flowers. Then there was the glass-enclosed back porch, filled with luxuriously blooming gloxinias, African violets, begonias, and indoor plants of all kinds. Her prized rose bushes bordered the sidewalk leading up to the porch in front.

A trained wisteria twined around the southwest corner of the front porch, pruned grapevines lined the east side and then trailed along the south wall above the garage. In June, the blooming wisteria would delight with its purple fragrance, and in the fall, the sweet smell of ripening grapes would waft through the open windows.

In 1958, Eric, wanting to expand his horizons, enlisted in the U.S. Army for a period of three years.

Sent to keep the peace in Korea, Eric was soon homesick. Who could forget the moving opening line of his initial letter home from that far-away place: "Dear folks," he wrote. "How are things back in God's own country?"

With Eric now gone, the farm obviously needed a muscular person to replace him. Papa ended up hiring, especially during the summer months, a series of mostly city boys with little or no prior experience at farm work and who did not share our family's strong work ethic. The behaviors of these young men would soon become the subject of many an amusing "hired man" story, as each brought his own unique personality, his foibles and misdeeds to the equation – lazy, peculiar, dishonest, or not too bright.

When Eric returned from his one-year stint in Korea, he married a local girl from Bethel, and by the time he was discharged from the Army in 1961, he had already fathered a son.

Eric enjoyed farming, and after his Army discharge he could easily have returned

to the farm where his help was sorely needed. It was his decision whether to help on the farm or to seek employment elsewhere. (As a wedding present, he and Lillian had been given an acre of land next to Nancy to build on…)

But even with the best of intentions, he could no longer put up with the treatment he received at his father's hands – worse than that of an army drill sergeant! One fine day, not long after he had gotten out of the Army, he and Rudy were up in the barn, cleaning out some old moldy corn stalks. Choking on the thick dust, Eric stepped outside for a breath of fresh air when he heard his father approach.

"Git your lazy, good-for-nottin *Arsch* back in dere und git to verk!" is all that Eric got for his trouble. Obviously, he had forgotten that taking a break was a concept to which "the old man" did not subscribe.

But why would Eric put up with such bull when he could choose not to? His mind made up, he went into the house, took a shower, got in his car, and drove away. Eric was quickly snatched up by RCA's (Thomson Consumer Electronics) plant in Lancaster from where he would eventually retire, some forty years later, after a successful career in electronics.

In spite of his workload, Alfred found time for his hobby: cultivating grapes. Where earlier in his life he had brewed his own beer, he now was into making wine. Agnes would have

Christmas, 1958. Eric (21) in uniform, Alfred, Frieda, Onkel Karl and Tante Helene. Front row: Agnes (seated) Margaret, Ruthie and Dorle

Wedding of Eric Ernest (Ernst-Erich) Fritz and Lillian G. Berger (February 20, 1960).

preferred to can grape juice from the ripening Concord grapes, but each September would find Papa with his barrels at the ready and barefoot Ruthie and I stomping on the grapes to release their juices. I assume he didn't properly control the fermentation process, because for some reason, every year the result was the same: the wine would become vinegar or undrinkable.

"Next time, use more sugar!" Agnes would volunteer. But Papa always saved on sugar, and the wine was always sour.

Often frugal to the point of absurdity, a lifetime of poverty had left its mark, and Papa could no longer change his ways. He had to save on everything, would sooner sit in the dark than turn on a lamp, and we children learned never to leave a room without turning off the light. Papa's frugal ways could often be quite annoying in a modern, hygienic American household. For example, even though plentiful, water was always to be used sparingly, since turning on the faucet would cause the pump to run, and electricity cost money! When Papa washed up, he used barely a trickle of water, but after soaping up and not properly rinsing, he would make such a mess at the kitchen sink that it would take twice as much water usage just to clean up after him!

Agnes knew how to make expenses palatable to her husband. For example, if some small, necessary item cost ten dollars, Agnes would quietly pay for it and later, in order to spare herself the ordeal of her husband's reaction, would simply tell him that it had cost only half as much. Even so, Papa would still have a fit at the cost.

My parents talked everything over, but it was Mama who kept the books and held the purse strings, and Papa came to rely more and more on her solid money management skills.

Agnes' hobby was gardening. If you couldn't find her in the kitchen or elsewhere in the house, then you were sure to find her working in the garden or tending to her flowers. Blessed with a green thumb, Agnes could make anything grow. She enjoyed vegetable gardening, but raising flowers was her passion. She grew flowers everywhere, filling even the barn windows with geraniums. Later, as one of the founding members of the Rehrersburg Flower Club, she often took first prize at regional flower shows for best floral arrangement or best specimen plant in bloom. Whenever we had company, they were invariably taken on a tour of the garden, and admiring visitors never went home without a few cuttings.

Agnes never rested. She never sat down, much less took a nap. She worked from dawn to dusk, and even a younger person could not keep up with her. She would help with the chores in the morning, feeding the chickens, getting breakfast for everyone, making certain the children got off to school, collecting and grading eggs, in summer working in the garden "before the sun got too hot," then preparing a big noon meal, then the dishes and the clean-up, perhaps some housework or more grading eggs, then making supper, then evening chores, then working in the garden again, in summer the endless days of harvesting and preserving the fruits and vegetables coming from the garden. And when the housework and the canning and the gardening were finally finished, and everyone's needs attended to, she would fall exhausted into bed only to be up again at the crack of dawn.

Nor could Agnes stand to see someone doing nothing. Daytime was for working; we were not allowed to just sit around until after the evening chores were done. Agnes subscribed to "*Die Hausfrau,*" a German language monthly, but the only time I recall her sitting and reading was on Sunday afternoons. She and Alfred would study the *Farm Journal* and *Pennsylvania Farmer* when they had a chance. They subscribed to the *Lebanon Daily News* and the Sunday edition of *The Reading Eagle*, and, of course, they regularly skimmed through the local *Merchandiser.* But not until retirement would they find the time to sit and read, or, in Agnes' case, to take up the fancy needlework at which she had once been so adept…

Dairy farming is tough. It is not a job that one leaves behind at quitting time, because there is no quitting time. The work is never done. The cows have to be milked twice a day, seven days a week. If you go somewhere on a Sunday afternoon, you have to leave by four o'clock in order to be home to start the milking. In the summer, the cows must be rounded up and brought in for milking, then let out to pasture again, while in winter, the manure has to be hauled out daily. Dairying also means knowing each cow's idiosyncrasies, keeping records, knowing when each cow must be bred and when she will go dry and when she will calve. It means getting up in the middle of the night to aid in the birth of a calf. It is a year-round, round-the-clock business. There are no vacations, ever.

After they retired from dairy farming, Onkel Karl and Tante Helene took a trip to Germany to visit family there. After admiring Karl's brand new Mercedes, a young relative stated he wished he could afford such a fine car. "Well," Karl replied, smiling. "You have to milk a barn full of cows twice a day for twenty-five years, never taking a vacation, and then you can buy a Mercedes!"

In 1944, when Alfred first acquired the farm, he could never have imagined all the changes to come. He may well have envisioned a more modern dairy barn and a larger, more profitable dairy herd, but farming as an agricultural money-making enterprise, rather than as a way of life, was probably not in the picture at the time. In fact, quite the opposite, as Rudy claims that when he and Nancy were young, Papa encouraged them to finish with the evening chores by six o'clock. "Any farmer who is still in the barn after six o'clock," he maintained, "is an idiot!"

In the early years, Alfred even found time in the evening to visit the Bethel Fire Hall and enjoy a beer while listening in on the other men's conversations. At first, he scarcely spoke a word, since, true to his nature, he was not much of a talker, and he could think of nothing to say. He preferred to listen and observe, and he was tickled by the Pennsylvania Dutch dialect.

Alfred patronized the Fire Hall for the better part of a year before talking to anyone! One night, the subject turned to one with which he was very familiar – Bang's disease. That finally broke the ice. But Alfred never said much as a rule, preferring to listen and to observe. Since he didn't know how to make small-talk, he never spoke unless he had something important to say. Nor, true to his Swabian heritage, did he ever flaunt what he had or volunteer any information, preferring to feign stupidity rather than reveal any information about himself. Even if you asked him a direct question, you might or might not get an answer, eventually.

My father never rested, nor was he ever content. The more he achieved, the more he wanted. Gradually the idea took root in his mind that he could expand his operations and become a large-scale producer: Alfred Fritz & Sons. The idea did not appear overnight, nor will we ever know if it was there from the very beginning or if, almost certainly, it was forced upon him by circumstances.

The 1950s were a very profitable time for farmers, while at the same time, 'lazy' and inefficient farmers were going broke and being sold out. Alfred, because of habits of frugality and industry acquired in "the old country", and living within his means, was finally becoming prosperous. In fact, he saw that he was growing even more profitable than those who had inherited their farms.

"Ve inherited notting," he bragged to his two sons. "Me and Mum, ve shtarted vit notting!"

By the late 1950s, dairy farming was becoming more like a business enterprise. In order to sell your milk to a dairy or milk processing company that paid a good price, you had to meet a certain minimum of gallons of milk produced. In other words, in order to make it worthwhile for Freeman's Dairy to continue to pick up the milk, Alfred would have to expand his operations to become more productive.

It was the start of a vicious cycle. More gallons of milk shipped meant more cows, and more cows meant more work and longer hours, plus the need to invest in more land on which to grow the crops to feed the increased number of cows needed to make the "business" profitable. More land meant the need for modern, labor-saving but expensive farm machinery, and more milk meant the need to construct a larger milk house to accommodate a new, larger bulk milk tank.

The milk had also to be of a certain quality, and dairies began to place ever more stringent requirements on the producers. Freeman's Dairy, for example, would no longer tolerate the presence of any livestock other than cows – no chickens, sheep, horses, pigs, etc. Even the old outhouse had to be gotten rid of, although it was no longer in use!

Ever stricter sanitary standards were also imposed on the handling of the milk, the cleanliness of the milking equipment and the milk house itself, so that in the end, Agnes herself took charge of the cleanup of the milk tank and the milking machines, as Freeman's not only kept track of the amount of butterfat in the milk, but also the bacteria count, and there was constant apprehension whether our milk would meet the high quality standards.

The milk check, the sole source of income, became all-important. But barely had the monthly check arrived before it was already spent, any cash left over channeled back into the operation. Thus, although well-to-do on paper, Alfred and Agnes lived from milk check to milk check, with hardly more disposable income than before, but a lot more work and a lot more headaches.

They worked hand in hand. Agnes kept the farm management records and the herd books showing the breeding and calving dates, and many a summer evening I saw them walking the field road, discussing what crops should be planted, what fields rotated. As long as there were enough hands to help with the chores and the milking, Agnes remained in the house, but whenever there was a shortage on manpower, Agnes was sure to appear. She was a true farmwoman, and there was not much she could not do, except she never learned to drive a tractor. This was actually very smart on her part; I am certain she did it on purpose, knowing full well that if she got into that, she would never be able to finish her own work!

One winter, Agnes even substituted entirely for her husband. That was the winter when Papa came down with a strange allergic ailment – an allergy to hay dust, and had to stay out of the barn entirely! Mama's fingers became sore from the harsh chemical detergents used to clean and sanitize the milking equipment.

Ruthie and I, although much younger than our older siblings, were also an integral part of the farm and were given tasks from the time that we were small. Our main responsibilities were domestic in nature – keeping the lawn mowed and cleaning house. But we also drove tractor and helped with the evening milking, especially on Sunday evenings when Eric had off. Our help was indispensable during the three years when Eric was away in the Army, and Rudy would be working 2nd shift (at Bethlehem Steel).

As farm kids, we never gave it a second thought. After school, we automatically changed into our "barn clothes" and joined Papa in the barn – a warm, comfortable place, with the two rows of cows in their stanchions, softly munching away on their hay, warming the barn with their body heat. After all, what was not to like, what with the pungent smell of the corn silage, the fragrant smell of the hay and straw, the friendly barn cats, eager to be held and stroked while waiting for their ration of warm milk, plus the newborn calves waiting to be fed, wanting to suck my thumb?

Then it was time to get busy helping with the milking: wiping the cow's teats, draping the leather strap over her back from which the Surge milker would then be hung, under the cow's belly, just in front of the udder, and then hooking up the machine to her udders. The Surge milkers, when full, were too heavy for us to lift, but we were kept busy carrying the heavy buckets of fresh, warm milk out to the milk house and emptying them into the bulk milk tank. In between, we distributed the hay, and when done with the milking, we helped with bedding down each cow with fresh straw.

For a long time, the added cropland and pasture gained from the 1954 purchase were sufficient. But the more Alfred prospered, the more, it seems, he wanted. Those two "golden years" during which he benefitted from both grown sons working for him and when the farm really took off, may have gone to his head. He dreamed of owning even more land in order to grow his operation.

He began going to farm auctions, if only to get a feel for prices. One day, getting caught up in the excitement of bidding, he raised his finger "just for the fun of it" to increase a bid by one hundred dollars. But before he knew it, the auctioneer was hammering the farm sold to him – at $22,100, he was the highest bidder! Arriving home later that afternoon, Alfred faced an unsuspecting Agnes with the stunning news that he had purchased another farm!

His announcement came as a complete surprise. Agnes, in shock, couldn't believe her ears! Had her husband lost his mind? Just when they had finally managed to pay off the latest piece of expensive farm machinery! Just when everything was running so smoothly!

The following day, Alfred drove Agnes over to have a look at what was now "their" property, a 105-acre farm located on the road to Strausstown (now 372 East Rehrersburg Road) in Upper Tulpehocken Township. Alfred liked the looks of the place, the fact that the buildings were in good repair. He reassured his wife that he had made a good decision. They needed more land, and he and Rudy could just as well farm both places. Agnes liked the farmhouse; she especially liked the idea of providing Rudy and his growing family with a nice place to live.

The purchase of the "second farm" in April 1959 prompted Rudy to quit his job at Bethlehem Steel so that he could work full-time on the farm, becoming his father's right-hand man. As compensation, in addition to free rent, he would receive a weekly salary of fifty dollars, plus free meat, milk and eggs. (In addition to farming the land, Alfred planned to raise heifers, pigs and chickens on the second farm.)

It was a working relationship which would continue to have its share of ups and downs. There was constant friction between father and son. According to Rudy, "the old man" was a real slave-driver; you could never do enough to suit him. "You're fired!" Alfred would angrily announce, while at other times Rudy would be the one to call it quits. (Rudy already had a job lined up, working nights as a bartender.) Then Agnes, skilled at appeasement, would either make Alfred go fetch his son, or she would call Rudy on the phone and plead with him to return. How could they manage without him! At the end of the day, Rudy could not say "No" to Mama, the eternal peacemaker…

Now the work truly was never-ending. The two farms were located four miles apart; there was a lot of traveling back and forth. No sooner had Papa and Rudy finished at one farm than they had to pick up and haul their farm machinery over to the second farm. Instead of calling it a day after the evening chores, they would be out in the fields till dark overcame them. Rudy was chafing at the bit. How he wished he had stayed at Bethlehem Steel. He saw Tony and Eric and all his buddies leaving work at five o'clock, going home to their families. Rudy began to think of farming as a dead end, too much work for not enough pay; drudgery. Nor was Rudy the type to spend his evenings at home with his wife and children, perusing the latest edition of *Farm Journal* magazine. He much preferred frequenting the local fire house, enjoying a couple of beers, flirting with the ladies, and "shooting the bull."

In the summer of 1963, Alfred, now fifty-nine years old and ailing, decided it was time for him to gradually retire from farming. In preparation, he and Agnes purchased a small house along Old U.S. Route #22, close to Boltz's Corner, with the idea that Rudy would move into the main house and gradually take over operations – naturally with Alfred's continued support and oversight. It would be stressful enough for Alfred to relinquish control, to draw Rudy into his plans, to communicate…

I had returned from a year as an exchange student and was about to start college in the fall when Papa instructed me to draft a contract under which Rudy would agree to manage both farms in return for a monthly salary of four hundred dollars plus free rent, meat, milk, etc., and reimbursement for half the electric bill. The contract also spelled out that the house and yard were to be kept in good order.

Giving up the farm was not easy. Preparing for the move, Agnes thought back over the last two decades during which time they had poured so much effort into making the farm a success. How could those twenty years have gone by so quickly? Why, it seemed like only yesterday that she and Alfred had first come to this place which she had come to love so dearly. She had never wanted to move again! How could she possibly leave her garden, her flowers, her home? Would she be able to simply turn a blind eye when her son and daughter-in-law did not look after the place as she would have wished? Would Alfred be able to relinquish his hold on this farm, which was his life's achievement?

Agnes knew that it was time to let go. It was, after all, in accordance with (northern German) tradition that the farm should pass to the eldest son. Agnes pretended that she was relieved to be rid of the big old farmhouse and to move into a smaller house with a brand-new customized kitchen! But Ruthie and I did not quite believe her. How could Mama possibly enjoy giving up a spacious, lovely old farmhouse in exchange for a small, nondescript bungalow where most of our furniture wouldn't even fit! Besides, all our memories were tied to the farm.

The contract with Rudy, dated September 1, 1963, was on a trial basis, to be reassessed four months later. Just two weeks into the contract, however, when Alfred drove over to the farm one morning to help with the milking, he discovered that Rudy was gone – without a word of explanation, without saying goodbye.

Alfred knew, he must have known, the reason why Rudy had left so abruptly, taking his wife and children with him. Alfred alone knew what had brought about the final rift between him and his eldest son. But true to form, he kept it to himself, and so Agnes never knew why her eldest son left so suddenly without even so much as saying goodbye...

Rudy's unanticipated departure changed everything. Alfred was stuck. Like his father, Christian, before him, he was now left with only two children at home – two young girls at that, with Ruthie (16) still in high school, and me (19) just starting college!

Alfred's plans for "Alfred Fritz & Sons" failed because, in the end, neither of his sons could tolerate his difficult personality. He was unable to communicate, much less be friends with them. Instead, he demanded work, and more work, without sharing with them his plans or allowing them to feel that they were an integral part of the operation. As long as you worked, you were "good enough." But Rudy and Eric, no longer boys but grown men, knew of a world where people laughed and joked, even while working, and they were certain there was a workplace where their knowledge and contribution would be appreciated and they would be well compensated for a job well done, and where there was a fixed quitting time, a time to call it a day, when you could go home to your family and relax.

In dealing with his sons, Alfred had repeated the very same mistake his father had made – exploiting his sons to the max instead of treating them with respect and drawing them into his plans, thereby succeeding only in alienating them, in driving them away.

It would prove a very tough fall and winter. Agnes and Alfred only "slept" in their new home; Agnes helped with both the morning and evening milking, and Alfred spent his days looking after both farms. The following spring, after graduating from high school, Ruthie agreed to spend the summer helping Papa on the farm before starting business school in the fall, but this would prove a touch-and-go situation "for all the usual reasons"…

In the meantime, Alfred had employed a full-time tenant farmer, although this arrangement would not prove to be a satisfactory, long-term solution either, since Alfred could not bear to observe, much less tolerate, how other men went about their work, nor was he any better at dealing with his hired farmer than he had been at communicating with his sons.

Annoyed and frustrated, Alfred, now sixty-one, arthritic and worn out from a lifetime of hard work, decided to put the family farm up for sale. And so it came to pass that two decades and a year after he first began moving his handful of cows over to the farm, in 1944, a resigned Alfred now looked on as his youngest daughter, Ruth, led his present herd of registered Holstein dairy cows, one by one, to the auction block – all thirty-five of them.

Alfred had reached the pinnacle of his life's work. How then to part with it? How difficult the decision to sell the family farm, to let go of what had once been his dream, his very goal in life! Of course, he still owned the second farm, but with that property, there was no close, sentimental bond, no emotional attachment.

Ruthie had been such a good little worker about the farm, and thus Alfred, still trying to devise a way to keep the farm in the family (again, according to German tradition), in a last-ditch effort, offered (was he serious?!) to sell the farm to Ruthie and her fiancé, Jim Frantz. Jim, about to be drafted and sent to Viet Nam, was so astonished at the offer that he didn't know what to say. A trained mechanic, he had never pictured himself as a farmer! Of course, the two young people did not have the financial means, nor did Ruthie wish to be a farmer, so Alfred's offer was quickly dismissed.

The story might have had a very different ending. At the time, Ruthie's fiancé, a direct descendant of the Christian Frantz family, had no idea that "our" farm was the Frantz family's original homestead. Had he known, he might have at least considered Alfred's offer. Possibly, the extended Frantz clan would have stepped in to "reclaim" their heritage, to offer financial support, to figure out some way of making it work. But at the time, who knew? The book detailing our farm's historical significance, *The Genealogy of the Matthias Frantz Family of Berks County*, would not be published until 1972.

PUBLIC SALE
Of Valuable
DAIRY HERD,
FARM EQUIPMENT, ETC.
Thursday, November 4th, 1965
At 12:00 Noon

1 1/2 MILES SOUTH OF BETHEL AND ROUTE #22 ALONG WINTERSVILLE BLACKTOP ROAD IN TULPEHOCKEN TOWNSHIP, BERKS COUNTY, PA.

DAIRY HERD

35 Large Holstein Cows In Various Stages Of Production, Some Fresh By Sale Day. All Good Producers, Herd Is Area Tested Individual Charts Will Be Furnished.

DAIRY EQUIPMENT

Majonnier Milk Sputnik, Surge Model SP-22 Milk Compressor And Three Units.

FARM EQUIPMENT

Ford Model 801 Diesel Tractor, Power Steering, Live PTO, Etc., Like New; International Model 350 Tractor, Fast Hitch Etc.; Farmall BN Tractor; MC 7' Fast Hitch Mower; MC Three Bottom Three Point Plow; New Idea 7' Mower; Ford 3-P Cultivator; MC Fast Hitch Cultivator; Dearborn 3-P Corn Planter, John Deere #14-T Hay Baler With Kicker; MC Crusher; New Holland Forage Harvester With Corn And Pickup Headers; John Deere Field Chopper; David Bradley Silo Blower; MC 125 Bushel PTO Manure Spreader, Used 1 Year; Allis Chalmers Rake On Rubber, Trailer Mounted Weed Sprayer; Ontario Grain Drill; Tractor Disc, Like New; Grove Front End Unloading Silage Wagon, Farm Trailor With False Front End Gate; Bale Elevator; 20' Smoker Bale Elevator; King Wyse Drag Elevator; Cement Mixer; Feed Carts; 1950 Chevrolet Truck; Scrap Iron; Plus Other Items Not Mentioned.

NOTE: Farm Equipment Sells First, Hardly No Small Wagon Items. Be On Time.

Sale On Farm Of:
ALFRED K. FRITZ

Ralph W. Zettlemoyer, Auctioneer
Phone: 215 285-2267

Public auction was held on November 4, 1965. (The average herd size of a dairy farm in 1964 was 40 milking cows.)

Thus the moment passed, and the idea was never mentioned again. Today, Jim regrets that the farm is no longer in the Frantz family, that the opportunity was missed. But he likes to tell the story of how he and Ruthie "almost" became farmers! As it turns out, they did eventually purchase – not the farm, but the house at Boltz's corner.

Alfred was certain he could get at least sixty thousand for his well-kept dairy farm, but at the time, and at that price, there were no takers. After sitting empty over the winter, the property was purchased by a realtor, Hiram Hershey, in March 1966 for forty-five thousand dollars, who then sold it to Roy Ziegler in August 1968 for just five hundred dollars more. (Alfred, of course, had no way of knowing that in just a few years, in the 1970s, land values would skyrocket. It was a bad time for my father to sell, but again, who knew?)

With the farm now sold and the second one rented out, Alfred and Agnes, for the first time in their lives, could take it easy! What a strange feeling, not to have to milk cows! Agnes could only shake her head and marvel at how much time she now had on her hands. But still she never rested. She spent her days gardening – planting flowers, shrubs and trees, transplanting the cuttings she had brought along from the farm. Soon, the little house at Boltz's corner began to feel more like "home." Besides, Ruthie, her "baby," was still at home, and I came home on the weekends, so she still had our company, someone to cook for besides Papa.

Agnes took pleasure in her grandchildren. While still on the farm, she would welcome Nancy's children when they came walking across the field (to check if Grandma had any leftover pancakes!), and Rudy's little girls would visit regularly. At Boltz's corner, when Eric and his family stopped by for *Kaffee und Kuchen* on a Sunday afternoon, she joyously anticipated their arrival and would be waiting at the door to greet his two little boys.

"I never had time to enjoy my own children," she would remark with a sigh. "There was so much work. I was always too busy."

Agnes' sister had visited from Germany the previous summer, in 1965. Eager to reciprocate, the following summer Meta invited Agnes, especially since I was now in Germany spending my junior year abroad in Marburg.

And so it happened that Agnes saw her wish come true – a wish that she had made thirty years earlier, in February 1938, on her way back to America with little Nancy and baby Erich, seasick and miserable, as third-class passengers packed like sardines in the very bowels of the ship. It was during that storm-tossed voyage when she had dared to dream that she might one day be able to cross the Atlantic in comfort and style…

Alfred, not surprisingly, refused to accompany his wife, proclaiming that he had no desire to set foot on German soil. Thus it was that in the summer of 1966, Agnes, now a "woman of leisure," embarked by herself on a trip down memory lane,

Agnes took pleasure in her grandchildren.

sailing from New York to Bremerhaven aboard the majestic SS United States, a luxury liner. This time she crossed the Atlantic "in comfort and style", was treated like a lady, and had a fabulous time.

In Bremen she was met by Adelheid and husband Leo. Then she visited Meta in Hamburg and from there, she and Meta travelled to their home town of Sittensen, where Meta had organized a reunion of childhood friends and where Agnes spent several days basking in their warmth and affection. Continuing on by train, she then stopped in Marburg for a few days to visit with me before continuing her journey south by train to visit Alfred's relatives in Stuttgart area. It was there, in the south of Germany, that she was most at ease, especially visiting with Tante Emma, her sister-in-law who had shown her such kindness during a very dark and uncertain period in her life, and with Emma's daughter, Gretel Fenchel, in the Schwarzwald.

Wherever she went, Agnes was received warmly and made to feel welcome. Not since her childhood had she experienced such open love and affection! She was able to reconnect with so many people who had been a part of her life. And yet, she was not too sad when her visit came to an end. She had enjoyed herself, but she was ready to go home. Germany was indeed beautiful, but it was no longer the Germany of her youth, nor in its modernity was Germany the country she recalled from the 1930s.

But then, Agnes was not the same person either. She was no longer a poor immigrant girl, nor were she and Alfred a couple struggling desperately to survive or to stay financially afloat. Through hard work and determination, they had "made it" in America, a country where everyone could get ahead if they worked hard. And

Agnes, after having lived in so many different locales, having been exposed to so many different cultures, milieus and types of people, and having had to adapt to so many different situations in her lifetime, was able to see through and rise above that certain smallness and pettiness which she had occasionally encountered during her visit, in particular among her well-meaning but smug *petite bourgeoisie* sisters in the north – one of them childless and the other an old maid. Used to American openness, she had seen and experienced too much in her life to ever fit into their narrow world again.

Agnes was eager to relate all that she had seen and experienced during her visit to Germany. But once home, those around her were no more interested in Germany than before, and a dour Alfred, in one of his resentful, self-pitying moods and at his sullen best, refused to talk to her for days.

Agnes had been exposed to a whole different world. But back home, nothing had changed.

"Hier ist alles beim Alten," she wrote to me in Marburg, the meaning of which I readily grasped. My mother was writing from the very depths of her soul: one more letdown in a lifetime of letdowns…

"What a life, if you don't weaken!"

Agnes and Meta with childhood friends in Sittensen (July 1966)

*Agnes with
Alfred's brother,
Rudolf, in
Heutensbach
(July 1966)*

And yes, there were many times when my long-suffering mother might have weakened, might have become disheartened, when any ordinary woman would have crumbled and given up. But Agnes, thanks to her resilience and determination, always bounced back. Strong and tough, she had endured the hardships of poverty, the drudgery of hard, continuous physical labor, and the unpredictable moods of her partner in life. And even when bickering, strife and a lack of family harmony might wear her down emotionally, when events might have appeared to get the best of her or when things didn't go as planned, she always kept her back straight and her head held high, in the firm belief that in the end, all would be well.

Mama was always the picture of health. (Agnes in 1964)

CHAPTER 11

The days of man are but as grass; for he flourisheth as a
flower of the field. For as soon as the wind goeth over it,
it is gone; and the place thereof shall know it no more.

— Psalms 103: 15-16

THERE WERE only a few times in my growing up years that I can recall my mother ever being ill. The first time I was still a small child. I retain an image of her sitting in the corner behind the wood burning kitchen stove, a white rag wrapped around her jaw and tied at the top of her head. She was unusually quiet, not at all her usual bustling self. (That afternoon, she had been to a dentist and had all her remaining teeth pulled...)

The second time I was in grade school. Coming home from school one afternoon, Mama was not there! She was in the hospital (Ruthie and I were not told why) and would have to remain there overnight. After the evening milking, Papa drove Ruthie and me to the hospital, but children were not allowed inside. So we stood on the sidewalk, looking up at our mother as she waved from her hospital window. On the way home, Papa treated us to an ice cream cone.

The third time I was in my early teens. It was a Saturday morning, and Mama had not gotten out of bed. This had never happened before! If anything, Mama was proud of never being sick and always claimed that we children were spoiled because we didn't know what it was like to have an ailing mother. But on that memorable day, she never left her bed, while Dr. Ansbach paid a house call. We were all at a loss. Told to prepare the noon dinner, I didn't have a clue. The kitchen was Mama's domain; she had never taught me how to cook! Thank goodness she only stayed in bed one day!

Thus, as far as we children knew, our mother was always healthy. She never complained of not feeling well. She never took a nap and very seldom even sat down to rest. She could work circles around anyone. Having endured so many hardships in her life, she had no use for weakness in herself or in others. A daughter-in-law recalls how, when she asked for an aspirin, Mama simply told her that she didn't keep aspirin in the house. "Get busy and find something to do!" she advised the astonished girl. "Work is the best cure; it will soon make your headache go away!"

Two occasions made 1967 a memorable year for our family:

In April, Ruthie married her high school sweetheart, Jim Frantz, who had recently been drafted into the Army.

Six weeks later, at the end of May, I graduated from college, the first in my family to do so. Mama wanted me to pursue a teaching career. In her mind, there could be no better profession, with summers off to go traveling! Proud of my academic achievements (I graduated at the top of my class, summa cum laude), she was deeply disappointed when instead I stubbornly insisted on returning to Germany.

A delighted Agnes poses with the bride and groom. Wedding of Ruth Elise Fritz and James Easton Frantz (April 15, 1967)

Agnes and Alfred at Frieda's college graduation (May 1967)

When Jim was sent to Vietnam several months later, Ruthie moved back home. Agnes was glad for her company, and the following spring, in April, when Ruthie went to the hospital to give birth to a baby girl, Agnes accompanied her. How wonderful to welcome another new grandchild (her eleventh!) into the world!

Alfred wanted to move to a warmer climate. For years, he had been complaining that he couldn't bear the cold any longer. Agnes, on the other hand, had no desire to move. She was perfectly content to stay where she was. But she did like to travel and was curious to see what Florida was like. They visited Florida twice before Agnes relented and agreed to move there, to Spring Hill, a new housing development north of Tampa.

Everything was falling into place. Jim had returned safely from Vietnam, and he and Ruthie were willing to purchase the house at Boltz's corner. In January 1969, Alfred and Agnes purchased a two-bedroom home that sat on a large corner lot (430 West Kelvin Court) in Spring Hill. With interest generated from the sale of the farm, income from renting out the second farm, plus Ruthie and Jim's house payments, they had sufficient means to live comfortably. Alfred's health seemed to improve, and Agnes went about making new friends and acquaintances.

They returned to Pennsylvania that August to collect their few remaining belongings. Since I had planned my visit to coincide with theirs, the plan was for me to share the long drive back down to Florida and then spend the remainder of my vacation with them in Spring Hill.

For some months, Agnes had been experiencing abdominal pain, so while she was in Pennsylvania, she quietly stopped by to consult Dr. Anspach in Bethel about her discomfort. A doctor was a doctor, or so Agnes thought. But Dr. Ansbach completely misdiagnosed her symptoms, advising her that she should come back when the pain got worse!

Agnes chose to accept Dr. Ansbach's diagnosis that most likely she had strained her abdominal muscle from heavy lifting. Not one for running to a doctor anyway, it never occurred to her to have a gynecological examination. Most women of her age group had never done so. If only she had mentioned her (classic) symptoms to her daughters!

Agnes sensed that something was wrong, but then, complaining had never been her style. She had no cause for alarm. She had been hale and hearty all her life, and at sixty-three, she was still the picture of health, and proud of it! Alfred, on the other hand, was always moaning and complaining about one ailment or another, although he seemed to do much better in the Florida heat. So Agnes had gone along with the Florida move, for her husband's sake. She had a brand new house in Spring Hill, and new acquaintances, but how she missed Pennsylvania – Nancy and Eric and their children, Ruthie and the baby, as well as all her friends! She felt so cut off in Florida, alone with Alfred, who hardly spoke. And there was nothing to keep her busy – that little bit of housework, and Alfred liked to take care of the yard…

Agnes waited for the pain to subside, but instead, it became almost incessant. In Spring Hill, on our evening walks around the neighborhood, I noticed something amiss.

"What's wrong?" I prodded her. "Why are you walking so slowly?"

"I must have strained myself working in the garden," she replied, dismissingly shrugging off my concern.

She and I were busy running around, selecting new furnishings, decorating, visiting new acquaintances and even entertaining weekend guests – Papa's young niece and her husband visiting from Nebraska.

Florida was hot and humid in August. It was all you could do to stay cool. But by October, the heat was less intense, and Agnes would frequently walk over to the large, man-made lake nearby where neighbors would notice her, sitting quietly, staring pensively out across the water…

Agnes and Alfred at home in Pennsylvania (August 1968)

Agnes and Alfred at home in
Spring Hill (August 1969)

By the time she sought medical help "from a real doctor," it was too late. Even after undergoing aggressive surgery, not all the cancer could be removed. It was early January when we children learned of the seriousness of her condition.

"COME HOME YOUR MOTHER IS DYING" read the telegram my brother-in-law Jim sent to me in Marburg.

She lay in the hospital in Gainesville near death. In those days, radiation was used as the main treatment for ovarian cancer after surgery to destroy cancer cells left behind. But apart from the terrible side effects of the full blown radiation treatments she had to endure, Mama was not responding to the treatment. Her white blood cell count was dangerously low, and with her immune system suppressed, her body was beginning to shut down.

Rudy flew in from California, Nancy and Ruthie from Pennsylvania, and I came from Germany. (Eric decided to hold off unless it was absolutely necessary.) With us gathered around her, Mama seemed to revive. Her emotional state improved; she wasn't so alone and frightened anymore. Thus it was decided that I (being single) would stay behind in Florida. I would take a room close to the nursing home where Mama would be staying while she resumed treatment on an outpatient basis. That way, I could see to her needs, accompany her to the hospital for radiation treatments, make certain that she was eating, and keep her company.

Six weeks later, she had once more to be admitted to hospital for a week to lie in bed while radioactive isotopes were implanted into her. Only nurses wearing special protective gear were allowed to enter her room. Being young and clueless at the time, I was certain that this final targeted cancer treatment would "cure" her. (I now realize it was merely palliative in nature – to relieve pain or to control the symptoms of advanced ovarian cancer.)

Standing outside the examination room, I remember cringing, hearing my brave, long-suffering mother screaming in pain as the doctors performed a final pelvic exam, during which the isotopes were removed. After that, Mama was discharged and allowed to go home under a doctor's care. We were both led to believe that she had every chance of getting better....

Back in Spring Hill, Alfred had been looking forward to the day when his wife would finally come home and things would return to normal. His weekly trips to the hospital and the nursing home in Gainesville had left him lonely and confused – and frightened! The growing pile of medical and hospital bills was threatening to eat up the entire proceeds from the sale of the farm!

With Agnes home again, at least for a few precious days at the end of March, the house in Spring Hill came "alive" once more, and Alfred could imagine how wonderful life could be, if only…

Since I had now been in Florida for nearly three months, I was understandably eager to get back to Marburg, where my job was being held for me and where my fiancé was waiting. At the same time, Mama obviously needed looking after. And so it was decided that I would accompany her to Pennsylvania while Papa remained in Florida to take care of the house and yard. Once Mama's health improved, she would return. Being the person she was, Mama made certain that I left the house in Spring Hill immaculate, and she gave Papa strict upkeep instructions so that she would not be greeted by mildew upon her return!

At the airport in Tampa, Mama was so weak that she could barely manage the stairs leading up to the plane's entrance. It was her first ride ever in an airplane! At the Philadelphia airport, a wheelchair and Eric were waiting! "Erich!" she cried out in delight, ever so glad to be back in Pennsylvania and ecstatic at the sight of her son!

The plan was for Mama to divide her stay between Ruthie, Eric and Nancy during her convalescence. As strange as it seems, up to this point, nobody believed that Mama would die. She had been a fighter all her life. And she loved life! Surely, the radiation treatments would have cleared up any remaining cancer and she would live to enjoy her retirement years and to see her grandchildren grow up!

When it came time for me to say goodbye, I found her sitting on the sofa in the living room, weeping. Taken aback, I assured her that she would certainly get better, and that instead of being sad, she should be glad, as I was returning to Germany to prepare for my upcoming wedding in July. Like all children, I could not imagine my mother dying. I could not fathom a world without her. She would always be there. Leaving her in Pennsylvania in good hands, I was convinced that Mama, of all people, would certainly be a cancer survivor!

But as the weeks passed and spring turned into summer, it became apparent that she was not getting better. After Agnes was admitted to the hospital in Lebanon, Alfred was summoned. He came by Greyhound bus, but didn't stay long. In his helpless, confused state, he was completely useless in comforting this dying woman with whom he had spent nearly forty years of his life and whom, until recently, he had merely taken for granted. It was incomprehensible that Agnes would die! And since he was quite unable to identify with anyone else's feelings, having never even bothered to stop and consider them, it was impossible for him to change at this late date.

Thinking only of his own predicament, instead of offering words of encouragement and comfort, all he could say to his wife when they were left alone together in her hospital room was "Mom, what is going to happen to me when you die?"

After he had gone, Nancy and Ruthie found her crying.

"Is it true?" she asked. "Am I going to die?"

Alfred insisted on returning to Florida because he had to "mow the grass," as he phrased it. After all, he owed it to Agnes to look after their Florida home. Besides, keeping busy was all he knew and was his only escape. He was smart enough to sense that he was not welcome 'up north,' at least not by Nancy and Ruthie, who, filled with a profound sense of injustice, could not even stand the sight of him, especially after this latest pitiful example of his inability to love and comfort their mother.

"Why does Mom have to die; why not him instead?" they both wondered out loud. It was so unfair. "If only she could have had more out of life than working for that old man!"

Meanwhile, Alfred, in desperation, turned to others for help. Having heard that there were additional, non-FDA approved drugs to treat cancer, he pleadingly wrote to me in Germany, asking me to try to obtain certain anti-cancer drugs not available in the United States. When questioned, however, the German pharmacists only shook their heads, so that, being still in the dark about Mama's rapidly deteriorating health and the gravity of her condition, I matter-of-factly wrote back to him that I was unable to obtain the drugs in question and so he should just continue to have faith in the care Mama was receiving at the hands of her U.S. doctors.

Mama did not wish to remain in the hospital, so Nancy was granted permission to take her home. Nancy rented a hospital bed, placing it in the living room, where Mama could be with family. She seemed to especially enjoy the company of Kathy, her oldest grandchild. Kathy, then fifteen, would talk to her, hold her hand, and sometimes feed her...

During the next eleven days, Nancy learned to administer morphine shots, three or four times a day, whenever the pain became unbearable. And it was during these same eleven days that Ruthie gave birth to a baby boy (Agnes' twelfth grandchild) and I was married. It is uncertain whether Agnes, in her morphine-induced state of reduced awareness, was actually aware of either of these events.

Her mind wandered. She cried a lot. Often Nancy would find her crying for her mother. She asked for her sister many times. Nancy would tell her that Meta was coming, because by morning, she would have forgotten. She also asked for Emma. Nancy didn't quite know who Emma was, but apparently, Emma was a very old woman, and Nancy was not allowed to let her go home. She would have to sleep on the couch overnight. By morning, Emma would be gone. There was also someone named Mary; she called everyone Mary for awhile. It didn't last long...

Poor Nancy put on a brave and cheerful face and cared for her dying mother as best she could. On the morning when the ambulance came to take her back to the hospital, Mama seemed to revive, if ever so briefly, smiling and waving goodbye to Nancy and the children.

Two days later, during Nancy's daily visit to the hospital, Mama recognized her. Nancy fed her lunch, which Mama threw up. When she asked if she could go outside, Nancy promised that she could go outside the following day. Nancy left around 3 o'clock, since Mama had been given a shot, and that always made her sleepy.

"I'll see you tomorrow," Nancy called to her as she left, and Mama smiled.

That evening, around 9 o'clock, the doctor called Nancy with the news that her mother had died, peacefully. He hadn't expected it for at least two more weeks…

Mama died of ovarian cancer on Thursday, July 16, 1970. She had just turned sixty-four. A grief-stricken Nancy proceeded with the funeral arrangements, selecting her mother's favorite hymns for the organist to play. Papa was on his way, and on the afternoon of Monday, July 20th, there would be one last gathering of Agnes' friends:

> From New York: Agnes' cousin Anna McGuinness, with Winnie Schmiemann's son, Henry Schmiemann, and wife Marilyn. (Henry, a policeman, would die four years later of gunshot wounds after being shot.)
>
> From Philadelphia: Päule Haegele and Karl and Päule Schwab.
>
> From Reading: Päule Esenwein and her husband, Paul Schanzenbach.
>
> From nearby: Old friends Karl and Katren Jancsics, with daughter Catherine; Onkel Karl and Tante Helene with daughter Dorothy; dear friends Eliza Kline and Anson Gettle; neighbors Dawson Harnish and Mr. & Mrs. Elam Burkholder; Flower Club members Anna Moyer, Elsie Knoll and Edna Gingrich; Justice of the Peace and Mrs. Lewis Frantz; Reverend and Mrs. Backenstose; Leah Althouse; Mrs. Amos Frantz; Mrs. Paul Ziegler and Mrs. Alvin Forry; the parents of Jim and Tony, and Eric's mother-in-law. All came to pay their last respects.
>
> Pallbearers were son Eric, sons-in-law Tony Wenger and James Frantz, brother-in-law Karl Fritz, and close friends Karl Jancsics and Anson Gettle.

It was a beautiful funeral – fourteen large floral bouquets from relatives and friends near and far, plus a casket spray of red roses. During the service, people wept as they sang "Nearer, My God, to Thee" and "I Come to the Garden Alone." At the end, the grandchildren approached the open coffin and each placed a long-stemmed red rose inside. Agnes loved flowers, and in death, she was surrounded by them.

Rudy, having flown to Florida in January and having made peace with his mother while she was still alive, was unable to attend her funeral.

As for me, Jim's telegram bearing the devastating news reached me on Saturday, July 18, one week after my wedding:

"YOUR MOTHER HAS PASSED AWAY."

CHAPTER 12

The days of our years are three score years and ten;
and if by reason of strength they be fourscore years,
yet is their strength labor and sorrow; for it is soon
cut off, and we fly away.
– Psalm 90: 10

TWO DAYS AFTER the funeral, Alfred returned to Florida to mourn. For nearly four decades, Agnes had been his constant companion and support. Now he was all alone. In his grief and despair, he wrote to Agnes' sister, Meta, in Germany: "Warum musste Agnes so früh sterben? Sie war doch so gut!" ("Why did Agnes have to die so young? She was such a good person!")

And that was indeed the general line of thought. Agnes had died so quickly – just nine months after being diagnosed. It was so unfair that she should have died so young, before having a chance to enjoy retirement. She, who had been so healthy and full of the joy of life, and then there was Alfred, moody, irritable, forever complaining about his aches and pains, and who seemingly found little joy in living!

Besides feeling sad and lonely, Alfred was frightened. What would he do without Agnes? How would he manage on his own? Desperately in need of someone to look after him, as Agnes had always done, he soon made somewhat of a spectacle of himself by indiscriminately proposing marriage to a number of female acquaintances, both past and present. He even wrote to Meta to ask if she wouldn't like to come and live with him! Päule Haegele, now widowed and also residing in Spring Hill, felt sorry for Alfred, whom she had known since childhood. An excellent cook, Päule frequently invited him over for dinner (Sauerbraten and Spätzle!), but when Alfred inevitably popped the question, she delicately declined.

Who was Peggy? She was the one woman who was willing to marry him! Apparently they met at a singles club for senior citizens. My father, who in the past had never wanted to go anywhere, was now frequenting a singles club?

If a woman were smart, she would know better than to marry my father, and if Alfred were smart, he would know better than to marry Peggy. Quite a few people, including Päule Haegele, warned him away from her. Rumor had it that Peggy was a "professional" widow; she had been bereaved three times and had a reputation of outliving her husbands.

In early April 1971, nine months after Agnes' death, Alfred returned for a short time to Pennsylvania to put his "second" farm up for sale. When Rudy (in California, working in the aerospace industry) caught wind that the farm where he had once lived was to be sold, he begged his father to sell it to him, but Alfred apparently had misgivings and refused.

The second farm, totaling a hundred and five acres, sold for $55,000. With such a tidy sum sitting in the bank, Alfred was now considered a very good catch indeed. In fact, after placing a lonely hearts ad in the German language magazine *Die Hausfrau,* he received over seventy replies! But before he even had a chance to write back to some of the nice German ladies who had replied to his advertisement, Peggy tossed all their letters into the trash! (Peggy was good at tossing things; years later, an alert neighbor would rescue the framed aerial photograph of our family farm from a dumpster...)

They were married in New Port Richey on February 3, 1972. Alfred was smitten! And as for Peggy, perhaps she was truly fond of him. In any event, as a way of announcing the marriage to his children, my father did a wondrous and astonishing thing: In a remarkable gesture of reconciliation, he sent each of us (my four siblings and me) a cashier's check for a thousand dollars, explaining that he was dividing the original amount that he had paid for the family farm back in 1944 ($5,000) among his five children.

Peggy's small house in Spring Hill was heavily mortgaged, so after she and my father were married, she simply returned it to the bank, shipped all her furniture and household goods to her daughter in Michigan and moved into my father's fully paid for and newly furnished home, using all my mother's things. Papa later informed me that the only thing Peggy brought into the marriage were the clothes on her back and a record playing stereo console – the one piece of furniture my parents did not possess!

Only once did I meet Peggy, a few months after she and my father were married, in the summer of 1972. I happened to be visiting from Germany at the same time they stopped by Pennsylvania on their way to visit Peggy's daughter in Michigan. I was curious to meet my 'stepmother.' What kind of woman, I wondered, could get along with my father! But Peggy seemed nice enough, and they seemed to get along, so why not give her the benefit of the doubt? Besides, their relationship did not affect me.

In a way, it was a blessing that Papa had found someone to look after him, and in my father, I am certain that Peggy had gotten more than she had bargained for. Just two years into their marriage, Alfred, who had previously been diagnosed with high blood pressure and hardening of the arteries (atherosclerosis), suffered a series of light strokes, which left him barely able to walk. In Spring Hill, Peggy could be seen pushing him along the sidewalk in a wheelchair...

Since he could no longer physically maintain his house, Alfred decided to sell it. In August 1974, he purchased a small, two-bedroom attached villa (102 Cambridge Trail, #233) in the newly developed, age-restricted, gated community of Kings Point in Sun City Center, south of Tampa, where, thanks to daily dips in the warm indoor pool and the hot tub, it was not long before he was able to walk again, his health significantly improved.

With the passing of the years, the two of them became more and more reclusive. Perhaps it was Alfred's personality rubbing off on Peggy, for, unlike Agnes, who had always been determined to make friends in spite of her unsociable husband, Peggy was not an outgoing, hospitable person. In Spring Hill, she had managed to alienate Alfred from everyone. She had been especially keen on avoiding Päule Haegele!

By then, Alfred's younger brother Karl had also retired from farming. He and Tante Helene now enjoyed spending the cold winter months in Florida. But even Onkel Karl found it difficult, if not impossible, to pay his brother a visit. Peggy seemed dead-set on avoiding him! No sooner would Karl and Helene ask the guard at the entrance gate to announce their visit, than Peggy and Alfred could be seen driving off in the opposite direction!

They were a strange pair indeed, and in the end, we children, busy with our own lives, were glad that they had each other so we could put them from our minds. Other than the odd telephone call, there was little or no communication. Ruthie maintained a semblance of contact, as she and Jim had to mail their house payment each month, and Eric occasionally took his family to Florida on vacation and would stop by to visit.

Then, in mid-February 1981, nine years into their marriage, Peggy suffered a stroke. With Peggy now in a nursing home, Alfred, after two months of being alone, was beginning to act bizarrely and becoming somewhat of a nuisance, to the point where his neighbors in the adjacent villas decided to notify Eric, as they had been instructed. Eric, however, either could not or would not be bothered. Frustrated, and not knowing to whom else to turn, the neighbors were somehow able to contact Onkel Karl.

Onkel Karl and Tante Helene, wintering about an hour-and-a-half drive north of Sun City Center, arrived to find Alfred unkempt and confused, his table piled high with unopened mail, bills, past-due notices, etc. It was apparent that things had gone neglected for some time. Onkel Karl then turned to me (now divorced and living in

Chicago), insisting that someone had to come and take charge, and, since none of my siblings was willing to do so, I reluctantly agreed to take a week's vacation from the law firm where I was employed to fly down to Florida and straighten things out.

I had not seen my father in nearly a decade, and then only briefly. Now, seeing him again, I marveled at the change that had come over this man who was barely a shadow of his former self – the father whom I had both feared and respected. He seemed now a pathetic figure indeed, an old man, deteriorated in mind and body.

Senility is how we referred to it back then. Dementia is how the symptoms are diagnosed today. At the time, I thought that Papa was just getting old and senile. Perhaps I simply did not want to acknowledge the extent to which his 'senility' had progressed.

Looking back, all the classic symptoms of dementia were there: Papa was no longer able to perform simple, familiar tasks, much less balance his checkbook. He still had his car, but had given up driving. He was easily confused, could not even distinguish between his medications, erroneously assuming, for example, that he was applying prescription eye drops for glaucoma when actually he was using over-the-counter drops for dry eye. Since he had always had mood swings and bouts of anger, I attributed any stubbornness to Papa being his usual ornery self. When he couldn't recall something or was unable to comprehend, I assumed he was just pretending.

Of course, there were also moments of good judgment and lucidity and even tender moments, like on that first night after my arrival, when, due to the "smell" in my (Peggy's) bedroom, combined with the realization of the enormity of the task awaiting me, I was unable to fall asleep. Finally, in the middle of the night, I decided to get up. It was then that Papa, himself anxious and unable to sleep, came out of his bedroom and poured me a half-glass of whisky, after which I was finally able to fall asleep on the living room sofa.

And so, since he was my father and I loved him and I knew how he was and always had been, I was slow in grasping the severity of the situation. In the days to follow, whenever he was stubborn or slow to comprehend, I just assumed that he was a bit overwhelmed and that if I could just explain things sufficiently, all would be fine. But moments of lucidity would soon give way again to confusion, and thus I was eternally grateful for the presence of Onkel Karl, who not only respected me and my capabilities, but whose advice and counsel my father trusted.

Where to start? I knew that my parents had drawn up a Will back in September 1967, appointing Eric as Executor and specifying that after their deaths, their estate should be divided equally among their children. Agnes especially, having grown up in a society where only the eldest son inherited and the remaining siblings were not always provided for, was determined that each of her children should be treated the same. Plus, she and Alfred had experienced first-hand the infighting that could result for lack of a valid will! Thus, well before moving to Florida, the ever efficient Agnes had taken care of two important details, both of which at the time seemed utterly premature: The purchase of a cemetery plot, and the drawing up of a joint Last Will and Testament. In seeing to both, Agnes felt she was saving everyone a lot of trouble.

"Share and share alike," she dictated to the testator, with the express intention that each of us children should receive an equal share in our parents' estate. It was a phrase she liked to repeat...

After Mama's death, and after the sale of his second farm, Papa had the foresight to have the Will updated. As soon as he returned to Florida, in April 1981, he had the old joint Will revoked and made a new Will stipulating the same terms, thus securing his remaining estate for his children: *"All of my estate of whatsoever kind and nature and wheresoever situate, I give, devise and bequeath unto my children ... in equal shares, share and share alike."* And again he appointed his younger son as Executor; though Eric would later claim he did not know!

And so, with Mama's words, "Share and share alike!" still ringing in my ears, I determined to salvage and preserve what was left of my parents' estate. The morning after my arrival, Papa and I, together with Tante Helene and Onkel Karl, met with an attorney who advised us on how to secure any remaining funds so that Papa would not exhaust his savings on Peggy's nursing home care and instead would be able to retain his hard-earned money for his own future care.

Papa was so relieved to have company again. He seemed a broken man – lonely, confused, and clearly misplaced. In retiring from farming, he had given up not just his life's work, but a whole way of life. In Spring Hill, he had taken care of the yard and garden. But now there was nothing for him to do. His garden tools – hoe, rake, spade and shovel – were propped against the shower stall, unused, since landscaping was included in the monthly assessment fee, and even the watering of the grass was done automatically.

Thus, even though the move to a landscaped gated community may have been the right thing to do at the time, Papa was totally out of place in Sun City Center, an old farmer who did not fit in, and who, for example, on his daily trip to the clubhouse and pool, stubbornly refused to follow the walk around the perimeter of the golf course, since for him, walking across the "field" seemed a logical shortcut. Never mind the irate golfers who had to wait to tee-off until that crazy old-man Fritz had finished crossing over the fairway!

Inside, the condo was in complete disarray and unsanitary: Rancid butter melted inside the kitchen cabinets; rotting meat in the refrigerator; urine-soaked carpeting in Peggy's bedroom, and the unwelcome site of dried feces on the bathroom rug. Peggy had suffered a stroke, and Papa had left her lying on the floor, not mentioning the situation to anyone, until he could not evade the neighbors' insistent queries any longer.

"Where is Peggy?" the neighbors in the adjoining villas persistently inquired, while Papa all the while (characteristically) avoided answering.

"She's in there and won't get up!" he finally blurted out.

The shocked neighbors found Peggy on the floor of her bedroom, where she had been lying in her own excrement for the last three days!

The first thing I had to do was put my father's finances in order. Searching through his important papers, I managed to track down the financial institutions (hopefully all?) to the north where Papa had savings accounts and where, upon paying each a visit, I learned, much to my dismay, that in his diminished mental capacity, Papa had failed to renew his CD's. Thus, during a period of sky-high interest rates, his certificates of deposit had lain dormant for years, not earning any interest at all!

It was while sifting through mounds of paperwork that I discovered that Peggy had her own savings! Thus, my next step was to contact Peggy's daughter in Michigan, informing her that since Peggy would require long-term skilled nursing home care, and since she was uninsured (Peggy had allowed her Medicare coverage to expire!), she might want to make alternative arrangements (perhaps in Michigan?) for her mother's care. (It was apparent to me that Peggy's children (a son and a daughter) had for some time neglected their mother's deteriorating physical and mental health.) In any event, I made it clear that going forward, Peggy would have to use her own funds to pay for her care, as my father was not in a financial position to do so.

By the end of my 'vacation' week, I had consolidated my father's CD's, providing for a steady monthly income flow while at the same time growing his principal so that he would have sufficient funds to provide for his own future care. I had hired a neighbor, a retired accountant, to manage Papa's checkbook and pay his bills, and a housekeeper to clean and to look after him a few times a week, to cook breakfast, to take him grocery shopping, and, more importantly, to keep him company. I had also subscribed to "Meals on Wheels" so that Papa would have at least one hot meal a day.

In-between, I de-cluttered and cleaned the house and, on my last day in Florida, went shopping with Papa to buy him some sorely needed new clothes, naturally over his protests! Even inside the store, he continued to object. Luckily for me, he was now old and I could more or less make him cooperate. In his younger years, that never would have been possible. I tried to employ the same tricks that Mama had perfected through years of experience. The only way to get him to part with the 'rags' he was wearing was to dispose of them when he wasn't around. True to form, Papa still hated to part with his money, insisting that he didn't have enough, not even for groceries. Left to his own devices, he would sooner have starved than spend money on nutritious, quality food.

Thus, by the end of the week, I had managed both to secure my father's financial situation and to provide for his physical needs. But I could not stay to provide for him emotionally – to keep him company, to ease his loneliness.

"Now I am all alone again," he reproached me on the morning of my departure.

My heart went out to him. Living by myself in Chicago, I understood perhaps better than most what it meant to be lonely. But what could I do? I could not give up my job in Chicago just to keep him company!

"I have everything set up so nicely for you, Papa," I assured him, "and you now have plenty of income to live on. Try to make friends, the way Mama always did, and then you won't be so lonely!"

But I can never forget that moment, and despite my best efforts to set things up for him and to manage his care during the months that followed, I still feel ashamed that I left him there alone. Nor did I ever make time to visit him again, instead managing his care from a distance.

It is said that a man's immortality can be found in his children, but at least in my father's case, this kind of immortality seemed rather illusory in nature. Here was a man who had raised five children, and yet not one of us was really there for him. All of us had taken on lives of our own, and in the meantime, we had become strangers to him, and he to us. How was Papa to achieve immortality through his children, who ignored him, much less so through his grandchildren, who didn't even know him?

I admit that I was curious about my 'stepmother,' about my father's relationship with her. During the week that I spent with him in Florida, and in the months that followed, Papa constantly vacillated between either wanting to divorce Peggy or missing her terribly and wanting her to come home. I don't think that my father and Peggy had the same close-working partnership relationship as that of my parents; their attachment seems to have been based more on physical closeness and attraction. What I do know is that, unlike my mother, Peggy did not put up with any patriarchal nonsense, nor did she cater to Papa's every whim or make a special effort to please him, for example, by preparing his favorite dishes, even though it is common knowledge that "Kissin' don't last, cookin' do!" In fact, one of Papa's pet peeves was that Peggy refused to make him a lemon pie, even though there was an abundance of lemons growing on the tree outside!

Whatever their relationship, I am certain that Peggy did not have an easy time of it. Perhaps in the course of the years, they had subdued each other, both attracted to and annoyed by each other in a kind of "love-hate" relationship. Papa wanted her home again, and yet she seemed to irritate him, and was he in his demented condition simply delusional, or was I to take him seriously when he told me that Peggy was trying to finish him off?

My father was not certain what he wanted anymore. His life was over, as far as he was concerned, and yet he feared death above all things, was terrified at the very thought of it. Papa, at the end of his life, was terribly alone. Nearly everyone he knew from his past was gone. As a sad reminder, he kept a list of those siblings and their spouses, plus old friends from the past, who had already passed away…

How, then, was he supposed to find any purpose in life, especially now, alone, in failing health, and in his confused state of mind? There was nothing left to give his life meaning. "If only I could have a small farm, a few acres of land, a cow!" he confided his yearning to me. Papa was a farmer, for goodness sake! But he no longer had a connection to the earth, and nothing to do that made sense!

Shortly after returning to Chicago, on April 30, 1981, I wrote to my siblings, apprising them of the situation in Florida and that I now held a Durable Family Power of Attorney, which would allow me to manage Papa's financial affairs. Since nobody voiced any objection, I determined to proceed with the arrangement that I had worked out with Papa and his attorney and to closely monitor the situation, albeit from a distance.

In May, Onkel Karl died, unexpectedly, of a heart attack – devastating news, especially for Papa, as Karl was the brother to whom he had been the closest. Onkel Karl, like Agnes, had been a happy person, and now, like Agnes, he also had died too young. Knowing that my father would want to attend his brother's funeral, I made arrangements for him to fly "home" to Pennsylvania.

Onkel Karl was laid to rest on a beautiful spring day. As his brother's coffin was lowered into the ground, my father, standing beside me, sobbed uncontrollably.

"I wish that I could exchange places with him!" I heard him say to his grief-stricken sister-in-law. And I know he truly meant it.

During the months that followed, the arrangements I had made for my father's care seemed to be working out; he was being well looked after in his own home. But regardless of what I or others tried to do for him, he was never happy, never content, frequently confused, unappreciative and uncooperative, and I knew that I would have to find an alternative option for his care. The problem was that Papa's social security income and the interest from his invested principal were not sufficient to place him in a good home where his savings would soon be exhausted.

In mid-October, Rudy decided to fly to Florida to check on his father's situation. Rudy saw that Papa had a good life and agreed that financially it would be preferable if Papa could remain in his own home. But at the same time, Papa did not enjoy living alone, no matter how good the arrangements for his care. After checking out several residential retirement hotels in the area, Rudy's only comment was that "he wouldn't put a dog in there!" Instead, he suggested selling the condo to help finance a good retirement home. Once sold, he would take Papa to California and then look for an affordable retirement home there. I reminded Rudy that the proceeds from the sale would have to be split with Peggy, as the condo was in joint ownership...

In mid-December, after undergoing cataract surgery, Papa's mood and cognitive function worsened, He became increasingly confused and disoriented. Since he had difficulty adhering to his post-operative eye drop regimen, a neighbor kindly volunteered to administer his drops several times a day.

But in his confusion and anxiety, Papa took to knocking on neighbors' doors in the middle of the night, not wearing any clothes, and not knowing where he was.

Depressed and disoriented, he tried to set his home on fire, melting all the pots and pans on top of the stove and inside the oven. One day, obviously hallucinating, he insisted on walking to the top of the hill in order to join the other people gathered there, only there was no hill, and instead, he was wading into the lake! At that point, his neighbors finally summoned the police. It took two officers to restrain him.

It was early January when he was admitted to the on-site nursing home, Trinity Lakes, where disruptive behavior, however, was not tolerated. In the end, he was institutionalized in Northeast Florida State Hospital in Macclenny, where, after a week-long futile attempt to trace his whereabouts, I finally was able to locate him and to speak with the social worker attached to his case, who assured me that my father was doing much better. Once Papa was able to leave, in a week or so, the social worker would help me find a good nursing home...

Papa died on January 30, 1982 at the University Hospital of Jacksonville. He died of cardiac arrest as a consequence of a massive stroke (cerebrovascular accident) which left him unconscious and paralyzed. He was seventy-seven years old.

He died all alone. His dream, the one that he had confided to me – his yearning to have a small farm, a few acres of land, a cow – would go unfulfilled.

But in life, he had more than achieved his dream. Possessing the traits characteristic of his Swabian ancestors, my father had more than fulfilled that proverbial Swabian saying: "Schaffe, schaffe Häusle baue!" As a true descendant of that prudent race, through hard work and thrift he had built his "Häusle." Looking back on his life, he could surely take pride in all that he, as an immigrant, had achieved.

Farming had been my father's life, and thus I choose to envision that at the end, as his poor distraught mind allowed the life to slowly fade from his body, Papa was able to find himself back home in Pennsylvania again, back on the farm, where, finished with the evening milking, he closes the barn door one last time, behind him the sound of contented cows munching away on their hay...

Stepping from the warm barn, he momentarily pauses, and, inhaling deeply the cool night air, he glances briefly up at the heavens filled with stars, and in that moment of reflection realizes that he has indeed accomplished his dream. Feeling strangely at peace, joyful at last, his heart full of gratitude, he begins walking towards the farmhouse, where the kitchen light is on, and where he knows that Agnes is waiting.

EPILOGUE

MY FATHER'S BODY was shipped back to Pennsylvania, where Nancy, Eric and Ruthie attended the brief, private, closed-coffin funeral service that Nancy had arranged.

After his death, my father's Florida condominium, including its contents, automatically passed to Peggy. His financial estate, however, had been preserved.

A little over a year later, after all financial obligations had been met, my job finally came to an end. With a frustrating sense of not having done enough, and yet with a profound sense of satisfaction at having made certain that my parents' wishes, as laid out in their Last Will and Testament, had been carried out, I was able to distribute their remaining assets equally between their children (all five of us) – share and share alike!

Alfred and Agnes' final resting place in the cemetery of Salem United Church of Christ in Bethel, Pennsylvania. From their gravesite overlooking the Blue Mountains (a view that Agnes loved), you can view in the distance a portion of the land they once farmed.

ACKNOWLEDGEMENTS

The idea for this book began to grow several months after my father's death when I visited his older brother in Nebraska. Unlike my parents, Onkel Theo was eager to talk about the past. His wonderful stories now fill the pages of this book, along with those of his sister, Tante Elise, and the recollections of my maternal aunts, Meta and Adelheid, who, though reticent to bring up the past, would often let slip more than they intended.

I am especially indebted to Tante Helene, an aunt by marriage. Without her encouragement and assistance, this book might never have been written.

Scattered cousins, here and in Germany, eager to help, scoured their attics for photographs and memorabilia, stuff their parents had saved and that the next generation would most likely have consigned to the trash.

Many others also helped to make the story of Alfred and Agnes possible.

Erich Bauer, archivist of the *Alt-Archiv der Gemeinde Allmersbach* in Heutensbach, unearthed fascinating details about my father's 19th century ancestors and validated my efforts with his enthusiastic support.

Professor Hans-Heinrich Seedorf, of Springe, served as my introduction to my mother's (and his) home town. Wilhelm Gohde of the *Heimatverein der Börde Sittensen* (Sittensen Heritage Society) and Erika Jaschinski of the Sittensen Touristikbüro provided generous assistance, and genealogist Ewald Albers, of Zeven, traced my mother's ancestors far back in time and shed light on their lives.

I became friends with Roy and Jean Fritz of Germantown, Wisconsin, authors of the "Fritz Family Book," and with Elberta Brummet of Lexington, Nebraska, who shared her knowledge of the Naumann and Tobaben families of Eustis. I was lucky to make the acquaintance of Irene Bleiweiss, a distant cousin by marriage and an amateur genealogist who loves a puzzle. Without Irene's diligence, several family lines would have remained 'lost' forever. My story is much richer, thanks to her.

Special thanks go to my friend, Heidi Friedrich, for her excellent editing skills, and to David Darian at www.darianphotoart.com for cover design and expert photo restoration work throughout.

I am also grateful to nieces April Frantz and Lois Snelson for their help and support – especially Lois, who read and commented on every page and whose unflagging enthusiasm kept me on track.

And finally, my thanks to all those not mentioned here by name who helped me in my effort to uncover the story of Alfred and Agnes.

— CHILDREN OF —

CHRISTIAN FRITZ
(11. 3.1868 – 6.24.1933)

&

LUISE PAULINE FRITZ, nee Kopf
(3.29.1871 – 12.23.1946)

	Name	Born	Died	Buried
* 1	CHRISTIAN Gottlob	6/13/1894	06/17/1894	
2	RUDOLF Wilhelm + Helene Schiefer	09/18/1895	08/27/1970	
** 3	Luise FRIEDA + Paul Kleinknecht	03/06/1897	04/09/1938	NE
** 4	Hermann THEODOR + Dora Meyer	11/09/1898	04/04/1985	NE
** 5	Anna BERTA + Emil Heller	12/06/1899	03/01/1981	NE
6	Pauline EMMA + Hermann Ettle	03/31/1901	11/10/1976	
** 7	Mathilde HEDWIG + Wilhelm Gottlob Schwarz	08/21/1902	06/12/1965	NY
** 8	Karl ALFRED + Agnes Anna Bredehöft	07/19/1904	01/30/1982	PA
* 9	HELENE	06/14/1906	01/02/1907	
** 10	KARL Johann + Helene Emma Jung	08/29/1907	05/16/1981	PA
* 11	CHRISTIAN	11/12/1908	01/02/1913	
** 12	ELISE Helene + Henry Frank Wagner, Sr.	03/18/1910	10/30/2004	CA
13	JOHANNA Helene + Albert Krauter	03/20/1912	12/16/1978	
14	Helene ERIKA + Gottlob Wilhelm Werf	02/10/1914	06/09/2008	
15	MARGARETE (Gretel) Helene + Karl Eugen Stirm	08/04/1916	02/27/2007	

*   Died in infancy/childhood
** Emigrated to America

— CHILDREN OF —

JACOB BREDEHÖFT
(1.5.1872 – 4.16.1929)
&
META ADELHEIT BREDEHÖFT,
nee Bartels (7.14.1871 – 11.23.1926)

	NAME	BORN	DIED
1	JACOB HINRICH ("JONNY") + Frieda Puls + Johanna Rolfes, nee Hünecke	Jan 5, 1904	Dec. 1962
2	META MARIE SOPHIE	May 3, 1905	July 5, 1985
**3	AGNES ANNA ERNESTINE + Karl Alfred Fritz	June 4, 1906	July 16, 1970
* 4	ERNST JOHANN	May 29, 1909	June 29, 1910
5	ADELHEID MARGARETE KATERINA + Leo Frank	Oct. 14, 1911	April 30, 2013

* Died in infancy/childhood
** Emigrated to America

— DESCENDANTS OF —

ALFRED KARL FRITZ
(7.19.1904 – 1.31.1982)

&

AGNES ANNA FRITZ,
nee Bredehöft (6.4.1906 – 7.11.1970)

Children	Grandchildren	Great Grandchildren
RUDOLF ALFRED 12.31.1933 + Louellyn Driscoll (3.01.1937)	LOIS ANNA (1.6.1957) [div.] Jeffrey Lynn Brock + Don Earl Snelson .... LINDA DEE (6.19.58) [div.] Richard Allan Langston LAURA BONNIE (7.31.61) + Bartly Jay Libsock RUDY ALFRED (9.26.65) [div.] Dana Sue Hazelwoood	Jennifer Lynn (2.6.76) Jason Michael (3.3.77) Jeffrey Lynn, Jr. (8.9.79) Donna Oranda (10.27.88) Lois Anna (9.26.91) Melissa Marie (10.5.79) Richard Paul (7.19.81) Chase Rudolf (5.19.98) Oranda Louellyn (1.18.02) Jillian Marie (6.25.93) Kelly Ann (5.4.98-9.25.10)
NANCY META 4.6.1935 + Anthony Christos WENGER (8.24.1930)	KATHY LYDIA (1.31.55) [div.] J. Robert Hummer RENEE ANNA (3.2.56) [div.] Dennis Elwood Fulk.... [div.] Henry Walter Clair...... WENDY TONI (5.25.58) + Scott Sachs ANTHONY NORMAN ALFRED (3.30.63) + Jennifer Louise Corcoran	Robert Anton (12.14.83) Megan Anna (6.6.85) Justin Michael (11.26.82) Brett Cody (5.21.85) --- Kristen Emily (5.24.90) Rebecca Abigail (7.25.94)
ERIC ERNEST 12.17.1937 + Lillian G. Berger (4.30.1938)	STEVEN ERIC (11.10.60) + Kay D. JERROLD KEVIN (3.26.65)	Hannah E. (1992) Austin Eric (1994) ---
FRIEDA ANNA 7.9.1944 [div.] Eckart STIEHL (2.10.1939)	---	
RUTH ELISE 5.28.1947 + James Easton FRANTZ (12.30.1947)	APRIL ELISE (4.20.1968) + Michael Scott Doyle JAMES JEFFREY (7.6.1970) + Michelle Lynne O'Neill	--- Kaylee Rae (1.31.93) Andrew James (9.12.94) Lauren Elise (8.3.96)